THE MEANING OF THE EUCHARIST

VOICES FROM THE TWENTIETH CENTURY

REV. DENNIS BILLY, C.SS.R.

En Route Books and Media, LLC

St. Louis, MO

⊕ENROUTE

Make the time

En Route Books and Media, LLC
5705 Rhodes Avenue
St. Louis, MO 63109

Cover credit: TJ Burdick

Library of Congress Control Number: 2019949748

ISBN-13: 978-1-950108-44-2
ISBN-10: 1-950108-44-9

DEDICATION

In loving memory of
Joanne Miniscalco Apothaker
(1944-2016)

Epigraph

Taking part in the eucharistic sacrifice, the source and summit of the Christian life, they offer the divine victim to God and themselves along with it. And so it is that, both in the offering and in the Holy Communion, each in his own way, though not of course indiscriminately, has his own part to play in the liturgical action. Then, strengthened by the body of Christ in the eucharistic communion, they manifest in a concrete way that unity of the People of God which this holy sacrament aptly signifies and admirably realizes.

Second Vatican Council,
Lumen gentium, no. 11

Contents

Voice Twenty-Eight

Introduction

This book is the third volume of my voices on the Eucharist series. In the previous two volumes, I covered the early Church Fathers and many of the saints and mystics who followed them in subsequent centuries.[1] The present volume looks at one of the richest periods of reflection on the Eucharist in the history of the Church and is aptly entitled, *The Meaning of the Eucharist: Voices from the Twentieth Century.*

My purpose in this volume is to highlight some of the major theological voices from the past century who contributed to a deepening of the Church's understanding of the significance of this great sacramental mystery and whose efforts came to fruition in the teachings of the Second Vatican Council. Each of the authors treated within these pages has a distinct voice that blends with the other voices of the Church's rich theological tradition. The result is a beautifully nuanced harmony of meanings that challenges the mind and moves the heart to wonder.

Twentieth-century Catholic theology embraced many streams of thought that existed in tension with one another and vied for influence in the larger ecclesiastical world. These tensions came to a head in the Second Vatican Council, a watershed moment in the life of the Church that brought it out

---

[1] See Dennis Billy, *The Beauty of the Eucharist: Voices from the Church Fathers* (Hyde Park, NY: New City Press, 2010; Idem, *The Mystery of the Eucharist: Voices from the Saints and Mystics* (Hyde Park, NY: New City Press, 2014).

of its defensive, fortress mentality and encouraged the faithful to engage the world on every level. The aim of this Council was *aggiornamento*, a long overdue "updating" of the Church that would allow it to enter into dialogue with every facet of human society, both religious and secular, in order to serve as a leaven for the cultures it encountered and transform these realities from within. The Council's documents present the Eucharist as an essential resource for this process of inculturation. They call it the "source and summit of the Christian life," which "both signifies and realizes the unity of the People of God."[2] It is through this great mystery of faith that "the work of our redemption is accomplished"[3] and "by which the unity of the Church is both signified and brought about."[4] Although the Church respects all religions and rejects nothing of what is true and holy in them,[5] it has an inherent duty "to proclaim without fail, Christ who is "the way, and the truth, and the life" (Jn 14:6). The Eucharist lies at the heart of this proclamation and forms an integral part of the Church's efforts of evangelization.

The Second Vatican Council, however, did not take shape in a vacuum. It became possible only because of the efforts of theological renewal in the decades both preceding and immediately following the close of the Second World War. Pope John XXIII's call to "throw open the windows of the church and let the fresh air of the Spirit blow through," came after years of

---

[2] The Second Vatican Council, *Lumen gentium* (The Dogmatic Constitution on the Church), no. 11.

[3] The Second Vatican Council, *Sacrosanctum concilium* ("The Constitution on the Sacred Liturgy"), no. 1.

[4] The Second Vatican Council, *Unitatis redintegratio* ("The Decree on Ecumenism"), no. 2.

[5] See The Second Vatican Council, *Nostra aetate*, (The Declaration on the Relation of the Church to Non-Christian Religions"), no. 2.

groundbreaking efforts to return to authoritative sources by the proponents of Ressourcement theology (also known as the Nouvelle Théologie). The purpose of "Ressourcement," which was not so much a theological school as it was a particular way of responding to the issues of the day, was to retrieve the Christian faith in order to respond to the critical needs of the times. Unfortunately, the response to these efforts was not always positive. The theologians of "Ressourcement" were sometimes met with suspicion and, at times, even silenced by those who felt threatened by the voices of change. In time, however, their message was heard and sincerely taken to heart. The documents of the Second Vatican Council represent the Church's response to these efforts for renewal. In continuity with the teachings of past councils, they represent a decisive attempt to engage the world through constructive dialogue.

The voices in this volume represent a wide spectrum of Catholic theological opinion, ranging from monastic theology, to Thomism (both neo- and transcendental), to Christian panentheism, to analytical philosophy, to ressourcement theology, and others. Some of these voices actively promoted the Nouvelle Théologie. Others were influenced by it. Some simply ignored it. Still others spoke out, in varying degrees, against it. For all their differences, however, it soon becomes clear when reading these authors alongside each other that, whatever their philosophical or theological point of view, they all shared a deep love for the Church and its sacraments— especially the Eucharist. With few exceptions, all were born in the seventy-five year span between 1850 and 1925 and, for the most past, wrote their major works either before the Second Vatican Council or shortly thereafter. Their lives span an arc of almost 150 years, and their writings impacted the theological world of the twentieth century and beyond.

For the most part, the chapters have been arranged in chronological order according to the years of the authors' births.

Some are converts to the Catholic faith. All but one are voices from the Latin rite. Although there are a few laymen and women, most are priests, some who were diocesans and many others who belonged to religious orders such as the Benedictines, Dominicans, Oratorians, Jesuits, and Redemptorists. Some of these priests were eventually consecrated bishops; some were even made cardinals; one was even elected pope. What brings these voices together in a single volume, however, is not their ecclesiastical dignity or state of life, but their distinctive contribution to twentieth-century thought on the Eucharist.

Notably absent from this volume are the Eucharistic writings of most of the popes of this time period. This lacuna was intentional, since to include such magisterial voices as Pius X, Pius XI, Pius XII, John XXIII, Paul VI, John Paul I, and John Paul II in a volume of this kind would enlarge its pages considerably and run the risk of drowning out the other significant twentieth-century Eucharistic contributions. The aim here was to separate the theological voices from the magisterial ones in an effort to highlight the former's contributions to Catholic Eucharistic theology, while in no way undermining the Church's authoritative teaching body. The one exception, here, is the inclusion of the voice of Josef Ratzinger, whose Apostolic Exhortation, *Sacramentum caritatis*, which he wrote and promulgated as Pope Benedict XVI, represents a beautiful synthesis of Church teaching after the Second Vatican Council and stands as the magisterium's most articulate presentation of the theology of the Eucharist to this day. Since each of the previous two volumes in this series ends with a chapter dedicated to the thought of a pope—*The Beauty of the Eucharist: Voices from the Fathers of the Church* with Pope St. Gregory the Great, and *The Mystery of the Eucharist: Voices from the Saints and Mystics* with Pope St. John Paul II—it is fitting that this present volume should conclude the thought of someone, like Benedict XVI, who was both a major theological voice in his day and a successor to the chair of Peter.

The Catholic thinkers chosen for this volume represent only a sampling of the many voices on the Eucharist in the decades leading up to the Second Vatican Council. They were selected because of their creative thinking, their loyalty to the tradition, and their desire to move it forward. They were also chosen, at least in part, because of the controversies their thought engendered within the Church and, at times, even among themselves. Such tensions, to my mind, are a sign of the vitality of the Catholic tradition and its capacity to integrate different perspectives without diluting the Gospel message or compromising its effectiveness.

Each of the twenty-eight chapters (or "voices,") begins with a brief biographical sketch of the Catholic thinker under consideration and a summary of his or her spiritual and/or theological outlook. A presentation of his or her teaching on the Eucharist follows with accompanying observations, a conclusion, and a series of reflection questions. This loose underlying structure unifies the whole, while at the same time allowing each chapter to stand by itself and, if need be, read alone. The reflection questions in particular are meant to encourage readers to explore the issues raised by these thinkers and to find their relevance for their own lives. My hope is that such reflection will deepen the readers' understanding of the theology the Eucharist and help them to find its significance for their lives.

The authors in this volume represent the best of theology as *fides quaerens intellectum* ("faith seeking understanding").[6] They approached the Eucharist as a mystery of the faith and understood that none of their theological formulations could

---

[6] See Augustine of Hippo, *De trinitate,* 8.5.8; Anselm of Canterbury, *Proslogion,* 1.

ever hope to fully exhaust its meaning. At the same time, they were propelled to ponder the sacrament's significance, because they knew that this great mystery embodied the whole of the Gospel message to be proclaimed throughout the ages. They saw the Eucharist as a continuation of Christ's redeeming action, one that freed humanity from the bondage of sin, healed it from within, and elevated it (along with the rest of creation along) to newer and greater heights. Their thinking on the Eucharist developed within the context of a living faith and was guided by it to probe the depths of God's love for humanity. The Eucharist, they believed, embodied this love in every respect. They understood that, whenever it was celebrated, God entered our world, gave himself to us completely to the point of dying for us, became nourishment for us, and a source of hope. Eucharist, for them, was the "Sacrament of Love." Those who partook of it were called to go forth and live what they received. Even today, their insights continue to speak to our hearts and inspire us to take up their steps.

At some point in our lives, each of us, regardless of our occupation, state of life, level of education, or cultural background, needs to ponder the meaning of the Eucharist and discover its significance for our lives. We are called to do so within the context of a living faith in search of understanding that seeks to probe the significance of Jesus' Last Supper with his disciples the evening before he died. This task involves an effort of both mind and heart and, although it can be burdensome (even tedious) at times, it promises to bear much fruit. The wealth and vitality of the theological insights in this volume encourage us to set out on our own path of theological inquiry. They remind us that the Eucharist is, first and foremost, the "Body of Christ, " the glorified presence of the Risen Lord, who enters our midst, nourishes us, transforms us, and carries us into the presence of the Father.

The voices within these pages give witness to the palpable

(albeit, ever elusive) presence of the God who calls himself, "Emmanuel, which means, God with us" (Mt 1:23). The words they speak suggest that no theological formulation, however probing or innovative, can exhaust the mystery that the sacrament brings into our midst and invites us to partake of. To ponder the meaning of the Eucharist, in other words, requires an open mind, a humble heart, and a willingness to explore the darkened pathways of the soul that only Jesus, the "Light of the World," can illumine. Their voices encourage us to ponder the mystery of the sacrament, discover its significance for our own lives, and to add our voices to theirs. In doing so, perhaps we may hear faint echoes of the heavenly chorus of saints and angels that continually renders glory, praise, and thanksgiving to God for the myriad wonders he has wrought in the lives of those who believe in him and call upon his name.

Voice One

Dom Columba Marmion:
Food of the Soul

Our first voice wrote in the early decades of the twentieth century and was one of the most influential and widely read spiritual writers of his day. Dom Columba Marmion (1858-1923) was a Benedictine abbot and renowned author in the early decades of the twentieth century. He was born in Dublin of Irish and French decent and given the name Joseph Aloysius at birth. He entered Dublin's diocesan seminary in 1874, completed his theological studies in Rome, and was ordained in 1881. After ordination, he was curate for a short time in Dundrum, before becoming a professor at the major seminary in Cloniffe and a chaplain for a both a monastery of nuns and a women's prison. In 1886, he received permission from his bishop to become a Benedictine monk at the monastery of Maredsous in Belgium, where he became a novice, embraced the monastic way of life, and professed solemn vows in 1891.

Soon afterwards, Marmion took part in the founding of the Abbey of Mont César in Louvain, eventually became its Prior, and in 1909 was elected Abbot of Maredsous, a position which he held until his death. A close friend and confidant of Cardinal Désiré Mercier, the Archbishop of Mechelen, he was a very influential voice in Belgium and beyond in the early decades of the twentieth century. A popular retreat master and spiritual director, he gave many conferences on the spiritual life, which were eventually prepared for publication and appeared as *Christ, the Life of the Soul* (1917), *Christ in His Mysteries* (1919), *Christ, the Ideal of the Monk* (1923), and *Christ, The Ideal of the Priest* (published posthumously, 1951). His teaching on the Eucharist reflects his Benedictine love for liturgy and contemplation and lies at the heart of his spiritual outlook.[1]

Dom Marmion's Spiritual Outlook

Marmion's spiritual outlook has its roots in the Benedictine tradition, which seeks conversion of life through work, prayer, and spiritual reading. The *Rule of Benedict* sought to create a "school for God's service" that would sanctify the day through a community life dedicated to liturgical worship, study, the fostering the interior life, and the care of souls.[2] Steeped in this spiritual tradition, Marmion placed Christ at the center of all things and provides in his writings a vision of the Christian life with appeal for Catholics from all walks of life.

Christ, for Marmion, is the author of our redemption, the efficient cause of all grace, and the head of a Mystical Body that imparts his Spirit to his followers and gives life to the soul. Faith in Jesus, which lies at the very heart of the Christian life, comes to us through baptism and opens for us the possibility of sharing in his divine life. We begin this sharing at baptism when we are immersed in Christ's paschal mystery and born again as adopted sons and daughters of the Father. As a result, we are

---

[1] This biographical information comes from *L'Osservatore Romano*, Weekly English Edition (September 6, 2000), http://www.vatican.va/news_services/liturgy/saints/ns_lit_doc_2 0000903_columba-marmion_en.html.

[2] See *The Rule of St. Benedict*, prologue, trans. Anthony C. Meisel and M. L. del Mastro (Garden City, NY: Image, 1975), 45.

made dead to sin and empowered by the Spirit to live for God and not ourselves.[3]

For Marmion, everyone is called to live for God. We live for God by participating in the life of the Church, especially by sharing in the sacraments and seeking to grow in our relationship with Christ through prayer and our love for God and neighbor. This supernatural growth in Christ comes by leading lives of continual conversion that foster the life of theological and moral virtues. "The sacraments," he maintains, "are the principal sources of growth of the divine life within us. They act in our souls by the efficacy of their very operation, *ex opere operato*, as the sun produces light and heat; it is necessary only that within us no obstacle stand in the way of their operation."[4] "The Eucharist," he goes on to say, "is the one [sacrament] which most increases the divine life in us, because we receive Christ in Person, we drink at the very source of the living waters."[5] Marmion sees the Eucharist as the food of the soul and "the Sacrament of Life par excellence;" it is the major means by which we grow in the love of both God and neighbor.[6] Through it, we are conformed to Christ's life and empowered by his Spirit to grow in his love and to live our lives centered totally on God and others. It provides us with food for our spiritual journey, gives us access to the transforming grace of Christ redemptive action, and lies at the heart of his spiritual outlook.

---

[3] Columba Marmion, *Christ, The Life of the Soul*, trans. Alan Bancroft (Bethesda, MD: Zaccheus Press, 2005), 60, 83, 107, 130, 167, 195, 242, 294..

[4] Ibid., 296.

[5] Ibid.

[6] Ibid., 95, 98.

Marmion's Teaching on the Eucharist

Dom Marmion is quick to point out our own inability to bridge the gap between the human and the divine: "[A]ll the efforts of human nature, left to itself, at a distance from Christ, are not able to advance us one step in the achieving of that union, in the birth and development of the life it brings forth. It is God alone who gives us the seed-germ and the growth; we care for the plant, we water it: that is necessary, indispensable ... but the fruits are produced only because God causes the sap of His grace to rise within us."[7] The Eucharist, in his mind, is the principal means God uses to bridge that gap, nourish our souls, and transform us into his adopted sons and daughters.

How does this happen? In the Eucharist, Christ immolates himself as an eternal offering for our sins. This Eucharistic sacrifice is a mystery of faith that cannot be fully captured in words. The Mass, for Marmion, is a true sacrifice where Christ is both victim and high priest and where the blood sacrifice of Calvary is made present in an unbloody manner. The same Christ who was immolated on the altar of the cross is immolated at the sacrifice of the altar. As high priest, Christ is the mediator between God and man. He is the "anointed one," who bridges the chasm between divinity and humanity. He possesses an eternal priesthood, which he shares with others in different degrees and for varying purposes.[8]

For Marmion the sacrifices of the Old Testament are only vague figures of the immolation that took place on Calvary. This sacrifice possesses infinite value and is the only way in which we can reestablish the communion with the divine that we lost on account of our sins. The immolation of Christ on Calvary, in his mind, is reproduced and renewed at the sacrifice of the altar:

---

[7] Ibid., 330.

[8] See Ibid., 332-34.

"[T]he Mass is not just a simple *representation* of the Sacrifice of the cross; it is not just the value of a simple remembrance. It is a true Sacrifice, the same as the Sacrifice of Calvary, which it reproduces and continues and the fruits of which it applies."[9]

In Marmion's eyes, the Mass gives us access to the same fruits as the cross. It is an act of perfect worship, for it represents the selfless offering of Christ Himself on our behalf. For this reason, it is a source of confidence and pardon; it is a true propitiatory sacrifice in which Christ, the divine victim, appeases God and makes him favorable to us. It is also an act of petition and supplication, whereby those worshiping seek light, strength, and consolation. When at Mass, we participate in the oblation of the altar by identifying ourselves with Christ, the High Priest and Victim. Receiving Holy Communion, in his mind, is the most assured way of maintaining the divine life within us. In this banquet, Christ gives himself to us as the Bread of Life. He becomes food for our souls and offers us His divine friendship so that He dwells in us and we in Him.[10]

Through the Eucharist, Christ transforms us into himself: "In receiving Jesus Christ, we receive Him whole and entire: His body, His blood, His soul, His humanity, His divinity. Christ makes us enter into His thoughts, share His feelings; He communicates His virtues to us, but above all He enkindles in us that 'fire' He came to cast upon the earth, the fire of love, of charity; *that* is the purpose of this transformation produced by the Eucharist."[11] To receive these fruits, however, we must be properly prepared to receive them and take care to remove any obstacles that would hinder their proper functioning in our lives. "As food is only given to the living, so the Eucharist is only

---

[9] Ibid., 335.

[10] Ibid., 342-44, 346, 349, 357-58, 361.

[11] Ibid., 365.

given to those who already possess the life of grace."[12] We must take care to prepare ourselves properly to receive it by rooting out sin in our lives and seeking to adhere more closely to God's life in us. For Marmion, the distinctive fruit of the Eucharist is "the identification of ourselves with Christ, through faith and love." If we receive the body of Christ well, we become what we receive.[13] The Eucharist, in this respect, "is the food of the soul that *maintains, restores, increases,* and *gladdens* the life of grace in the soul, because it gives to it the very Author of grace."[14]

Marmion also sees the Eucharist as the "sacrament of union with Christ as Head of the mystical body."[15] The sacrament, in his mind, "makes the faithful enter more fully into that plenitude of the supernatural order which makes Christ and us one incomparable unity."[16] When we receive holy communion we come into contact with Jesus and submit ourselves to his gentle rule of love: "In the sacrament, Jesus touches, sanctifies, and takes possession of the soul. He casts His rays upon it from the glorious shelter of the Eucharist. As long as the sacred species remain unaltered, the soul receives the benefit of this *contactus virtutis*; it becomes more dependent on the action of the Lord, more profoundly united to His mystical body. But when the sacramental presence ceases, the faithful Christian, as a member of the mystical body, remains still under the influence of the Savior."[17] Marmion bids us, moreover, not to place any obstacles in the way of receiving the fruits of Holy Communion:

---

[12] Ibid., 369.

[13] Ibid., 388.

[14] Ibid., 360.

[15] Columba Marmion, *Christ, The Ideal Priest*, trans. Matthew Dillon (St. Louis, MO: B. Herder Book Co., 1952; San Francisco: Ignatius Press, 2005), 249.

[16] Ibid.

[17] Ibid., 250.

"Christ cannot unite himself to a soul which is not humble, to a heart which does not receive Him unreservedly, which neglects the duties of its state, or above, all, which is closed to its neighbor for lack of charity or the spirit of forgiveness."[18]

Some Further Insights

This brief exposition of Don Marmion's teaching on the Eucharist shows the central place it holds in his spiritual outlook and emphasizes his understanding of the sacrament's importance for the Church's life and worship. The following observations develop some of the implications of his view of the sacrament and their relevance for today's Catholics.

To begin with, Dom Marmion roots his teaching on the Eucharist firmly in the tradition of the Church. He employs quotations from Scripture, the ecumenical councils (especially Trent), and the Church fathers, as well as distinctions from scholasticism, and the monastic emphasis on experience to offer a synthesis of the Church's teaching on this central sacramental mystery. His teaching is comprehensive, thorough, and well-rounded, one that goes to the heart of the sacrament, while at the same time respecting the limits of human knowledge and our inability to exhaust the full meaning of this central mystery of our faith. His knowledge of the tradition enables him to present the Eucharist in a way that fosters faith across a wide spectrum of the faithful, from those who are well along in their spiritual journey to those just starting out. His influence as a spiritual director and retreat master stems, at least in part, from his ability to stress the essentials of the faith in a simple and relatively easy manner. His audience extends far beyond his monastery walls and has a certain universal appeal to the Catholic faithful.

---

[18] Ibid., 252.

Dom Marmion emphasizes the sacrificial nature of the Mass and its intrinsic connection to the Jesus' death on Calvary. This immolation of Christ at Mass is the same as his immolation on the cross, the only difference being that the first occurs in an unbloody rather than bloody manner. While this teaching comes straight from the Council of Trent,[19] Marmion uses it to expound the mysterious connection between the sacrament and the faith of the believer. Through the eyes of faith, the believer is immersed in the saving mystery of Christ's passion and death: the cross of Calvary becomes one with the consecrated bread and wine; those who eat and drink of Christ's body and blood and are immersed in his redemptive self-emptying. His oblation becomes their oblation, and theirs, his. Marmion brings new life to the Church's traditional teaching by highlighting the experiential nature of the sacramental mysteries. By eating Jesus' Eucharistic body and blood, believers unite themselves in an intimate way with Christ and his journey to the Father.

Dom Marmion describes the Eucharist as the sacrament that most increases the divine life within us. It does so because it puts us directly in touch with the person of Christ and his paschal mystery.[20] At the altar of sacrifice, our meager offerings of bread and wine are transformed into Christ's Body and Blood to become food for our souls that nourishes and strengthens us for our spiritual journey. The Eucharist, in this respect, has a transformative effect on our lives; it conforms us to Christ and empowers us to love as he loves. By means of the Eucharist we enter into communion with Christ and share in his divine life. This supernatural ordering of our persons to Christ is accomplished primarily through grace and only secondarily

---

[19] See Council of Trent, Session 22, chap. 2 (Denzinger, 43 ed., no. 1743).

[20] See Marmion, *Christ, The Life of the Soul,* 296.

through our willful cooperation. The most we can do is purify our hearts by repenting of our sins and opening our hearts to the work he wishes to accomplish in us. The purpose of the Eucharist is to foster the divine life of Christ within our hearts so that our thoughts, feelings, words, and actions might be in concert with the promptings of his Spirit who dwells within us.

Dom Marmion emphasizes the importance of our being properly prepared to receive the Eucharist. For the grace of the sacrament to bear fruit in our lives, we must take care to remove any obstacles that might get in the way of its operation. The stream of divine grace cannot enter a vessel whose mouth has closed by sin and hardness of heart. Repentance of our spiritual and moral failures is necessary before the redemptive and transforming grace of the sacrament can touch our lives and bring about its desired effect. It is wrong simply to presume God's forgiveness without taking advantage of the means God has provided for us to confess our sins and receive forgiveness. There is an intimate relationship between the Mass and the sacrament of reconciliation, and the faithful must take care to seek forgiveness for their serious sins before receiving Holy Communion. The bread of angels has no positive effect on those who have embraced the dark side of their human nature and do nothing to free themselves from the hold it has over them.

Dom Marmion emphasizes not only the sacrificial and nourishing dimensions of the Eucharist, but also the reality of Christ's real presence: "Through Holy Communion, Christ dwells in us and we in Him."[21] When we receive the sacrament with the proper dispositions, our humanity enters into close, intimate contact with the humanity of the glorified Christ, who embraces us, dwells within us, and transforms us from within. Through the Eucharist, Christ transforms us into Himself and empowers us to give a complete gift of ourselves to God and

---

[21] Ibid., 361.

others.[22] For this reason, every action of our lives should be oriented toward receiving Holy Communion and maintaining this deep, intimate relationship with Christ. Jesus' real and abiding Presence in the sacrament demands special reverence, because it points to his real and abiding presence in our own lives and the transforming effect it has on the members of his mystical body. When seen in this light, the Eucharist in its various dimensions—as sacrifice, banquet, and presence—represents the primary means by which we participate in Christ's paschal mystery and share in the fruits of his redemptive action.

For Marmion, Christ is both priest and victim at the Eucharistic sacrifice, and we have been given the privilege in sharing in his redemptive life. Because of Christ's passion, death, and resurrection, we have become a priestly people who offer ourselves to God the Father through Christ's mediation. Christ takes the burdens of our weak and sinful humanity onto himself and suffers the penalty of death on our behalf in order to free us from our sins and allow us to enter into right relationship with His Father. His Holy Spirit is the bond that unites us to him and makes us members of his mystical body. Christ is alive today and continues to live his paschal mystery in the members of his body, the Church. He dwells within us and conforms us to himself by living his passion, death, and resurrection in and through us. Because we share in paschal mystery in such an intimate way, we too become both priest and victim in the sacrificial offering of ourselves at Mass and in the living out of the fruits of the Eucharist in our lives.

Finally, the Eucharist for Marmion is both the "sacrament of unity" and the "sacrament of thanksgiving."[23] Through it, we celebrate our communion with God and one another and give

---

[22] Ibid., 364, 371.
[23] Ibid., 346, 361.

thanks to God for the gift we have received as a result of Christ's sacrificial offering of self. Through the sacrament, we are immersed in the mystery of Christ's paschal mystery and become one with his mystical body. This mystical reality has repercussions on the way we relate to ourselves and to one another. The sacrament is a concrete reminder that we are no longer isolated individuals wandering haplessly about in search of meaning for our lives, but people with a clear identity: brothers and sisters of Christ and adopted sons and daughters of the Father. The sacrament unites us to Christ in a way that deepens our bonds with one another and enables us to offer our lives as a living sacrifice of praise and thanksgiving to the Father. The Eucharist is a "sacrament of unity" because it is a "sacrament of thanksgiving"—and vice versa. The two dimensions are intimately related.

Although these observations barely scratch the surface of Marmion's insights, they highlight the centrality of the Eucharist for his thought and overall spiritual outlook. They also reveal his desire to explain the profound truths of the faith in a way that is both easy to understand and that touches the experience of ordinary believers. His legacy is rooted in his eagerness to convey the truths of the Catholic faith in a comprehensive and uncompromising manner for the people of his day and for generations of believers to come.

Conclusion

Dom Columba Marmion was an Abbot of a renowned Benedictine monastery and one of the premier spiritual authors of his day. His writings cover nearly every aspect of Christian spirituality and represent a return to the fundamentals. He places Christ at the center of the spiritual life and, in all his teachings and writings, never veers from that one basic truth. Marmion believes Christ is central to the spiritual life, because the opportunity to become adopted sons and daughters of the Father comes only through him. Without Christ's selfless sacrificial gift from the cross, we have no possibility whatsoever of entering into communion with God, let alone relating to him as a son or daughter.

The Eucharist, for Dom Marmion, is the way Christ chose to continue his redemptive action in the hearts of his followers. Through it, Christ nourishes our souls and transforms them into living members of his mystical body. He sees the Mass as an unbloody manifestation of the one bloody sacrifice of Calvary, thinks of the Eucharist as an essential spiritual food for the soul, and believes those who consume it receive the body and blood of the glorified and risen Lord. Holy Communion, for him, is an intimate and living contact with the person of Christ. Those who do not put any obstacles in the way of the working of God's grace, can be assured of a growing intimacy and friendship with the divine.

The Eucharist, for Dom Marmion, is the primary means by which the divine life takes root in our souls and by which we grow in love for God and neighbor. It is the sacrament of love, the sacrament of unity, and the sacrament of thanksgiving. It lies at the heart of Catholic theology and imbues every aspect of the spiritual life. This food for the soul enables Christ to be the life of the soul. Dom Columba Marmion dedicated his life to making this fundamental truth of the spiritual life known to as many people as possible, both within and without the walls of his monastic cloister. Beatified by Pope John Paul II on September 3, 2000, his spiritual legacy is well established and his writings continue to provide sound direction and solid food to many of today's faithful.

Reflection Questions

- Dom Marmion maintains that the Eucharist is the

principal means God uses to bridge that gap between the
human and divine. Have you ever thought of the
sacrament in this way? How have you experienced this
gap in your life? Have you ever tried to bridge it by
yourself? With others? Why is God alone capable of
bridging it?

- For Dom Marmion, the Eucharist nourishes our souls
  and transforms us into God's adopted sons and
  daughters. What does being an adopted son or daughter
  mean to you? Do you think of yourself in this way? What
  does this relationship to God the Father ask of you?

- Dom Marmion sees the Eucharist as the "sacrament of
  unity." How does this sacrament draw people together?
  Has it ever kept them apart? What kind of unity does it
  form? Have you experienced the Eucharist to be a source
  of unity or division in your life? Why is the Eucharist
  sometimes a point of contention among Christians?
  What can Christians do to overcome their divisions?

Voice Two

Karl Adam:
Community Act

Our next voice is that of a well-known German scholar who taught at several European universities during his long academic career. Karl Adam (1876-1966) was one of the great Catholic thinkers of the twentieth century. Born in Bavaria to a large Catholic family, he received his early education at Amburg, studied philosophy and theology at Regensburg, was ordained a priest in 1900, and took his doctorate in theology at the University of Munich in 1904. After a few years in a parish, he was allowed to focus on scholarly interests and a career in the academy. He became a professor at the University of Munich in 1915, assumed the chair of moral theology at the University of Strasbourg in 1917, and took over the chair of dogmatic theology the University of Tübingen in 1919.[1]

An expert in historical and systematic theology, Adam was especially noted for his lectures on the Church and his knowledge of the theology of Augustine and the Church fathers. In the years leading up to the Second World War, he initially (and somewhat naively) tried to reconcile his Catholicism with

---

[1] "Foreword" to Karl Adam, *The Spirit of Catholicism* http://www.ewtn.com/library/THEOLOGY/ SPIRCATH.HTM.

the National Socialism, but eventually criticized the Nazi party's heavy-handed tactics and its endorsement of neo-pagan worship and practices. Heavily influenced by the German neo-romantic tradition, he is best remembered for books such as *The Spirit of Catholicism* (1924), *Christ Our Brother* (1927), and *The Son of God* (1933). His thinking influenced a generation of Catholic thinkers and had an impact on the proceedings of the Second Vatican Council, especially in its emphasis on the Church as *communio*. His teaching on the Eucharist flows from this organic theological vision of the Church as community.[2]

The Spirit of Catholicism

Adam's theological and spiritual outlook shines through most clearly in *The Spirit of Catholicism*, an influential work that has been translated into several languages and often reprinted in English.[3] Acclaimed as one of the best introductions to the Catholic faith of its day, this book aims "to provide a calm, dispassionate, clearly written consideration of the fundamental concepts of the Catholic faith which would explain to all, Catholic and non-Catholic alike, exactly what the Catholic Church is."[4]

In this book, Adam seeks to capture the essence of the diverse yet unified reality known as Catholicism. He points out that Catholicism, in its very heart, affirms the existence of an intimate union between Christ and his Church. This bond

---

[2] Ibid. For Adam's dealings with Nazi Germany, see Robert A. Krieg, "Karl Adam, National Socialism, and Catholic Tradition," *Theological Studies* 60(1999): 432-56.

[3] All future citations from this book come from Karl Adam, *The Spirit of Catholicism* (London/Sydney: Sheed and Ward, Ltd, 1929; 8th impression 1969).

[4] "Foreword" to Karl Adam, *The Spirit of Catholicism.* http://www.ewtn.com/library/THEOLOGY/SPIRCATH.HTM.

reflects the Pauline mystery of the Body of Christ and permeates every aspect of Catholicism's dogmatic and moral teaching, as well as its life of worship. The Church's dogmatic theology centers on Christ; her moral teaching seeks to transform believers and make them like Christ; she conducts her worship through, with, and in Christ. The Church, according to Adam, is a visible and invisible community of believers. This idea of community is fundamental to the Church's self-understanding and expression. Like a body, the Church is a unified organism with different functions differentiated among its various members. The authority of the Church's hierarchy flows from this underlying unity and is a service to it.[5]

According to Adam, Catholicism has its roots in the affirmation of the intimate relationship between God, Christ, and His Church. Christianity, for him, is "more than a system of thought," but "a living stream of divine life flowing out from Christ and bearing His truth and His life, pure and uncontaminated, down the centuries."[6] The Church is a living organism that mediates this life to the world in a visible way through her sacramental life and mission. Its organic life is both visible and invisible with a hierarchical structure that insures the purity of the faith and a sacramental system offering visible signs of invisible grace. The Church is one, holy, catholic, and apostolic. It is a union of believers at various stages in their journey into God and the fullness of life. Mary, the Mother of the Church, holds a special place in our prayers and devotion, because she is the first to experience the fullness of her Son's redemptive mission.[7]

Adam goes on to describe the Church's vital role in the

---

[5] Karl Adam, *The Spirit of Catholicism* (London: Sheed and Ward, 1929; eighth impression 1969), 15-33.

[6] Ibid., viii.

[7] Ibid., 51-70, 122-30, 162-82.

process of salvation. Christ's body exists for one reason and one reason alone: to sanctify humanity by carrying out its missionary mandate of going forth and making disciples of all nations. It sanctifies by the power of the Holy Spirit in virtue of the creative power of the Father and the redemptive love of the Son. By proclaiming God's Word and celebrating the sacraments, it immerses those it reaches in Christ's paschal mystery. For this reason, all true Christians are oriented toward the Church and their invisible union with it must someday become a visible union. In this respect, the Church has an important educative task to lead the human family to God through her teaching and moral discipline. Its sacramental action is the primary way by which it fosters the spread of the Gospel and continues Christ's redemptive action in the world.[8]

Adam admits that a gap exists between the vision the Church seeks to embody and its lived historical reality.[9] He recognizes certain tensions existing between theology and divine mystery, authority and freedom, liturgical formalism and personal piety. Because of these tensions, the need for the Incarnation becomes ever clearer, since through it (and only through it) will humanity ever find its way to God. This mystery extends far beyond Word becoming flesh in the person of Jesus of Nazareth. If Jesus is "the way, and the truth, and the life" (Jn 14:6), the Eucharist is the continuation of the incarnational principle through time and the way God has chosen to continue his redemptive and sanctifying mission in the world. As St. Athanasius reminds us, "God became human so that humanity might become divine."[10] By becoming the very food we eat, God promises to transform humanity by the divinizing power of Christ's redemptive grace.

---

[8] Ibid., 203-41.

[9] Ibid., 242-63.

[10] Athanasius of Alexandria, *De incarnatione*, 54.3.

Adam's Teaching on the Eucharist

Adam's teaching on the Eucharist flows from his sacramental understanding of the Church and its sanctifying mission."[11] "[T]he sacraments," he maintains, "breathe the very spirit of primitive Christianity" and "are the truest expression and result of that original and central Christian belief that the Christian should be inseparably united with Christ and should live in Christ."[12] Through Catholic sacramental practice and piety, "Christ is faithfully affirmed and experienced as the Lord of the community, as its invisible strength and principle of activity."[13] For him, the sacraments express "the fundamental nature of the Church, the fact that Christ lives in her."[14]

For Adam, "there is no sanctity in the Church which is not sacramental, and there is no sacramental act which is not at the same time a striving for sanctity."[15] The seven sacraments, in his mind, embrace all of human life and make every aspect of it holy: "The soul at peace with God is sanctified in Confirmation and Holy Eucharist; the soul burdened with sin in Baptism and Penance; the afflicted soul, in the awful hour of death, in the Last Anointing. The community life is also sanctified by the sacramental blessing: on its social side by the sacrament of Matrimony, on its religious side by the sacrament of Holy Orders."[16]

Adam goes on to describe the sacramental realism at the heart of the Church's life and mission: "It is before all else the realism of its sacramental thought which give the sacramental

---

[11] Adam, *The Spirit of Catholicism*, 22.

[12] Ibid.

[13] Ibid.

[14] Ibid.

[15] Ibid., 213.

[16] Ibid., 213-14.

worship of the Church its religious and moral value. The Church does not attenuate the sacrament into an empty symbol, or into a sign of grace which obtains all its efficacy from subjective faith."[17] The sacraments are thus "a real expression of our Lord's gracious will, a sign of Christ (*signum Christi*), and as such it already ensures the presence of His grace through itself, through its actual performance."[18] He highlights here an underlying truth of Catholic sacramental doctrine: "A sacrament is not fulfilled by the fact that one believes in it, but by the fact that it is performed."[19]

For Adam, "[t]he Sacrament of the Altar is the strongest, profoundest, most intimate memorial of the Lord, until He comes again. And therefore we can never forget Jesus, though the centuries and millennia pass, and though nations and civilizations are ever perishing and rising anew."[20] As a result, "there is no heart in the world, not even the heart of father or mother, that is so loved by millions and millions, so truly and loyally, so practically and devotedly, as in the Heart of Jesus."[21] He understands "that in the sacraments, and especially in the Sacrament of the Altar, the fundamental idea of the Church is most plainly represented, the idea, that is, of the incorporation of the faithful in Christ."[22]

Adam also highlights the beauty of the Eucharist and the way it inspires creative and artistic endeavors: "The life and activity of the Church are irradiated with innocent joy, serene brightness, devout gladness. The source of all this devout happiness is the Tabernacle, belief in the beneficent presence of

---

[17] Ibid., 214.
[18] Ibid.
[19] Ibid.
[20] Ibid., 21.
[21] Ibid.
[22] Ibid., 21-22.

eternal Love."[23] Catholic churches, by their very nature, are Eucharistic in orientation: "They have sprung from a living faith in the sacramental Presence of our Lord. And where this faith has departed they lose their deepest meaning and are left without the idea which created and inspired them. They are beautiful but dead, bodies without a soul."[24]

The Church, for Adam, is the living mystical body of Christ; the Eucharist, the transforming, nourishing food that feeds its members with the life-giving body and blood of its Divine Master. As such, "[t]he Mass is never an individual act, but always essentially a community act."[25] This is true not merely in the sense that the whole community should take part in it, but also and emphatically in the sense that participation in the one Bread gives the community its true cohesion and unity, and builds it up into the supernatural organism of the Body of Christ in which form it is presented to the Father by the hand of the divine High Priest."[26]

This communal dimension of the Eucharist lies at its very heart and forms the basis of the Church's identity: "The ultimate meaning of Holy Communion is not union with the uncreated Word, with the pure Godhead, as some ancient Greek theologians erroneously held; nor is it more than a half-truth to say that its meaning is union with the living Christ. The full truth is that it is union with Christ and through Christ with all his members, in whom, in mysterious yet real manner, he achieves his fullness. The Eucharist is not the sacrament of the personal Christ alone; it is also at the same time and for that very reason

---

[23] Ibid., 220.

[24] Ibid., 220-21.

[25] Karl Adam, "Through Christ Our Lord," trans. Justin McCann, www.americancatholicpress.org/Karl_Adam_Through_Christ_Page 2.html.

[26] Ibid.

the sacrament of the mystical Christ. It is a community thing, through and through."[27] In this respect, the Eucharist lies at the very heart of the Church—and vice versa.

Some Further Insights

Although these insights do not exhaust the richness of Adam's teaching on the Eucharist, they provide a general sketch of its main contours and invite careful scrutiny. The following observations seek to bring out some of the ramifications of his teaching with special emphasis on their relevance for the Church today.

To begin with, Adam is a sacramental realist who sees the Eucharist not merely as a sign or symbol pointing to a transcendent spiritual reality, but a continuation of the incarnational principal by which the Word of God became human in the person of Jesus and now divinizes our humanity by means of his Eucharistic body and blood. In this respect, Adam echoes the traditional Eucharistic teaching of the Church with its threefold emphasis on the Eucharist as presence, sacrifice, and banquet. The *real* presence of Christ in the sacrament is rooted in the *real* sacrificial offering of the Mass, which is a *real* but unbloody manifestation of the one sacrifice of Calvary and a *real* (albeit sacred) meal in which we receive nourishment that incorporates our humanity into Christ's. His teaching shows how these elements are themselves intimately related and co-inhere in such a way that one cannot be dropped without doing damage to integrity of the sacrament. His sacramental realism challenges today's believers to ponder the deeper meaning of the Eucharistic mystery and the central role it plays in their ongoing redemption.

Adam sees the Eucharist as embedded in the community of

---

[27] Ibid.

the faithful. This ecclesiological dimension lies at its very heart of the sacrament and captures the very reason for its existence. The Eucharist exists for the supernatural organism that is the Church and is the primary means by which it continues its sanctifying mission in the world. If the members of the believing community are members of Christ's mystical body, the Eucharist provides the transforming, sanctifying nourishment by which they remain in Christ and perform the unique functions within his body. In this respect, the Eucharist is primarily a communal sacrament, one that unites the members of the body, rebuilds them so that they may properly perform their functions within the body, and energizes them for their mission in the world. This important communal dimension of the sacrament supports personal Eucharistic piety and, when proper understood actually deepens it. Authentic Eucharistic devotion leads a person to a deeper love for and celebration of the liturgy. Believers find their true identities within the communal celebration of the sacrament and, through it, give glory and honor to God in their personal lives.

Adam understands that the Church, as a living, unified organism, continually changes over time and yet remains the same. The body of Christ developed from its roots in primitive Christianity in much the same way that a seed grows into a tree or a child matures through to adolescence and adulthood. That her understanding of herself deepens and matures through history has concrete implications for theology in all its various aspects, including its sacramental theology. For this reason, Adam understands that the Church will never be able to capture the fullness of the mystery of the Eucharist through theological concepts and must remain open at least to the possibility of more profound theological presentations that capture the mystery more fully while remaining in continuity with those tried and true expressions that have gone before. The Church's positive theological understanding of the Eucharist, in other words, can adequately convey certain truths about the mystery of the sacrament, but will never fully exhaust it. Adam sustains a realistic view of what theology can and cannot do. Its purpose is to sustain the living organism of the Church, not reduce it to a closed system. His teaching on the Eucharist reflects this important theological nuance.

When viewing the Eucharist in its relationship to the other sacraments, Adam highlights its important sanctifying role in the Church's life and mission. When the faithful approach the sacrament with the proper dispositions, the grace of the Spirit conforms them more closely unto the image of Christ. This transformative, divinizing function of the sacrament deepens the faithful's communion with Christ and empowers them to follow him more closely and partake more deeply in his mission. The Eucharist, in this respect, is intimately related to the Church's mandate to "make disciples of all nations" (Mt 28:19). Communion with Christ empowers the members of his body to proclaim his message through their words, deeds, and their very lives. Communion with Christ inevitably leads to mission with Christ. As Adam so eloquently points out, the Eucharist is a sacrament of the Mystical Christ, and Christ is ever arising anew in the life of the community of the faithful. His insight echoes the words of the Apostle Paul, "I have been crucified with Christ; and it is no longer I who live, but it is Christ who lives in me" (Gal 2:20).

Adam highlights the impact the Eucharist plays on the imagination of the faithful. He emphasizes the creative role it has had in inspiring many of the world's great masterpieces in the areas of music, art, literature, sculpture, and architecture. It does so because its inherent beauty has inspired believers to capture something of its mystery and wonder in the work of human hands. These attempts are the artist's way of paying homage to God, the master artisan and craftsman, who in the sacrament has given the world a living memorial of his Only

Begotten Son. The Eucharist has sometimes been called the "Icon of Christ." As a living icon, it offers a window through which the faithful can gaze and ponder eternity. As the sacrament of the Mystical Christ, it continues to this day to cultivate the imagination of the faithful and inspire them to create new works of beauty that touch the hearts of believers and non-believers alike. If the Eucharist embodies the hope in the final transformation all of human existence itself, then the beauty of the art it has inspired points to the divine metamorphosis that the imagination itself yearns for and will one day undergo.

Adam points out the eschatological orientation of the Eucharist by calling it "the strongest, profoundest, most intimate memorial of the Lord, until He comes again." In doing so, he highlights the sacrament's role as both the visible presence of God's kingdom in our midst and a visible sign of its fullness in the world to come. The Eucharist, in this respect, is the sacrament of the new creation: it both realizes the kingdom in the here-and-now and points to its fruition at the end of time. It embodies in a concrete, visible way the "already-but-not-yet" character of the historical manifestation of the kingdom which is both "in our midst" and "yet to come." As an eschatological manifestation of the Messianic banquet, it exists both in and out of time. Its historical manifestation, moreover, while rooted in past events, makes the love of God palpably present, and instills in the community of the faithful a hope that God's reign will one day be fully realized. When seen in this light, the Eucharist points to God's redemptive action in the past, his continuing presence in the community of the faithful, and his coming in glory at the end of time.

Finally, Adam's thought on the communal nature of the Church and its implications for the Eucharist had a direct impact on the ecclesiology of the Second Vatican Council with its emphasis on the people of God and the Eucharist as "the source and summit of the Christian life."[28] His writings on the Church as the Mystical Body united in Christ as a unitary organism of the faithful contributed to the renewal of Catholic theology and prepared a way for the Council's emphasis on the Church as *communio*. Writing at a time when personal piety permeated much of Catholic spirituality, his emphasis on the Church as a mystical communion of believers encouraged the faithful to look beyond their private devotional practices and to see that they worshiped God first and foremost as a people united in Christ as members of his body. Communion in Christ, for Adam, goes to the very heart of the Church and underlies every aspect of its visible and invisible dimensions. Although he was not the only Catholic theologian focusing on such issues in the decades leading up to the Council, his voice was clear, rooted in the tradition, prominent, and influential.

While these observations touch only a part of Adam's many profound insights into the Eucharist, they highlight the centrality of the sacrament for his thought and the key role it plays in his vision of the Church. They also reveal his desire to probe the truths of the Catholic faith and make them as accessible as possible to the community of believers.

Conclusion

Karl Adam is remembered as an insightful thinker who was able to translate Catholicism's rich theological and spiritual tradition into terms that engaged a wide reading audience, both intellectual and popular. He had the ability to convey the most difficult of theological concepts in a way that would both captured the imagination of his readers and engage their understanding of what it meant to be a member of Christ's Mystical

---

[28] Second Vatican Council, *Lumen gentium* (The Dogmatic Constitution on the Church"), no. 11.

Body. This ability led him to produce a body of writing that would impact a generation of theologians and lay much of the important groundwork for the Second Vatican Council.

Adam's insights into the communal nature of the Church touched a sensitive cord in the hearts of his readers, one that challenged them to ponder their place in the community of the faithful and rethink what, in his day, was an overly individualistic approach to Catholic piety and devotion. His efforts to depict the Church as a vital, living organism of many members working for the common task of proclaiming the Gospel in the concrete historical circumstances of daily life resonated with the tradition and challenged believers to find way of implementing the message of Christ. That his own implementation of these insights, at times, fell short should encourage the community of the faithful to redouble their efforts to allow Christ's paschal mystery to quietly weave its way into their lives.

Adam's teaching on the Eucharist is timely, well-argued, traditional, and profound. He places the sacrament at the heart of Christ's body, the Church, and draws keens insights into the meaning of communion with Christ and his mission to the world. The Eucharist, he held, was the Church's lifeblood, for it gave believers access to the life-giving Body and Blood of Christ and incorporated them ever more deeply into his redemptive mission. Adam was a sacramental realist and the Eucharist, for him, was the sacrament of redeemed reality, a visible sign of the new creation and an eschatological symbol of a reality yet to come.

Reflection Questions

- For Adam, the Eucharist is a transforming, nourishing food that feeds us with the life-giving body and blood of our Lord and Master. In what ways have you experienced this nourishing and transforming food? What areas in your life remain in need of such nourishment? What areas in your life have you kept out of reach from God's transforming power?
- Adam highlights the beauty of the Eucharist and the way it inspires creative and artistic endeavors. Can you point to any specific creative and artistic works that have been inspired by the beauty of the sacrament? Can you point to any recent endeavors? Has the Eucharistic inspired you in any creative and artistic ways?
- For Adam, the Eucharist is a sacrament of the mystical Christ. What does it mean to be a member of Christ's mystical body? Do you consider yourself a part of this body? If so, what role do you play? What role does the Eucharist play? What meaning do you attach to the words "the Body of Christ" when the priest gives you Holy Communion?

Voice Three

Reginald Garrigou-Lagrange:
Sacramental Immolation

Our next voice was one of the great Thomistic thinkers of his day. Reginald Marie Garrigou-Lagrange, O.P. (1877-1964) was a professor of ascetical and mystical theology at the Pontifical University of St. Thomas (also known as the Angelicum) in Rome and one of the foremost Catholic theologians of the twentieth century. He was born in southwest France and grew up in a strong Catholic environment. A conversion experience sparked by reading the French philosopher Ernest Hello led him to a deeper embrace of the Catholic faith and eventually the decision to abandon his medical studies at the university of Bordeaux and join the French Dominicans. After his religious formation and theological studies, he taught for a time at Le Saulchoir in France before moving to the Angelicum, where he taught from 1909 to 1960. In 1917, the Angelicum established a special chair of ascetical and mystical theology for him, the first of its kind in the world. A leading figure in what has come to be called "strict observance Thomism," he wrote against modernism and the Nouvelle Théologie movement, worked for the Holy Office, helped shape Pius XII's *Humani generis* (1950), and served on the preparatory commission for the definition of the Assumption of Mary. A prolific author and renowned teacher who educated generations of priests and religious from all over the world, he was a master at finding the ramifications of Neo-Thomistic thought for the spiritual journey of the faithful. The author of many books and numerous articles, he is probably best remembered for his masterful, *The Three Ages of the Interior Life* (1938). His teaching on the Eucharist has a central place in his spiritual outlook and is intimately bound up with his understanding of these three ages.[1]

Garrigou-Lagrange's Spiritual Outlook

Garrigou-Lagrange believed that every Christian was called to the mystical life. In his mind, infused contemplation, long considered the dividing line between ascetical and mystical prayer, belonged not to a select few, but to all members of the faithful. Such contemplation, in his mind, was the normal outcome of the daily Christian life. He believed that everyone was called to holiness and that such a life normally ended in a mystical, face-to-face encounter with God.[2] In this respect, he opposed those who drew a sharp distinction between the ascetical and mystical lives and who acknowledged two separate paths to union with God by making the latter accessible only to a select spiritual elite. This sharp distinction between the ascetical and mystical developed relatively late in the history of spirituality and was largely due to a growing suspicion of

---

[1] This biographical information comes from Reginald Garrigou-Lagrange, *The Three Ages of the Interior Life*, trans. Sister M. Timothea Doyle, 2 vols. (London: Catholic Way Publishing, 2013), 1: 552-53; Thomas Crean, "A Saint in Heaven," http://www.christendom-awake.org/pages/thomas-crean/saint-in-heaven.htm. For a complete bibliography of Garrigou-Lagrange's writings, see http://www.u.arizona.edu/~aversa/scholastic/garrigou-lagrange_bibliography.pdf.

[2] Garrigou-Lagrange, *The Three Ages of the Interior Life*, 1:51; 2:750.

mystical experience because of the latent effects of Quietism. This spiritual doctrine was a false, heretical mysticism popular in the Baroque spirituality of the late-seventeenth century that endorsed an utter passivity before God and even went so far as denying that a person should even will his or her own salvation.[3]

Garrigou-Lagrange countered this underlying mistrust of mysticism by synthesizing the speculative theology of Thomas Aquinas with the experiential-oriented writings of John of the Cross to show that the mystical life was simply living in the Spirit and allowing his gifts to manifest themselves and bear fruit.[4] Since the Spirit and his gifts are given to all Christians at baptism and strengthened when they are confirmed, the mystical life, for him, was an expected outcome of authentic Christian living. Garrigou-Lagrange's teaching retrieved an earlier understanding of the spiritual life, one that resonated deeply with the tradition. In many respects, it corresponds to the Second Vatican Council's teaching on the universal call to holiness in chapter five of *Lumen gentium*, "The Dogmatic Constitution on the Church."[5]

For Garrigou-Lagrange, holiness in the Christian life is intimately bound up with the threefold journey of purgation, illumination, and union. The "three ways," as they are commonly called, represent a broad pattern of the Christian's journey to God. They are sometimes presented as separate and distinct stages of a the spiritual journey, and sometimes as a upwardly spiraling and repetitive movement of purgation (which focuses on purging oneself from sin and vice), illumination (which involves a deepening of one's awareness of

---

[3] Ibid., 1:26-37; 2:337-348,732-58.

[4] See, for example, Reginald Garrigou-Lagrange, *Christian Perfection and Contemplation in Thomas Aquinas and John of the Cross* (1923; reprint, Rockville, IL: Tan Books, 2010).

[5] Garrigou-Lagrange, *The Three Ages of the Interior Life*, 1:553.

God's presence in one's life), and union (which speaks of the culmination of a person's journey to God in a life of intimate communion with Him).[6] Garrigou-Lagrange's contribution to the theology of the three ways involves his systematic and comprehensive rendering of this journey, the way he integrates it with the best insights of Thomas and John of the Cross, and his opening up of mystical experience to all believers within its broad, general framework. The Eucharist plays a central role in each of these stages.[7]

Garrigou-Lagrange's Teaching on the Eucharist

Garrigou-Lagrange believes that participation in the sacrifice of the Mass is our greatest means to holiness, since from this sacrament of the altar flow all the graces we need to foster our relationship with God. These graces help us in our journey and, in the course of our lives, carry us through the ascetical (i.e., purgative) and mystical (i.e., illuminative and mystical) stages of the spiritual life. For this reason, he maintains that we should value the daily participation in the Mass, have a deep awareness of its effect on our interior dispositions, and make every effort to unite ourselves to Christ's sacrificial offering in the Eucharist.[8]

Garrigou-Lagrange reiterates the Church's teaching on the Mass as an unbloody manifestation of the bloody sacrifice of Calvary. The only difference between them, in his mind, is their manner of expression: "whereas on the cross there was a bloody

---

[6] See Thomas D. McGonigle, "Three Ways" in *The New Dictionary of Catholic Spirituality*, ed. Michael Downey (Collegeville, MN: The Liturgical Press, 1993), 963-65.

[7] See Garrigou-Lagrange, *The Three Ages of the Interior Life*, 1:269-93, 476-500; 2:289-307.

[8] Ibid., 1:476-84; 2:289-99.

immolation, there is in the Mass, in virtue of the double consecration, a sacramental immolation through the separation, not physical but sacramental, of the body and blood of Christ."[9] For him, the soul of the Mass is the very same interior oblation of the heart of Christ that happened at Calvary. When we participate at Mass, we unite ourselves to this internal self-offering as members of his mystical body, the Church.[10]

For Garrigou-Lagrange, the quality of the faithful's participation in the Mass varies depending on where they are in their spiritual journey. Those in the purgative state seek to insure that they approach the sacrament in the state of grace. They try to root out evil from their lives by seeking forgiveness for their sins and making sure that they prepare themselves properly for Mass. They work hard to be attentive during Mass and pray that Holy Communion will strengthen them in their struggle to root out all habits of sin from their lives.[11] Those in the illuminative state go beyond these initial steps by immersing themselves in Scripture and opening their hearts to whatever words God may be speaking to them in the silence of their hearts. Holy Communion, for them, is an invitation to bask in the illuminating light of Christ's saving grace and to live with a deeper awareness of God's presence in their lives.[12] Those in the unitive state move beyond this illuminating light to rest in the joyful, intimate communion with him. They experience the transforming power of God's unconditional love for them and experience so deep an intimacy with him that the two seem as one. In each of these instances, the effect of Holy Communion depends on where they presently stand in their relationship with God. The grace of the sacrament will not be effective in

---

9 Ibid., 1:477.

10 Ibid., 1:478-79.

11 Ibid., 1:479-84.

12 Ibid., 2:289-99.

their lives if they are not properly disposed to receive it. For this reason, they must take special care to remove any obstacles that might stand in the way of God's grace.[13]

Garrigou-Lagrange's teaching reminds us that God does not force himself into our lives and that his grace will not be effective and bear fruit if we are not willing to cooperate with it. God, in other words, meets us where we are and leads us toward holiness according to our capacity to receive his grace. In most cases, this happens in small incremental steps by way of the three ways. Each successive stage, moreover, incorporates into itself all that went before it. Progress often occurs by revisiting earlier experiences and deepening one's awareness of the action of God's grace.[14]

Some Further Insights

Although this presentation of Garrigou-Lagrange's teaching on the Eucharist does not even scratch the surface of his profound spiritual doctrine, it does provide the main contours of his doctrine and summarizes succinctly its relevance for our journey of faith. The following observations seek to develop his teaching in more detail and highlight its relevance for today's believers.

To begin with, Garrigou-Lagrange's teaching on the Eucharist is rooted in the Church's spiritual and theological tradition, especially the teachings of the Council of Trent and the writings of Thomas Aquinas and John of the Cross. With Trent, he affirms the doctrines of the sacrificial nature of the Mass, transubstantiation, the real presence, and its significance as an eschatological sign of the heavenly banquet—to name but a few. With Thomas Aquinas and John of the Cross, he em-

---

[13] Ibid., 2:578-79.
[14] Ibid., 1:38-39, 551; 2:763.

phasizes the transformative power of the sacrament and its capacity to root out the weeds of sin from the life of the believer. He also is able to synthesize the speculative, often abstract, insights of Aquinas with John of the Cross' emphasis on experience to present a teaching on the Eucharist that is theologically sound, while at the same time spiritually attractive to the sensitivities of his day. In this respect, he stands as one of the most prominent orthodox Catholic spiritual writers of his day, whose impact is still strong even a half a century after his death.[15]

For Garrigou-Lagrange, participation in the sacrifice of the Mass is the greatest means to holiness and the prayer par excellence of the Church. All other prayer—private, communal, and liturgical—flows from it and ultimately goes back to it. In his mind, there can be no opposition between private devotions and the celebration of the Eucharist. The Mass lies at very heart of the Church's life and worship and any attempt to replace it with private devotions or para-liturgical practices must be seriously called into question. By their very nature, such practices seek to cultivate the relationship of the faithful with Christ and deepen their awareness of his presence in their lives. Although they may lead the faithful to Christ, however, the Eucharist is an action of Christ himself and lies at the very heart of the Church's identity. Something has gone seriously awry when such practices, although good in themselves, displace the Eucharist in the life of the faithful and become the focal point of their life and worship. It would be like mistaking a pond for an ocean or replacing a fountain with a cup of water.[16]

At the same time, Garrigou-Lagrange emphasizes the importance of having the proper dispositions for participating at Mass and receiving Holy Communion. Like all the

---

[15] Ibid., 1:476-500; 2:289-307.
[16] Ibid., 1:512-38.

sacraments, the Eucharist comes about from the work performed (*ex opere operato*), but depends on the interior
dispositions of those who receiving them (*ex opere operantis*).
Serious sin will block the graces of the sacrament to work
effectively in a person's heart; lesser sins will inhibit the person
from experiencing the full effects of the sacramental grace in his
or her life. Certain attitudes, in themselves are not necessarily
sinful, can dampen the effects of the sacrament in a person's life
and, if care is not taken, actually bring about negative effects.
Garrigou-Lagrange stresses the importance of good preparation
before receiving Holy Communion (e. g., confession in the case
of serious sin, fasting for the designated hours, prayer),
attentiveness at Mass (e.g., following the actions of the priest,
listening to the readings and sermon), and giving thanks to God
afterwards (e.g., remaining in prayer afterwards, resolving to
act more lovingly throughout the day). Such actions dispose the
soul properly to receive the sacrament and to allow its graces to
work in a timely and efficacious manner within a person's
heart.[17]

Garrigou-Lagrange's teaching on the Eucharist is
intimately bound up with the spiritual journey of the faithful.
The purpose of this sacrament is to bring the redemptive effects
of Christ's paschal mystery to the believing community as they
continue their journey to their heavenly homeland. The Mass
immerses those who participate in it into the mystery of Christ's
passion, death, and resurrection, an event, existing both in and
out of time, that carries the faithful to the foot of the cross, the
empty tomb, and beyond. This sacramental immolation of
Christ's body and blood releases the soul from the power of the
evil one and reestablishes the relationship between the human
and the divine. Without it, the faithful have no hope whatsoever
of finding their way to God. With it, they have the assurance of

---

[17] Ibid., 1:476-84; 2:289-99.

faith that they will find their way to God and that he will welcome them home and invite them to the heavenly banquet.[18]

In emphasizing the central role played by the Eucharist in the spiritual journey of the faithful, Garrigou-Lagrange demonstrates how Christ accompanies the faithful at every stage of their development. Those in the purgative stage recognize that, when properly disposed, they receive grace when they reverently assist at Mass, even when they are unable to receive Holy Communion. Christ's healing, salvific grace flows from the sacrifice itself and touches all who attend with an open heart. He underscores the important role of participation at Mass as members of Christ's body. As an action of Christ, the sacrificial offering of Christ involves not only the head, but also all of the members of the faithful. Although receiving Holy Communion represents the summit of the faithful's participation at Mass, he is quick to point out the many other ways in which the faithful can receive the spiritual fruits of Christ's sacrificial offering (e.g., reverent participation, attentive listening, spiritual communion). Christ, in other words, is always there to meet people where they are and accompany them along the way of conversion.[19]

Those in the illuminative way approach the Eucharist with a close intimacy with the Lord in both mind and heart. They approach it with a deep yearning for an even deeper intimacy and are drawn to the sacrament with a deeper consciousness of God's presence in their lives. According to Garrigou-Lagrange, the Eucharist enlightens the hearts and minds of those at this stage of the spiritual journey. It acts as a lantern or illuminating light which gives them a deeper knowledge of themselves, fills them with sanctifying grace, and enables them to respond more readily to the promptings of the Holy Spirit in their lives. At this

---

[18] Ibid.

[19] Ibid., 1:476-84.

stage of their journey, their prayer has become mystical, because the Spirit has gently moved from the background to the foreground of action in their lives. Holy Communion, for them, is the sacrament which deepens their knowledge of themselves, others, and God himself. The Spirit's action in their lives has become palpable and they are filled with gratitude for the deeper level of consciousness with which they have been blessed.[20]

Those in the unitive way can hardly distinguish the difference between themselves and God. So close is their intimacy with the divine that they feel as though they have been absorbed into the divine and the boundaries between themselves and God seem, at least from their perspective, to have become temporarily blurred. Garrigou-Lagrange points out that the Eucharist affirms their experience of union with Christ, as well as the other persons of the Trinity. Holy Communion signifies not only receiving the body and blood of Christ, but also entering into the intimacy of the Trinity itself. In this respect, the Eucharist is the sacrament of union with the divine. It represents not only the primary means of holiness for the faithful, but also the primary means through which they share in the intimate life of the Trinity. The Eucharist, in this respect, is the vehicle through which they attain the heights of intimacy with God. It invites them to become like little children and, by means of their lives lived in the Spirit, encourage others to do the same.[21]

---

[20] Ibid., 2:289-99.
[21] Ibid., 2:505-12.

Conclusion

Reginald Garrigou-Lagrange was a world-renowned theologian, teacher, and spiritual writer who introduced several generations of Catholic seminarians, priests, and religious to the intricacies of the spiritual life. He attracted students from all over the world to study under him and profit from his wisdom and profound learning concerning the spiritual life. His influence, moreover, extended not only throughout the world, but also to the highest levels of authority within the Church. To name one prominent example: when studying at the Angelicum, Karol Wojtyla, the future Pope John Paul II, wrote his doctoral thesis under his supervision on the topic of faith in St. John of the Cross.

Garrigou-Lagrange is remembered for his theological orthodoxy, prolific and comprehensive body of writings, and capacity to synthesize the abstract principles of Neo-Thomism with the experiential emphasis found in the writings of St. John of the Cross. He championed the idea that the mystical life was not for a select few, but was the normal outgrowth of the Christian life. He identified mysticism with intimacy with Christ leading to life in the Spirit and the expression of his manifold gifts and fruits. Mysticism, he believed, began in this life and ended in the next with the face-to-face encounter with God known as the beatific vision. He considered experiences such as ecstasy, interior visions and allocutions, and the stigmata as extraordinary graces given by God to someone for the good of the Church.

The Eucharist, for Garrigou-Lagrange, is the ordinary means to holiness established by Christ for his followers and the most reliable way to foster intimacy with Christ and his Spirit. It immerses those participating in it in Christ's paschal mystery and gives hope to those approaching it with faith and the right dispositions of one day seeing God face-to-face. For him, this intimate encounter takes place either in this life or in the world to come and involves a complete transformation of the believer so that a deep union might take place with the divine. In such a state, the person desires nothing but to do the will of God and rest in his presence. He or she is totally transfigured by sanctifying grace. Like Mary, the Mother of God, such a believer experiences the Gospel on a deep level of awareness. He or she proclaims the greatness of the Lord, glorifies him with praise and thanksgiving, and rejoices in the greatness of all that he has accomplished.[22]

Reflection Questions

- Garrigou-Lagrange believes the soul of the Mass was the same interior oblation of the heart of Christ that happened at Calvary. Do you think of the Mass in this way? Do you believe it manifests in an unbloody manner Christ's Good Friday sacrifice? What does this mean for your participation at Mass?

- Garrigou-Lagrange holds that the quality of our participation at Mass depends on where we are in our spiritual journey. Where are you in your spiritual journey? Do you consider yourself a beginner? Somewhere along the way? Nearing the end of it? How does your understanding of your spiritual life affect you understanding of what takes place at the celebration of the Eucharist?

- Garrigou-Lagrange maintains that the grace of the Eucharist will not be effective in our lives if we are not properly disposed to receive it. What does it mean to be properly disposed to receive the sacrament? What steps do you take to insure that you are? Do you examine

---

[22] Ibid., 1:147-58; 2:308-15, 559-67.

yourself before receiving Communion? Do you frequent the sacrament of reconciliation? Do you seek forgiveness from those you have offended?

Voice Four

Teilhard de Chardin:
Eucharistization of the Cosmos

Our next voice was one of the most creative (and controversial) Catholic thinkers of the twentieth century. Teilhard de Chardin (1881-1955) was born in the Château of Sarcenat at Orcines, studied philosophy and mathematics at the Jesuit college of Mongré, in Villefranche-sur-Saône, and entered the Jesuit novitiate at Aix-en-Provence in 1899. After earning a licentiate in literature in Caen in 1902, he taught physics and chemistry in Cairo, Egypt, at the Jesuit College of the Holy Family in Cairo, Egypt from 1905 to 1908, studied theology in Hastings, in Sussex (UK) from 1908 to 1912, and was ordained a priest in 1911. He worked in the paleontology laboratory of the *Museum National d'Histoire* in Paris from 1912-1914.

Teilhard served as a stretcher-bearer in the 8th Moroccan Rifles during World War I and received several citations for bravery. He pronounced his solemn vows as a Jesuit in 1918, studied natural science at the Sorbonne, lectured in geology at the Catholic Institute of Paris in 1920, and became a professor there after being granted a doctorate in science in 1922. He traveled to China in 1926 and would remain there for roughly 20 years, making from 1926 to 1935 a total of five geological research expeditions which enabled him to establish a geological map of China.

In addition to his scientific expeditions, Teilhard lectured extensively in Europe and the United States and was recognized for his groundbreaking insights into the dialogue between religion and science. His wide acclaim brought him to the attention the Vatican's Holy Office, which silenced him at various points in his career and prohibited him from publishing any works that would undermine the faith. His views on Christianity and evolution, once condemned, would be rehabilitated in later years by many mainstream Catholic theologians and authorities with close ties to the Holy See. A prolific author, he is probably best known to English readers for *The Divine Milieu* (1957), *The Phenomenon of Man* (1959), *Hymn of the Universe* (1961), *Christianity and Evolution* (2002), and *The Heart of the Matter* (2002). He wrote extensively on the Eucharist, because he believed it gave the world a clear indication of the spirituality of matter and marked the beginning of the recapitulation of all things in Christ, the Omega point of the universe.[1]

Teilhard's Theological and Spiritual Outlook

Unified and comprehensive in its outlook, Teilhard's thought underwent continuous development and is noted for a simplicity underlying its vast intellectual complexities. His anthropology is intimately connected to his cosmology, for he believes that human consciousness represents the culmination of the universe coming to a consciousness of itself. Man, for him,

---

[1] See Henri de Lubac, *Teilhard de Chardin: The Man and His Meaning*, trans René Hague. (New York: The New American Library, 1967), 13-21. For the stages of Teilhard's life and thought, see Emile Rideau, *Teilhard de Chardin: A Guide to His Thought*, trans. René Hague (London: Collins, 1967), 27-30. The dates after Teilhard's works refer to the appearance of the first English edition.

is both involved in the physical universe and transcendent to it. Our experience of isolation from the world results from an existential anxiety and fear of annihilation and can only be counteracted by a growing awareness that God is involved in a continuous creative process through which the orders of the natural and the supernatural converge.[2]

Christ is the initial point of contact between these two orders, the Omega point toward which humanity and, through it, all the universe are tending. Evolution is but a single aspect of a much larger process involving the movement of the cosmos to higher and higher levels of consciousness. Matter, in his mind, is a "matrix of spirit" moving toward ever higher and higher states of existence.[3] The biological, which he calls the "biosphere," is one such state; human life, which he associates with the "noosphere," yet another.[4] Both are tending toward yet another transcendent state, which he calls the "Omega Point."[5] This new level is both an immanent principle and a transcendent goal; it represents the inner dynamism behind all reality and the end toward which it tends. It is actual, stable, transcendent, and personal.[6] First localized in the person of Jesus of Nazareth, it gradually gathers all things to itself as it expands and opens itself up to the universal. For Teilhard, all things are being recapitulated into this universal, cosmic Christ.[7] With the exception of sin, everything forms a part of the movement of unbounded, and unconditional love at work in the

---

[2] Rideau, *Teilhard de Chardin*, 35-36.

[3] Ibid., 51-52.

[4] Teilhard de Chardon, *The Phenomenon of Man*, trans. Bernard Wall (New York, Harper and Brothers, 1959), 180-83, 190-211, Rideau, *Teilhard de Chardin*, 52-53.

[5] Rideau, *Teilhard de Chardin*, 57-60.

[6] Ibid., 58.

[7] Ibid., 60-62.

universe.[8]

Teilhard's theological, and spiritual outlook is rooted in the philosophical assumptions that the world as we know it is involved in a process of evolution toward ever higher and higher states of consciousness and that all matter is spiritual at its core and gradually being recapitulated into advanced forms of existence. This convergence of process and panpsychist (i.e, all reality participates in mind) thought leads him to construct a vision of the cosmos in which the orders of the natural and supernatural, while distinct, are in the process of converging into a unified, harmonious whole. A part of God's providential plan for the universe from time eternal, the movement toward this "New Creation" is working itself out in the universe's evolutionary movement through time. The mystery of the Incarnation represents a critical stage in this development and the doctrine of the Mystical Body of Christ points to its ever-expanding embrace. The Church and the sacraments, for Teilhard, are mediators of this divinizing process at work in the very fabric of the universe and the Eucharist is the concrete manifestation of this process becoming reality.[9]

Teilhard on the Eucharist

Teilhard was an ontological realist who believed that the sacraments operated not only "symbolically," but also "bio-logically."[10] The Eucharist, for him, is the sacrament of Christ par excellence and has a certain "devouring power" on those

---

[8] Ibid., 114-24, 138-40, 538n. 107.

[9] Christopher F. Mooney, *Teilhard de Chardin and the Mystery of Christ* (New York: Harper & Row, 1966), 68, 168.

[10] Joseph Fitzer, "Teilhard's Eucharist: A Reflection," *Theological Studies* 34(no. 2, 1973): 258.

who receive it.[11] Rather than our assimilating it through the process of digestion, it assimilates us and involves us in a process of divinization which he called "Christogenesis."[12] In this respect, it is the prototype through which God consecrates the universe and enters into a close, intimate relationship with it. This process entails a kind of *"eucharistization* of the universe," a process at work in the entire cosmos as it makes its way toward the Omega Point of the cosmic, universal Christ.[13]

Teilhard's teaching on the Eucharist hinges upon his unique interpretation of the mystery of the Incarnation and his analogous interpretation of the doctrine of transubstantiation. The Incarnation represents a stage in the evolution of the cosmos when matter itself sets out on a stage of being recapitulated into Christ. Cosmogenesis is subsumed into Christogenesis.[14] Christ in becoming man has initiated a much larger process of Christ becoming the entire universe. Although he does not go into great detail about how this process takes place or even how this insight conforms with traditional Catholic teaching, he is adamant in his assertion that as a result of the Incarnation matter itself is in the process of becoming incarnate.[15] In doing so, however, the cosmos is being divinized only in a derived and secondary sense; he seeks not to equate the universe with God or in some way dilute the substance of his divinity, but merely to show that God seeks to permeate the universe with his abiding and embracing presence.[16]

Teilhard correlates this innovative interpretation of the Eucharist with Catholic doctrine through an analogous

---

[11] De Lubac, *Teilhard de Chardin*, 61.

[12] Mooney, *Teilhard de Chardin*, 162.

[13] Fitzer, "Teilhard's Eucharist," 251.

[14] Ibid., 258.

[15] Ibid., 253.

[16] See De Lubac, *Teilhard de Chardin*, 27.

interpretation of the doctrine of transubstantiation.[17] While the bread and wine, are the primary analogates of the doctrine, the world is the secondary one. The bread are wine are transformed into the Body and Blood of Christ himself, yet point to an even greater change taking place on the level of the cosmos. Matter itself, according to this view, is being transformed into the presence of the universal, cosmic Christ. Teilhard is quick to maintain not only the importance of each of these understandings of transubstantiation, but also their close interconnection: "The center of Christ's personal energy is really situated in the Host. And, just as we rightly give the name of "our body" to the local center of our spiritual radiation (though that does not perhaps necessarily mean that our flesh is more ours than is any other matter) we must say that the initial Body of Christ, his *primary Body* is confined to the species of bread and wine."[18]

Although he has, at times, been accused of coming close to (if not embracing) a pantheistic view of the cosmos, a careful reading of Teilhard's thought shows that he is not so much pantheistic as panentheistic in his outlook. In other words, he holds a view that God penetrates every aspect of the universe, while at the same time extending infinitely beyond it. Teilhard has a difficult time rectifying the traditional Aristotelian matter/form categories upon which the doctrine of transubstantiation is based with a view of the Eucharist that falls more in line with a Neoplatonic understanding of the sacrament based on the notion of participation. As the cosmic Christ represents the universal form in which the historical Incarnate Word of God participates, so too the Eucharistic

---

[17] See Fitzer, "Teilhard's Eucharist, 255-59.

[18] Teilhard de Chardin, *Science and Christ*, trans. René Hague (New York: Harper & Row, 1968), 65; Fitzer, "Teilhard's Eucharist, 256.

sacrament of the world represents the universal form in which the consecrated species share. This underlying philosophical concept of participation enables him to extend the sacrament of the Eucharist beyond the eucharistic species of bread and wine to the entire cosmos.

In his *Hymn of the Universe*, Teilhard relates how his insight into the *eucharistization* of the cosmos stemmed from his inability to celebrate Mass during his scientific fieldwork and how he decided at one point to see the sacrifice of the Mass at work in the world at large: "Since...I have neither bread, nor wine, nor altar, I will raise myself beyond these symbols, up to the pure majesty of the real itself; I, your priest, will make the whole earth my altar and on it will offer you all the labors and sufferings of the world."[19] Through this expanded understanding of the Eucharist, Teilhard incorporates everything in the cosmos into the power, influence, and realism of the universal Christ. His subordination of the historical Jesus to the universal Christ is replicated in his understanding of the sacrament. Although the consecrated bread and wine are the primary analogates in this extension, the body of Christ in the world is, in his mind, the much deeper reality for it represents that towards which the sacrament tends.

Some Further Insights

Although this brief exposition of Teilhard's teaching on the Eucharist does not do justice to the complexity and various nuances of his thought, it highlights its relevance, for his overall theological vision shows how he sought to root his insights in the Church's traditional teaching on the Eucharist. The following observations develop some of the implications of his

---

[19] Teilhard de Chardin, *The Hymn of the Universe* (New York: Harper & Row, 1965), 19; Fitzer, "Teilhard's Eucharist, 252.

views and seeks to show their relevance for today's Catholics.

To begin with, Teilhard extends the meaning of the Eucharist in a way that seeks to preserve its sacramental integrity while, at the same time, accentuating its ramifications for the cosmic order. While the traditional Catholic teaching has no difficulty asserting the impact the sacrament should have on the spiritual and moral lives of the faithful, Teilhard takes a further step by extending its relevance to the ontological order. The sacrament, in this respect, embodies not only the transformation of bread and wine into the glorified body and blood of Christ, but also the transformation of the world of matter to a higher plane of spirit and consciousness, one that lifts it up into the very being of the universal Christ. One of the key difficulties in Teilhard's Eucharistic teaching concerns the way these two orders relate to one another and which of them takes precedence. From all indications, and despite heated claims to the contrary, Teilhard seems to opt for the priority (teleological if not historical) of the universal Christ and the Eucharistic world sacrament. This emphasis runs the risk of diminishing the importance of the original sacrament as the primary analogate or, in the very least, of shifting its preeminence to a secondary plane.[20]

Teilhard uses the concept of analogy to extend the meaning of the sacrament of the Eucharist to the cosmic order, identifying the bread and wine as the primary analogues and the world of matter as the secondary analogue in this sacramental extension. Analogy, however, always contains both a "likeness" and a "difference" and embraces different types, ranging anywhere from a simple metaphor to one involving proportionate likenesses and differences. Teilhard's failure to develop his analogical use of "transubstantiation" to any great extent leaves himself open to misinterpretation. Some critics

---

[20] Fitzer, "Teilhard's Eucharist, 255.

maintain that employing this analogy waters down the uniqueness of the sacrament as a eschatological sign of transcendence; others say he brings out the sacrament's hidden potential by connecting the order of the new creation to the world of matter. In addition to being a scientist, Teilhard, we must remember, was also a poet, theologian, and mystic. His vague and often imaginative use of language points to his own difficulty in finding appropriate concepts to convey his intuitions into the nature of the divine milieu.[21]

Teilhard's creative interpretation of the Eucharist caught the attention of the Holy Office on a number of counts and was at least partially responsible for his being silenced. By tying the sacramental order to the order of the cosmos, he could easily be accused, on the one hand, of collapsing the supernatural order unto the natural plane or, on the other hand, of extending the natural into the supernatural. Behind these accusations lay Teilhard's belief in the eventual convergence of the two orders in the Omega Point of the universal Christ. Also coming under suspicion was the seemingly facile way in which he ties the recapitulation of all things in Christ to the theory of evolution, as well as the way he uses the Eucharist as the means by which the world of matter is divinized and brought into the order of the New Creation. If these areas of concern caused the Holy Office to curtail the spread and general influence of these creative ideas, the rehabilitation of Teilhard's thought in later years has vindicated if not the orthodoxy of his ideas, then at least the Church's willingness to recognize in him a loyal son who sought to explore the boundaries and ramifications of some

---

[21] For an analysis of Teilhard's language, see Rideau, *Teilhard de Chardin*, 257-76. For Teilhard's general use of analogy, see De Lubac, *Teilhard de Chardin*, 161-68. For Teilhard's analogous use of "transubstantiation," see Fitzer, "Teilhard's Eucharist, 255-59.

of its most sacred teachings.[22]

The mystery of the Incarnation lies at the heart of Teilhard's extension of the Eucharist to the world. He believed that, by becoming man, God initiated a process of divinization that would ultimately extend to all humanity and the entire cosmos. In his *Hymn of the Universe*, he writes, "Through your own incarnation, my God, all matter is henceforth incarnate."[23] If this process begins in the mystery of the Incarnation, it is furthered at every celebration of the Eucharist and will reach its consummation when all matter is recapitulated into the universal Christ. This divine unfolding "in our midst" yet "still to come" emphasizes the return of all things to God while, at the same time remaining separate from him: "each of us is our own little microcosm in which the Incarnation is wrought independently with degrees of intensity, and shades that are incomemunicable."[24] The convergence of the natural and supernatural orders, in other words, does not bring about a fusion of the human and divine, but a dynamic union and harmony of wills and an ontological sharing in the divine.

Teilhard's teaching on the Eucharist has much more in common with a Platonic or Neoplatonic understanding of the sacrament than its classical Aristotelian/Thomistic counterpart.[25] As the universal Christ represents the form or pattern for the first historical realization of Christ in the person of Jesus of Nazareth, so does the universal sacrament of the Eucharist do

---

[22] For the controversies surrounding Teilhard's thought, see De Lubac, *Teilhard de Chardin*, 161-90.

[23] De Chardin, *The Hymn of the Universe*, 24, 26; Fitzer, "Teilhard's Eucharist, 253.

[24] Ibid., 28; 253.

[25] "...Teilhard's eucharistic fragments evidence, in and through the negativities of both decadent scholasticism and modern technology, an anguished yet joyful reinvention of a species of eucharistic Platonism." See Fitzer, "Teilhard's Eucharist," 263.

for the Mass. Teilhard, however, gives this Neoplatonic rendering of the sacrament a marked evolutionary flavor. Rather than the typical Neoplatonic framework of having lesser and lesser degrees of emanation flowing from the One, he equips the concrete localization of the Universal with an inner dynamism that moves it toward ever higher and higher degrees of complexity. The result is a hybrid model using Aristotelian/ Thomistic language (matter/form, transubstantiation), Neoplatonic ontology (participatory being), and Darwinian dynamism (evolution). Whether this represents a compre- hensive theory or a syncretistic blend of essentially incompatible concepts, it is clear that Teilhard's Neoplatonism softens his evolutionary bent and makes it more palatable to Christian sensitivities.

It has been said that, despite its analogous use of "transubstantiation," Teilhard's teaching on the Eucharist moves the sacrament away from this traditional under- standing of what takes place during the sacrament to a model of "transignification" that is more in line with the philosophical sensitivities of his time.[26] A change of "meaning," in other words, occurs rather than a change in "substance." Just as the bread and wine take on new significance in the light of Jesus' Last Supper with his disciples, so does the entire world of matter as the universal Christ celebrates his cosmic Mass and recapitulates all things in himself. While this approach to the sacrament solves the difficulties modern philosophers have with the notion of "substance," it is not at all clear that this is what Teilhard intends. "The Host," he states, is in the first place, and primarily, the fragment of matter to which, through transubstantiation, the Presence of the Incarnate Word attaches itself among us, that is to say in the human zone of the

---

[26] Ibid., 262.

universe."[27] Teilhard uses the term "transubstantiation" not merely out of respect for the tradition, but because he believes it conveys something unique about what takes place in the sacrament. For this reason, it would be better to say that he complements the traditional "transubstantiation" model with a "transignification" model to explain his understanding of the comic Eucharist.

Finally, Teilhard's teaching on the Eucharist cannot be fully understood apart from his devotion to the Catholic faith, his deep priestly fervor, and his formation in Jesuit spirituality. His scientific explorations and his attempt to bring them into dialogue with Catholicism stem from one of the fundamental principles of Ignatian spirituality: "to find Christ in all things." As a Catholic and as a priest dedicated to the administration of the sacramental mysteries, this meant, first and foremost, finding the Eucharist in all things—and vice versa. Even when silenced by the Holy Office, he saw this as an opportunity to bear the sufferings of Christ with courage the paschal mystery of the cosmic Christ manifested itself in the microcosm of his own life. No less a figure than Henri de Lubac has this to say about Teilhard's loyalty to the Catholic faith: "If this bold Christian sometimes, as has been said, came close to the edge of the precipice, it was his roots in the tradition, held firmly in place by his choice of unswerving fidelity, that saved him from a fall. We may, indeed, go further and say that it was from those roots that he drew nourishment for what we admire in him as being the most vigorously personal."[28] When seen in his light, Teilhard's teaching on the Eucharist represents an attempt on his part to remain faithful to the teachings of the faith while at the same time exploring new avenues of thought with a view

---

[27] De Chardin, *Science and Christ*, 65; Fitzer, "Teilhard's Eucharist, 255.

[28] De Lubac, *Teilhard de Chardin*, 13-14.

toward possible reformulations that would propel the tradition forward.

Although these observations barely skim the surface of Teilhard's profound insights into the Eucharist, they highlight the centrality of the sacrament for his thought and the key role it plays in his comprehensive vision of the cosmos. They also reveal his desire to probe the truths of the Catholic faith and to allow those truths to be questioned by the findings of empirical research. To a large extent, Teilhard's legacy is rooted in his eagerness to pursue this dialogue between religion and science, integrate his findings, and follow with persistence whatever path it set before him.

Conclusion

Teilhard de Chardin was a seminal Catholic thinker who sought to deepen his faith through the insights gained through scientific research. He was not afraid to let his empirical findings challenge his Catholic beliefs, since he held that the unity of Truth would not permit reason to undermine the doctrines of the faith. He used the insights of reason to explore the mysteries of the faith still further and to push the boundaries of orthodoxy to its limits. He is remembered as a foundational thinker whose unshaken faith in "the primacy of the Personal" led him to wed the insights of science, philosophy, and theology into a comprehensive vision of the universe.[29]

Teilhard was a pioneer in the dialogue between science and faith, a penetrating thinker who sought to synthesize the insights from a number of fields of inquiry into a unified, integral whole. His theory of the evolution of the universe—from the biosphere to the noosphere to the cosmic Christ—weds evolution to Christianity in a way never before imagined. His

---

[29] See Ibid., 26.

belief in the sentient nature of matter and the notion of the cosmic Christ recapitulating the entire universe led him to test the limits of Catholic orthodoxy and to pose new ways in which some of the most traditional doctrines of faith could be formulated. Even though he suffered for these innovative insights and took criticism from many directions, he remained intensely loyal to his Catholic and Jesuit moorings and followed the instructions of his superiors to the letter. He was a man who was ahead of his time and who unfortunately never lived to witness either the rehabilitation of his reputation or the vindication of many his most profound insights.

Teilhard's teaching on the Eucharist lies at the very heart of his thought. The "eucharistization" of the cosmos, as he calls it, has its roots in the mystery of the Incarnation and was extended by Christ to the world of matter when he celebrated his Last Supper with his disciples. This process of divinization continues every time the Eucharist is celebrated in the Church and will not relent until it converts the entire cosmos into the universal Christ celebrating the cosmic Mass at the Omega point, when all of reality will be recapitulated in his divine embrace. The Eucharist, for Teilhard, is the bridge between the historical Jesus and the cosmic Christ. It challenges believers to embrace a comprehensive vision of the cosmos, where the Lord of history converges with the cosmic Christ and where divinized creation offers itself as an eternal offering of love to the communion of divine love from which it came.

Reflection Questions

- Teilhard believes the Eucharist has a certain devouring effect on those who receive it. Have you ever thought of the sacrament in this way? Do you believe that the Eucharist assimilates those who receive it into itself through a process of divinization? Do you truly consider the Eucharist to be the "Bread of Life?"

- Teilhard has an analogous interpretation of the doctrine of transubstantiation, where matter itself is gradually being transformed into the presence of the universal, cosmic Christ. Does Teilhard's transformational view of the cosmos make any sense to you? What are its strengths and weaknesses? In what ways does it develop, complement, or depart from the traditional Catholic teaching?

- What do you think about Teilhard's notion of the *eucharistization* of the cosmos? Do you find it attractive? Does it challenge you to stretch your imagination? Does it make you feel uncomfortable? Does it fill you with wonder? Does it in any way affect your own spiritual outlook and the way you view the sacrament? What do theologians mean when they call the Eucharist the "Sacrament of the New Creation?"

Voice Five

Romano Guardini:
Sacrament of the New Creation

Our next voice has been called the "father of the twentieth-century Church."[1] Romano Guardini (1885-1968) was a German Catholic theologian whose writings on the Liturgy in many ways set the stage for the reforms of the Second Vatican Council. He was born of Italian parents in Verona, Italy, emigrated with his parents to Mainz, Germany at an early age, and became a German citizen in 1911. He was ordained to the priesthood in 1910, received his Ph.D. in theology in 1915, and spent the next five years in pastoral care and hospital work. In 1920 he began writing his *Habilitationschrift* in dogmatic theology, a second dissertation necessary to teach in a German university. In 1923 he began teaching theology at the Friedrich Wilhelm University in Berlin and continued in that position until the Nazis dismissed him in 1939. After the war, he accepted a position at the University of Munich in 1948 and taught there until his death in 1968. A prolific author, he wrote on a wide range of topics such as meditation and prayer, literature and art, education and philosophy, dogmatic and liturgical theology. His many writings include: *The Church and the Catholic* (1935), *The*

---

[1] See Silvano Zucal, "The Intellectual relationship between Joseph Ratzinger and Romano Guardini," at: http://www.ewtn.com/library/Theology/ratzinguardini.HTM.

Death of Socrates (1948), *The Lord* (1954), *The End of the Modern* World (1956), and *The Wisdom of the* Psalms (1968). His first book, *The Spirit of the Liturgy* (1918) offers much wisdom and insight into the nature of the Eucharist.[2]

Guardini's Spiritual Outlook

Guardini's spiritual outlook can best be understood by looking at the distinction he draws between personal and liturgical prayer. "Personal prayer and the Liturgy," he claims, "are the two main spheres of religious life, each one having its own roots and character and each its unique significance. In personal prayer man is alone with God and himself. The Liturgy, however, is a united prayer of the Christian community. In the Liturgy it is not *I* but *we*; and the *we* does not merely signify that many individuals are congregated. It is not a sum of individuals but a wholeness: the Church."[3] Man's spiritual life, in other words, possesses both personal and corporate aspects. As human beings, we relate to God both as unique individuals and as members of a corporate body, the Church. The Liturgy, Guardini maintains, is not the locus for personal prayer, but for the worship of the entire Christian community. Nor is it a mere gathering of individuals who come together to pray to God in

---

[2] The biographical information comes from Joanne M. Pierce, "Introduction" in Romano Guardini, *The Spirit of the Liturgy*, trans. Ada Lane (New York: Crossroad, 1998; originally published in German in 1918 as *Vom Gist der Liturgie*), 7-8. See also Robert A Krieg, "A Precursor's Life and Work," in Robert A. Krieg, ed., *Romano Guardini Proclaiming the Sacred in the Modern World* (Chicago: Liturgy Training Publications, 1995), 15-29.

[3] Romano Guardini, *The Art of Praying: The Principles and Methods of Christian Prayer*, trans. Prince Leopold of Loewenstein-Wertheim (Manchester, NH: Sophia Institute Press, 1957, 1985; originally published in German as *Vorschule des Betens*), 174.

their own private ways. It is a formal act of worship of the Church, the Body of Christ, who, united with the Glorified and Risen Lord, renders praise and adoration to the Father in heaven.[4]

This insight into the communal dimensions of the Liturgy permeates Guardini's spiritual outlook. Although he recognizes the dignity of each human being, he understands that this dignity is not denigrated, but elevated in the Church's liturgical worship. This idea may not seem new to those of us who have gone through the liturgical reforms of the Second Vatican Council. In his day, however, it was considered innovative, since the liturgy was popularly thought of as a personal matter between the individual and God and placed on the same footing as private devotions. That most of the faithful could not understand what was going on because Mass was said in Latin and because the priest recited the prayers *sotto voce* with his back to the people reinforced this tendency (at least in the popular mind) to look upon it as a work of the priest and a time when the faithful could concentrate on their own private prayers and devotions.

In his book, *The Spirit of the Liturgy*, Guardini focuses on the nature of the Church's liturgical worship. Written at a time when the Church was dealing with the secularizing tendencies the Modernist controversy, he takes pains to distance himself from this theological movement and seeks to preserve a sense of the sacred in Catholic belief and worship. For him, the prayer of the Liturgy "is the supreme example of an objectively established rule of spiritual life,"[5] the primary aim of which is not "the individual's reverence and worship for God. "[6] "In the Liturgy," he says, "God is to be honored by the body of the

---

[4] Ibid., 174-75.

[5] Guardini, *The Spirit of the Liturgy*, 18.

[6] Ibid., 19.

faithful, and the latter is in its turn to derive sanctification from this act of worship."[7] "Non-liturgical prayer," for him, "must take the liturgy for its model, and must renew itself in the liturgy."[8] The fellowship of liturgical worship, its universality in style, its potent symbolism, its measured playfulness, as well as its seriousness, are expressions of the entire body of believers mystically united to Christ by means of his redeeming action taking place in the liturgy.

In his spiritual outlook, Guardini also emphasizes "the primacy the of the *Logos* over the *Ethos*," meaning that the moral life has its roots in Truth and therefore presupposes a primacy of reason over the will.[9] "The Church," he maintains, "represents truth—dogma—as an absolute fact, based upon itself, independent of all confirmation from the moral or even the practical sphere. Truth is truth because it is truth. The attitude of the will to it, and its action towards it, is of itself a matter of indifference to truth."[10] The spiritual life, in other words, is not a matter of what the will says it is, but must be rooted in objective truth. "In the liturgy," he says, "the Logos has been assigned its fitting precedence over the will. Hence the wonderful power of relaxation proper to the liturgy, and its deep reposefulness. Hence its apparent consummation entirely in the contemplation, adoration and glorification of Divine Truth."[11] The Liturgy may seem removed from the troubles of everyday life, because it is primarily concerned with shaping what Guardini calls "the fundamental Christian temper."[12] Through the Liturgy, a person is led "to determine correctly his essential

---

[7] Ibid.

[8] Ibid., 20.

[9] Ibid., 85.

[10] Ibid., 91-92.

[11] Ibid., 94.

[12] Ibid., 86.

relation to God, and to put himself right in regard to reverence for God, love and faith, atonement and the desire for sacrifice. As a result of this spiritual disposition, it follows that when action is required of him he will do what is right."[13] The Liturgy renders glory and praise to God; in the process it shapes the Christian soul and move the person toward the good. For this reason, "[t]he Catholic liturgy is the supreme example of an objectively established rule of spiritual life."[14] This claim holds true especially for the Holy Sacrifice of the Mass.

Guardini's Teaching on the Eucharist

Guardini's views on the Eucharist flow directly from his understanding of the nature of the Liturgy. The Eucharist is the liturgical action of the Church *par excellence* and embodies all that the Liturgy is meant to be. By its very nature, it is a common act of the entire community of believers, living and dead. The worship of the Church is an action of Christ manifested in a formal, objective manner through his Mystical Body, the Church. The Eucharist is not the place for individual expression, but a sacred moment both in and out of time where the body of believers as a whole expresses its faith and offers its official worship to God. Ritual plays a very important role in the celebration of Eucharist: "From long experience...and by repeated examination and revision, the Church has shaped and reshaped the liturgical order. This order is more than a guide; it is a ruling which it is our duty to obey."[15]

As the corporate worship of the Church, the Eucharist manifests the depths of God's mercy, as well as the demands of

---

[13] Ibid.

[14] Ibid., 18.

[15] Guardini, *The Art of Praying*, 175.

his justice.[16] It manifests emotion, but under strict control so that it will speak to the body of believers as a whole and not to a select few.[17] As the sacrament of the New Creation, it builds on the created order. As grace builds on nature and as philosophy prepares the ground for theology, so does the Eucharist rely on civilization and all that it has to offer—poetry, literature, music, sculpture—to give voice to humanity's worship and praise to God. The Eucharist establishes a bond of fellowship. It gathers all that is genuinely human and places it in the hands of Christ to offer to our Father in heaven. It asks us to sacrifice our individuality, without denying it, and placing it in the service of community:[18] "The individual is, it is true, a member of the whole—but he is only a member. He is not utterly merged in it; he is added to it, but in such a way that he throughout remains an entity, existing of himself."[19] Such an action requires humility, the same humility manifested by Christ in becoming man and in becoming our food and nourishment.

The Eucharist, for Guardini, is a place where the natural and supernatural, the human and divine, meet and interact. As an offering to God, it takes the best of human culture and presents it as a symbol of our deep desire to give glory, honor, and praise to God. For this reason, it seeks to engage every aspect of the human person and lift him up to the level of the universal: "[T]he Church's directions on the adornment of the sanctuary, on vestments and altar vessels, with popular methods of decoration, and of dress on religious occasions; and the Gregorian chant with the popular hymn—we shall always find, within the sphere of the liturgy, that medium of spiritual expression, whether it consists of words, gestures, colors or

---

[16] Guardini, *The Spirit of the Liturgy*, 24.

[17] Ibid., 26.

[18] Ibid., 38.

[19] Ibid., 41.

materials, is to a certain degree divested of is singleness of purpose, intensified, tranquilized, and given universal currency."[20] The universal character of the Eucharist, its very catholicity, rests on its capacity to engage the person on this level. The Jesus of the Eucharist, for him, "is the Sovereign Mediator between God and man, the eternal High-Priest, the divine Teacher, the Judge of the living and of the dead; in his Body, hidden in the Eucharist, He mystically unites all the faithful in the great society that is the Church. He is the God-man, the Word made Flesh....He is truly and wholly human, with a body and a soul which have actually lived. But they are now utterly transformed by the Godhead, rapt into the light of eternity, and remote from time and space. He is the Lord 'sitting at the right hand of the Father,' the mystic Christ living on in His Church."[21]

As a genuine and effective symbol, the Eucharist, Guardini maintains, rises above the purely individual to deal with life in all its wholeness.[22] The bodily movements, actions, and material objects involved in its celebration have real significance, for they go beyond the particular and speak to the universal meaning of human destiny.[23] It is, at one and the same time, both playful and serious. Its purpose is to put those participating in touch with the basic questions of human existence and to place them face to face with the Risen and Glorified Lord. In doing so, it immerses us in a spiritual world where our souls can live and flourish: "The liturgy means that the soul exists in God's presence, originates in Him, lives in a world of divine realities, truths, mysteries and symbols, and really lives its true,

---

[20] Ibid., 46.
[21] Ibid., 48-49.
[22] Ibid., 57.
[23] Ibid., 60.

characteristic and fruitful life."[24] It also gives expression to the inner life of the believer: to "the assimilation, through the Holy Ghost, of the life of the creature to the life of God in Christ; the actual and genuine rebirth of the creature into a new existence; the development and nourishment of this life, its stretching forth from God in the Blessed Sacrament and the means of grace, towards God in prayer and sacrifice; and all this in the continual mystic renewal of Christ's life in the course of the ecclesiastical year.[25] He goes on to say: "The fulfillment of all these processes by the set forms of language, gesture, and instruments, their revelation, teaching, accomplishment and acceptance by the faithful, together constitute the liturgy."[26] The Eucharist, for Guardini, represents all these things—and so very much more: "When we assist at Holy Mass, we must know that we are close to the font of all grace."[27] This sacrament, for him, is the primary means by which Christ and his Church shape the Christian temperament.

Some Further Insights

The above presentation of Guardini's teaching on the Eucharist, while in no way exhaustive, offers many unique insights into its meaning as a liturgical action and its significance for the community of believers. His views toward the liturgy as a whole, and the Eucharist, in particular, invite a number of remarks on the nature and scope of the sacrament.

Guardini's distinction between personal prayer and liturgical worship highlights the individual and communal dimensions of the human person. These dimensions are found

---

[24] Ibid., 66-67.

[25] Ibid., 82

[26] Ibid., 82-83.

[27] Ibid., 83.

in every Eucharistic celebration. When at Mass, each person participates in the corporate prayer of the Church without losing his or her identity. The highly individualistic character of modern Western culture makes it easy for believers to lose sight of the communal nature of the sacrament and to focus solely on their private, personal concerns. The Eucharist does not neglect the private concerns of believers, but elevates them by assimilating them into the concerns of the Church universal.

The communal nature of the Eucharist lies at the very heart of its identity. The sacrament, indeed all liturgical celebrations, are actions of the Risen Lord and his Mystical Body, the Church. Guardini brought this all-important dimension to Catholic sacramental worship back into focus and, in doing so, helped pave the way for many of the liturgical forms of the Second Vatican Council. When seen in this light, the Eucharist encompasses but goes far beyond an act of private worship. It is the corporate worship of the People of God who, with Christ as their Head, render thanksgiving, glory, and praise to God.

For Guardini, the Liturgy is an established rule of spiritual life rooted in the objective order that allows God's people to honor him and be sanctified by him. Of these two aspects of worship, the latter presupposes the first. That is to say that those gathering for Eucharist should not be concerned with what they receive or "get out of" the Mass, but concentrate instead on their participation in the corporate worship of the Church. The Eucharist is the worship of the Church *par excellence* and should not be diminished by placing it on the same level of private devotion, even those that focus more on adoration and praise. At the same time, it is the source of all genuine devotion—both personal and communal—for our voices are heard only because of the Redemptive action of Christ that is both memorialized and realized in its sacred action.

The Eucharist, for Guardini, makes us fully human by continuing in us the process of divinization begun in us at

Baptism. It embraces our deepest aspirations and transforms them into the something far greater than we could ever imagine. At Mass, the priest takes bread and wine, the work of human hands, and transforms them through the work of the Holy Spirit into the Body and Blood of Our Lord Jesus Christ. The gifts offered by the priest represent everything offered up by the believing community. God accepts the humble work of human hands and transforms them into something truly worthy of the Kingdom. As grace presupposes and builds on nature, so does the Eucharist build on the work of human civilization and transforms it. As the sacrament of the New Creation, it is an action of Christ and his body, the Church and continues in time and space the gradual process of turning the City of Man into the City of God.

For Guardini, the Eucharist's symbolism is a genuine expression of our human condition and the destiny toward which we are headed. It avoids any dualistic tendencies that would place matter in opposition to spirit or the material against the immaterial, and does so by embracing the material world and elevating it to a higher level, one that does not deny its material properties, but transforms and glorifies them. As such, it points to the ultimate transformation of humanity into a new humanity—one rooted in Christ, the New Adam— of Jerusalem into the Heavenly Jerusalem. The symbolism of the Eucharist effects what it signifies. When seen in this light, the Eucharist and the other sacraments represent the first fruits of the world's transformation in Christ.

Guardini claims that the Eucharist gives shape to the Christian temperament. Its goal is to root us in Christ so that his attitudes, dispositions, and attitudes become our own. The moral life flows from this gradual process of assimilating the mind of Christ. This process comes about not through human effort alone, but primarily by the grace of God. The Eucharist is a major means by which God's divinizing grace transforms us and molds us into a likeness of his Son. The moral life is not something we create through an act of the will, but the fruit of our participation in the divine nature, the *Logos*. The moral life, in other words, flows from life in Christ—not vice versa. The Christian moral life is all about putting on the mind of Christ and allowing him to act in and through us. We need to be aware of "putting the cart before the horse" and thinking that it is the other way around.

Finally, according to Guardini, the Eucharist makes sense only when viewed through the eyes of the Church's faith. Those who see it otherwise, may speak of its lack of utility and perhaps even complain that it is throwback from the past, and strangely out of place in today's workaday world. Its purpose, we might say, lies precisely in that it has no "this-worldly" purpose. It delves beneath appearances and puts us in touch with our deeper intuitions, which are so often buried beneath the concerns of daily life. It focuses on the one thing that matters— our relationship to God— and in doing so brings meaning to all of life's other activities. It looks to the questions of ultimate meaning, those related to the purpose of our existence, our origins, and our destiny. Its purposeful purposelessness allows it to be focused yet at rest, serious yet playful, in, yet out, of time.

These remarks represent just a few of the implications of Guardini's overall spiritual outlook and teaching on the Eucharist for today. They remind us to delve beneath the level of appearances and to ponder the meaning of this sacrament through the eyes of Christ. Most of all, they remind us of the sacrament's corporate nature and its hallowed position as the primary means by which the Church with Christ as its Head renders glory and praise to God.

Conclusion

Romano Guardini was a profound thinker whose ideas anticipated the reforms of the Second Vatican Council. In his earliest work, *The Spirit of the Liturgy*, he emphasizes the corporate character of the Church's liturgical celebrations and sets them apart from mere private devotions. As the corporate worship of the body of believers, the liturgy embraces the universal aspirations of humanity and emphasizes its objective grounding in the Truth. The Mass, for him, is the highest expression of the Church's formal worship and shapes the character and temperament of the believing community.

The Eucharist, for Guardini, has many facets: it is part of the official prayer of the Church; it engenders fellowship; it employs a style that highlights the universal aspects of the Christian message; it is rich in symbolism that effects what it signifies; it has an air of playfulness about it, yet is serious about the Truth it celebrates of humanity's redemption in Christ Jesus; it generates the *Ethos* of Christian morality; it exalts in all things the primacy of the *Logos*, who is Christ himself. These many facets combine to preserve its sacramental mystery and point to something that is, at one and the same time, both within its grasp and far beyond it. The Eucharist—the official, formal worship of the Church— is rooted in the objective order. The Church celebrates it, because it longs for the fullness of this order and the transformation of all humanity (and, with it, all creation) in Christ.

Guardini's views on the Eucharist remind today's believers that the liturgy is, first and foremost, a communal action whereby Christ and his Body, the Church, give glory, praise and thanksgiving to God, the Father. We go to Mass to worship God and to be sanctified by the redemptive grace made possible as a result of Christ's sacrificial offering. We go there not to get something out of it (although *that* we do), but to offer ourselves to the Father as members of Christ's Mystical Body. Guardini's views anticipated the liturgical reforms that took place in the Second Vatican Council and continue to this day. As a precursor of these reforms, he helped to shape Catholic thought for years to come and the trajectory it would take after his death and into the new millennium.

Reflection Questions

- Guardini emphasizes the corporate action of the Eucharist over the personal. How do you view the sacrament's relationship to these two dimensions? Do you participate in the Liturgy for your own personal spiritual needs or to take part in the communal act of worship? How are the two related? Which takes precedence in your spiritual life?
- The Eucharist, for Guardini, continues the process of divinization that begins in us at Baptism. What does it mean for human nature to become divinized? What manifestations does one look for? Have you experienced this process in your own life? If we can be divinized, is it also possible for the reverse process to take place?
- The Eucharist, for Guardini, gives to shape the Christian temperament. Does this happen automatically? What attitudes toward the sacrament must one have for the sacrament to do its work? What are the dispositions proper to this temperament? Has the sacrament enabled you to be a more loving and caring person? Has it helped you to grow in faith?

Voice Six

Ronald Knox:
Religious Drama

Our next voice was one of the most influential Catholic priests in the English-speaking world during the first half of the twentieth century. Ronald Knox (1888-1957) was born into a low Church Anglican family (his father was an Anglican bishop), he was educated at Eton, moved to the Anglo-Catholic branch of the Church of England at the age of sixteen, studied classics at Oxford, became an Anglican priest in 1912, served in army intelligence during the First World War, converted to Catholicism in 1917, and was ordained a Catholic priest in 1918. He tells the story of his conversion to Catholicism in his autobiography *A Spiritual Aeneid* (1918). A man of many talents—preacher, broadcaster, journalist, novelist, scholar, Bible translator—he was assigned to St. Edmund's College from 1919-1926 and was chaplain to the Catholic undergraduates at Oxford from 1926-1939. He became a Monsignor in 1936 and was offered the presidency of St. Edmund's College, Oxford in 1939, a position he refused thinking he was not a good administrator and that he could serve the Church in better ways.

In 1939, Knox resigned his university position to become the private chaplain to Lord and Lady Acton and devote his time to writing, preaching, and lecturing. At this point, he started working on a new English translation the Latin Vulgate, a task that would be one of his principal concerns for the remaining years of his life. A friend to other prominent Catholic literary figures such as Maurice Baring, G.K. Chesterton, Evelyn Waugh, and Hilaire Belloc, his literary corpus covered a wide range of genres: autobiography, essays, sermons, apologetics, translations, detective novels, literary criticism, satire, popular and academic theology, and others. In addition to his translation of the Latin Vulgate, he is most remembered for his radio broadcasts during the Second Word War, his codification of the rules of detective fiction, and such works as *Some Loose Stones* (1913), *Reunion All Round* (1914), *A Spiritual Aeneid* (1918), *The Belief of Catholics* (1927), *Caliban in Grub Street* (1930), *Heaven and Charing Cross* (1935), *Let Dons Delight* (1939), *Captive Flames* (1940), *The Mass in Slow Motion* (1948), *The Creed in Slow Motion* (1949), *The Gospel in Slow Motion* (1950), *Enthusiasm* (1950), *Stimuli* (1951), and *The Window in the Wall* (1956). His teaching on the Eucharist appears primarily in his works on religious themes, especially in his sermons and retreat conferences.[1]

Knox's Theological Outlook

Knox's theological outlook was shaped by a wide variety in internal and external influences: his training in the classics, his wide range of interests, his conversion to Catholicism from Anglicanism, and his friendships with a slew of like-minded Catholic intellectuals—to name but a few. Although he wrote

---

[1] The biographical information in this section comes from "The Ronald Knox Society of North America," http://www.ronaldknoxsociety.com. See this website also for a compete bibliography of Knox's writings. For an audio file of some of Knox's Eucharistic sermons, see *A Month of Sunday Sermons with Monsignor Knox* at ignatius.com.

across a wide variety of literary genres and conducted his priestly ministry in a number different contexts (e.g., university chaplain, apologist, lecturer, radio broadcaster, newspaper journalist, retreat master, novelist, preacher), everything he did was motivated by a devotion to Catholic orthodoxy and a desire to defend its truth, promulgate its message, and make it accessible to as wide an audience as possible, Catholic and non-Catholic alike. His radio broadcasts during the Second Word War, his detective novels, his English translation of the Latin Vulgate, his religious essays, sermons, retreat conferences, and many popular works of Catholic theology and spirituality point to his deep desire to serve God by means of the skill of the pen and the power of the spoken word.[2]

Although he did not have an extensive theological education and deferred to the opinion of qualified experts, Knox had a deep love for Scripture, a keen literary eye, and a resolute passion for the truth. His sermons and religious conferences display a unique talent for going to the essential truth of an issue and dealing with it in a way that persuaded both mind and heart. He was a master at employing images and metaphors that ignited the imagination to lead his readers and listeners into a deeper encounter with the truths of the faith and, ultimately, the Truth of the faith Himself, our Lord and Savior, Jesus Christ. Knox had an intense fervor for the Catholic faith that was typical of someone who converted at no small personal cost. He also brought to his newfound faith many of the sensitivities of his Protestant upbringing, not the least of which were his love for Scripture, his Christocentric focus, and his dedication to the ministry of the Word. The loss of many in his close circle of friends to the ravages of the First World War led him to take stock of his life and to look more deeply at previously unexamined aspects of his childhood faith. His journey to

---

[2] Ibid.

Catholicism was fueled by his passion for the truth and a desire to follow his conscience in matters of faith, regardless of the consequences. He displayed a breadth of interests comparable to that of G. K. Chesterton (1874-1936), his older contemporary whose writings and friendship had a profound influence on his life.[3]

Along with C. S. Lewis, Knox was one of the most popular and sought-after popular writers of his day. Although the two authors were not close friends and met only on a rare occasions, they shared a mutual respect for each other and wrote on similar topics, ranging from apologetics, to the person of Jesus Christ, the evidence for miracles, the nature of evil and suffering, the Church, prayer, and the last things. Lewis once described Knox as "possibly the wittiest man in Europe."[4] Although Lewis concentrated on what he termed "Mere Christianity" and focused more on themes common to all Christians, Knox wrote primarily within the Catholic tradition and tried to deepen his fellow Catholics' appreciation of the faith and help those outside the tradition to understand its significance and relevance for their lives. His writings on the Eucharist flow from his staunch Catholic viewpoint and deeply held belief in the centrality of the sacrament for the Christian life.

Knox's Teaching on the Eucharist

Knox's teaching on the Eucharist appears in his many of his sermons, which were written throughout the course of his career for various liturgical celebrations and popular devotions such as Forty Hours Devotion and the Feast of Corpus Christi,

---

[3] Ibid.

[4] Walter Hooper, "Foreword," in Milton Walsh, *Second Friends: C. S. Lewis and Ronald Knox in Conversation* (San Francisco: Ignatius Press, 2008), 9.

and in such popular works as *Heaven and Charing Cross* (1936), *Mass in Slow Motion* (1948) and *The Window in the Wall: Reflections on the Holy Eucharist* (1956). Although he wrote on a wide variety of themes, he generally focused on the doctrine of the Real Presence, the Sacrifice of the Mass, and the Eucharist and the Church. According to Milton Wash, "The Eucharist was at the center of Knox's life both as a Catholic and a priest; far from being tormented by the question "What is this?" he rejoiced in exploring the significance of the Body and Blood of Christ....Knox's sermons on the Eucharist present the profound doctrinal teaching of the Church in an imaginative, biblical way."[5]

This imaginative presentation of the Eucharist is seen very clearly in Knox's *The Mass in Slow Motion*, where he tries "to analyze ...the inwardness of my own Mass; talk about the odd bells that ring in my mind, the odd vistas that open up to my own view, to close again at once, in the hope that they may have some value for other people."[6] In this book, Knox offers twelve sermons that focus on the different parts of the Mass, from the prayers at the foot of the altar to the *Ite Missa est*. His purpose in going through the Mass in this way was to give his audience— school-girls at the convent school of the Assumption sisters—a clear understanding of what happens at Mass, especially at its most solemn moment. Of the consecration, Knox writes: "I ask that the bread and wine may be blessed; that they shall form a reasonable sacrifice, and therefore an acceptable sacrifice. We do not under the Christian dispensation, offer to God dumb animals or lifeless things, but it will be all right about the bread and wine, because, once consecrated, they will be built into the human Body of our Lord Jesus Christ. And, finally, I ask that

---

[5] Walsh, *Second Friends*, 247-48.

[6] Ronald Knox, *The Mass in Slow Motion* (New York: Sheed and Ward, 1948), ix-x.

they may be accepted. Then, with two more signs of the Cross, I ask God to perform this miracle of Transubstantiation."[7] The Mass, for Knox, is a kind sacred dance, a religious drama that captures the central features of the Catholic faith. Of course, he is explaining the Mass as it was celebrated in its pre-Vatican II form, which cultivated a mysterious, sacred aura, as the priest whispered Latin quietly with his back to the people. By going through it step-by-step, Knox seeks to convey the meaning of the deep symbolism of the Mass in a way that even school children could understand. In an earlier passage, he claims that adults can enjoy it only "by pretending to be a child. *Nisi efficiamini sicut parvuli.*"[8]

In *The Window in the Wall,* Knox presents the Eucharist as "the thing that matters," the Mass is the place where God restores his ancient mercies: "For us the immediate, dazzling truth is that here and all over the world Christ, in the person of the Christ, is offering Christ under the forms of Bread and Wine in perfect sacrifice to the eternal Father. If I am worthy, if I am willing, he gives himself for me, as for all mankind, his brothers; on earth, as in heaven, he is our High Priest and representative."[9] "And we Catholics," he further notes, "have the assurance that this is being done, whenever we go into a church and find a priest saying Mass."[10] In the Eucharist, Knox indicates that the priest celebrates *in persona Christi* and that this takes place by virtue of his priestly ordination, regardless of his personal holiness or what we think about him personally. Through the priest, the community of the faithful stretches out our hands and offers God gifts of Bread and Wine. God, in turn,

---

[7] Ibid., 109.

[8] Ibid., vii.

[9] Ronald Knox, *Window in the Wall* (New York: Sheed and Ward, 1956), 76, 78.

[10] Ibid., 77.

accepts these gifts and transforms them into the Body and Blood Christ. If we offer the direction of our lives to God, Knox assures us that we will come to know what it means to lead an ordered life, one in which our minds and hearts become whole, and we are made to live in holy communion with him.[11]

Some Further Insights

Although this brief exposition of Knox's teaching on the Eucharist does not do justice to the breadth of his knowledge or span of his imagination, it conveys his profound loyalty to the truths of the Catholic faith and his deep desire to convey them in a fresh new way to as wide an audience as possible. The following remarks seek to tease out some of the implications of Knox's teaching and highlight their relevance for today.

To begin with, Knox's conversion to Catholicism had much to do with the question of authority and doubts he entertained about the validity of Anglican Orders. As he writes in *A Spiritual Aeneid*, "authority played a large part in my belief, and I could not now find that any certain source of authority was available outside the pale of the Catholic Church."[12] It was divine authority that, for him, validated the Catholic priesthood and the celebration of the sacraments, especially the Eucharist. Knox's faith rests in the apostolic authority of the Catholic Church and the authenticity of its sacramental order. Since he sees the priesthood and the Eucharist as inextricably linked, it follows that the validity of one depends on the validity of the other. When seen in this light, Knox's faith in the Eucharist is preeminently apostolic. It flows from Christ's institution of the priesthood at the Last Supper and remains authentic through

---

[11] Ibid., 52.

[12] Ronald Knox, *A Spiritual Aeneid*, 2d ed. (London: Burns and Oates, 1950), 212.

an unbroken line of apostolic succession. His conversion to Catholicism has much to do with his understanding of the nature of the Church and the sacramental economy of salvation.

Knox also makes great use of the imagination to convey his Eucharistic teaching. His training in the great works of Western civilization gave him a deep appreciation for the stories and dramas that shape our lives to this day. He thinks of the Mass as a sacrament that immersed believers in the great drama of their salvation, and he uses images and metaphors that give his readers and listeners a deeper appreciation of what they are celebrating. The Eucharist, for him, is God's re-imagining of humanity, a creation disfigured by the ravages of sin and in drastic need of inner healing and transformation. By immersing the faithful into the great narrative of Christ's passion, death, and resurrection, it gives meaning to their lives and helps them make sense of their daily activity. He used the powers of the imagination to spread the Gospel message. The images and metaphors he employed were carefully chosen to attract attention (even curiosity) so as to impress upon the Catholic imagination the great significance of the Church's teaching.

The title of one of Knox's collection of sermons, The Window in the Wall, *gives an apt description of how he viewed the sacrament's importance for his spiritual life.* The phrase comes from *The Song of Songs* and refers to a lover whispering through a window in a wall to his true love saying, "Rise up, rise up quickly, dear heart, so gentle, so beautiful, rise up and come with me"(Sg 2:10).[13] The Eucharist, for Knox, was just that, a window in the wall where Christ whispers words of love to those who believe in him and love him. In this sense it is a portal, a window to eternity, a place in time and space that opens up to the eternal. The sacrament, in other words, helps the believer listen to the words of Christ and respond to them with the heart

---

[13] Knox, *The Window in the Wall*, 1.

of a lover. One falls in love with Christ by drawing ever closer to that window and listening to that voice and to its warm, endearing words. The Eucharist, for Knox, is closely linked to the voice of Christ. After all, Christ himself speaks through the priest every time he pronounces the words of institution. The Eucharist mediates the love of Christ to each member of the faithful. It does so for the believing community as a whole, as well as for each individual member.

Another of Knox's books, The Mass in Slow Motion, goes through the drama of the Eucharistic liturgy step-by-step. Using the analogy of a slow motion movie, he shares his own thought processes with his reading audience in the hope of giving them a more intimate sense of what takes place both in the external ritual of the Mass and within the priest himself as he celebrates the sacrament *in persona Christi*. By analyzing the inwardness of his own Mass, he hopes to bring the worshipper closer to the mind of the priest and, through him, to the mind of Christ himself. He does so not to draw attention to himself, for he is fully aware of his own human weaknesses and inadequacies, but to highlight the wonder of the Mass and the drama of Christ's paschal mystery that it makes present. The image of the Mass "in slow motion" has a twofold purpose: it connects the Eucharist to the movie technology of his day, making the sacrament more palatable to the sensitivities of the day; it also says something very profound about the relationship between historical time (*Chronos*) and sacred time (*Kairos*). For Knox, Time and Eternity touch during the drama of the Mass. We need to examine it "in slow motion" to grasp its deep inner meaning and relevance for our lives.

In keeping with the sacramental realism of the Catholic tradition, however, Knox sees the Eucharist not merely as a narrative representation of Christ's paschal mystery, but an actual presence of that timeless mystery in the here-and-now. He understands that Christ's passion, death, and resurrection happen both in time and out of time, and that the Mass is the sacrament instituted by Christ to put the faithful in touch with the culminating events of the history of salvation. The Mass is much more than a drama; it is salvation itself. It brings Christ's paschal mystery into the present moment and enables those who partake in it to wash themselves clean in the Blood of the Lamb. The Eucharist, for him, is Christ's saving mystery made present in the form of bread and wine. It extends Christ's offer of the fullness of life to all people, of every time, and in every place. It is the most universal of the sacraments and the most catholic.

Knox sees the Eucharist as a banquet, a presence, and a sacrifice. He sees it as a memorial of the Last Supper and a foretaste of the heavenly banquet. He also sees it as a sacred meal in which those present participate and of which they partake. This meal is celebrated by the priest *in persona Christi,* and indicates that more is happening than meets the eye. When seen through the eyes of faith, Christ himself is the principal celebrant who sits at the head of the table sharing food with his disciples. What is more, he is not only present in the person of the priest, but also in the very food that is shared   This real presence of Christ in the sacrament comes out more clearly when we see that the Eucharist is also a sacrifice and Christ its sacrificial victim. When the priest says, "Take and eat, for this is my body" and "Take and drink, for this is my blood," Christ himself offers himself as the sacrificial lamb for the sins of the world. For Knox, the events of Holy Thursday, Good Friday, and Easter Sunday are inextricably linked, and the Eucharist is the sacramental in which all of the events of this single mystery inhere.

Knox's view of the Eucharist is also intimately tied to the Church. As the Body of the Christ, the sacrament embodies the whole of the Risen and Glorified Christ, who continues to live in history through the members of his Mystical Body. The

Eucharist is the sacrament of Christ's Body and Blood. It is the food that binds its members together and gives them the spiritual and moral strength of followers of Christ. The Eucharist is a sacrament of the Church just as the Church is a sacrament of Christ. The Church exists for the Eucharist—and vice versa. Knox has a very keen sense of the sacrament's institution by Christ for his apostles and the community of believers. He recognizes that the Eucharist exists within the Church and for the Church. The sacrament makes sense only when seen through the eyes of faith, and it is the Church, the body of believers, that recognizes its true worth. The Body of Christ, in other words, recognizes the Body of Christ. The Eucharist is Eucharist, because the Church is Church.

Conclusion

Ronald Knox was one of the most prominent Roman Catholic priests of the twentieth century. Trained in Oxford's course in the classics (the so-called Greats), he was a man of many talents who used them to further the cause of the faith both within the Church and outside of it. Although his background was more in classical literature than in the nuances of theological reasoning, he wrote on a variety of religious issues to great effect, usually in the context of his preaching and retreat conferences.

Knox was a great communicator and employed his writing skills in a variety of literary genres (sermons, autobiography, apologies, novels, newspaper articles, radio broadcasts, translations, and others) that sought to engage the Catholic imagination and make it attractive to his readers and listeners. He used the images and metaphors as a way of engaging both mind and heart to lead his audience to a deeper awareness of the sacred lurking in the ordinary circumstances of everyday life. His impact on the Catholicism of his day went beyond the shores of Great Britain to the rest of the English-speaking world, and beyond. He had a deep love for the Church, a fondness for Scripture, a profound sense of the drama of the Mass, an unwavering belief in the Real Presence of Christ in the Blessed Sacrament, and a finely tuned awareness of the priest celebrating the sacrament *in persona Christi.*

In the final analysis, Knox's teaching on the Eucharist was informed by his own personal journey of faith and rooted in his deep respect for the authority of the apostolic tradition. It was traditional, easy to follow, imaginative, and comprehensive. In his many sermons and writings on the sacrament hardly a theme relevant to Catholic belief concerning the sacrament was left untouched. To this day, his writings are read, his teachings inspire, and his legacy endures. His impact on the Catholic imagination will likely continue for some time to come.

Reflection Questions

- Knox uses images and metaphors that give his readers and listeners a deeper appreciation of how the Eucharist immerses them in the mystery of salvation. What images come to your mind when you think of the sacrament? How would you explain the Eucharist to someone who asks why it is so central to the Catholic faith?
- Knox sees the Eucharist as a banquet, a presence, and a sacrifice. Do these three dimensions of the sacrament make sense to you? Do they have equal weight in your spirituality? Is one more important to you than the others? What aspect of the Eucharist is most important to you in your daily life?
- Knox's view of the Eucharist is intimately tied to the Church. How do you understand the relationship between Christ's presence in the sacrament and the body of believers? What is the relationship of each to the body of

the Glorified and Risen Lord? What happens when you receive the Eucharist? Why does the sacrament make sense only when viewed through the eyes of faith?

Voice Seven

Josef A. Jungmann:
Memorial Celebration

Our next voice was one of the leading catechists and liturgists of the twentieth century. Josef A. Jungmann, S.J. (1889-1975) was born in the South Tyrolia region of Austria, studied at Brixen, Innsbruck, Munich and Vienna, was ordained in 1913 and, after some years of pastoral experience, entered the Society of Jesus in 1917. He taught pastoral theology at the University of Innsbruck from 1925 until the Nazis closed it in 1939. He resumed his teaching duties when the university reopened in 1945 and remained there for the remainder of his academic career. In 1956, he was named professor emeritus of pastoral theology. He was a *peritus* at the Second Vatican Council and a member of the committee responsible for composing *Sacrosanctum concilium* ("The Constitution on the Sacred Liturgy," 1963). In 1972, he was awarded an honorary doctorate from the University of Salzburg. A prolific author, he is associated with the kerygmatic movement of catechetics and probably most remembered for his magisterial two-volume work, *The Mass of the Roman Rite: Its Origins and Development* (1948). The Eucharist is a recurrent theme in his writings.[1]

Jungmann's Spiritual Outlook

In his early years of parish ministry, Jungmann was struck by the stark contrast between the fear that permeated the minds of so many of his parishioners and the message of joy contained in the Gospel. His reflection on this discrepancy led to his work, *The Good News and Our Proclamation of the Faith* (1915), which emphasized the *kerygma* in catechetical instruction and sought to replace such fear with the joy of life in Christ. This focus on the *kerygma* led to a concentration on the liturgy, since it was through the Church's official worship that the values of the kingdom could best be communicated to the faithful. The Liturgy, in his mind, was a sacrifice of thanksgiving and a celebration of joy in the redemption of humanity accomplished through Christ's paschal mystery. The kerygma lies at the very heart of the Church's worship, and the Good News is a message of hope rooted in faith in Christ and the revelation of God's merciful love manifested through his sacrificial offering.[2]

In his Foreword to *The Rite of the Roman Mass*, Jungmann explains how he decided to research the origins and developments of the Latin Rite shortly after the University of Innsbruck and the Jesuit college were closed by the Nazis after

---

[1] The historical details come from Michael P. Horan, "Josef A. Jungmann (1889-1975), http://liturgicalleaders.blogspot.com/2008/09/josef-jungmann.html. See also, https://translate.google.com/translate?hl=en&sl=it&u=https://it.wikipedia.org/wiki/Josef_Andreas_Jungmann&prev=search.

[2] Ibid.

their invasion of Austria in 1939.[3] Freed from his teaching responsibilities, he thought a historical study of the Mass would be a worthy project to pursue: "I made up my mind to dedicate the time thus left free to me to an exposition of the Mass-liturgy. For that seemed to me to be the theme most useful to handle in a time of stress like this."[4] He was very much aware of the work's limitations and asked his readers to be mild in their judgment of it: "Do not think I am deluding myself with the belief that, for all this diligence, the work does not suffer certain weaknesses. It is a child of war; children of war have a claim to a milder judgment. It was difficult, and in some instances—even after the war—impossible, to procure the pertinent new literature from the foreign press. And manuscripts and *incunabula* for the whole period under consideration were for all practical purposes unavailable."[5] Limited though it may be, Jungmann offers his scholarship in the service of the Church and claims that his work is more than a historical study: "[T]his book is not meant to serve only for knowledge— but it is intended for life, for a fuller grasp of that mystery of which Pope Pius XII says in his encyclical *Mediator Dei*: 'The Mass is the chief act of divine worship; it should also be the source and center of Christian piety.'"[6]

Jungmann's dedication to scholarship was an essential part of his spiritual outlook. He considered his work potentially life giving, since a sound knowledge of the past was necessary for the decisions being made in the present. He liked to quote Cardinal Newman: "the history of the past ends in the present;

---

[3] Josef A. Jungmann, *The Mass of the Roman Rite: Its Origin and Development,* vol. 1, trans. Francis A. Brunner (New York: Benzinger Brothers, 1950), v.

[4] Ibid.

[5] Ibid., vii.

[6] Ibid., viii.

and the present is our scene of trial; and to behave ourselves towards its various phenomena duly and religiously, we must understand them; and to understand them, we must have recourse to those past events which lead to them. Thus the present is a text and the past its interpretation."[7] The focus of his scholarship, the Mass, was equally important to his spiritual outlook: "In Holy Mass the world beyond reaches down into our earthy world. In the power of this invasion, in the fire of this meeting of man with God, the iridescent form of earthly artistry is lost and entangled in the balanced rhythm of resonant human words."[8] The Eucharist, for Jungmann, lay at the very heart of Catholic spirituality. A knowledge of its origins, he believed, would provide the Church with a helpful historical context for its present celebration and ongoing renewal.

Jungmann's Teaching on the Eucharist

Jungmann treats the Eucharist in a number of places in his literary corpus, and it would be impossible to treat them in detail in an essay of this kind. In his work, *Announcing the Word of God* (1967), he offers a good summary of his essential insights. In it, he makes the point that prior the Second Vatican Council Catholic piety was generally delineated along three separate spheres: "it was quite common to find presentations of the doctrine of the Eucharist which spoke first of all about the sacrament, then about Communion, and finally about the

---

[7] Cited in Josef A. Jungmann, *The Early Liturgy: To the Time of Gregory the Great,* trans. Francis A. Brunner (Notre Dame, IN: University of Notre Dame Press, 1959), 2. See also John Henry Newman, "Reformation of the XIth Century, in *essays Critical and Historical,* 10th ed. (London, 1890), 250.

[8] Jungmann, *The Mass of the Roman Rite,* 4.

sacrifice of the Mass."[9] In his treatment of the Eucharist, he shifts the focus to another overlooked aspect of the Liturgy: "the celebration of the Eucharist is a sacrifice, it is true—the sacrifice of the New Covenant, but first of all it is a memorial. It is a memorial celebration of the redeeming Passion in the same way as Sunday is the memorial day of the perfected work of redemption. From the start Eucharist and Sunday have belonged together."[10] He claims that emphasizing the sacrificial dimension of the Mass to the exclusion of it being a *memoria passionis* was the result of the doctrinal controversies of the sixteenth century. He calls for a recovery of the true meaning of Sunday as "the eighth day, the day upon which the Creator continued the work of the seven days and completed it in Christ."[11] For this reason it was considered to be "the Christian conclusion and climax of the week."[12]

In his analysis, Jungmann also claims that the Mass is not only "the sacrifice of Christ, but at the same time the sacrifice of the Church, offered in union with Christ; in distinction to the sacrifice of the Church, it is primarily the sacrifice of the Church."[13] When seen from this perspective, it is our sacrifice: "it is our entering into the sacrifice of Christ; it is our affiliation with his oblation to the heavenly Father—so much so, that the symbols of his oblation, the offerings of his body and blood, are allowed to represent our offering also."[14] At Mass, we share in Christ's paschal mystery and unite our offering to his. He continues: "The primary function of the celebration of the Eucharist is not, as it is with the other sacraments, to produce

---

[9] Josef A. Jungmann *Announcing the Word of God*, trans. Ronald Walls (New York: Herder and Herder, 1967), 110.

[10] Ibid., 111.

[11] Ibid., 112.

[12] Ibid.

[13] Ibid. , 113.

[14] Ibid., 114.

benefits for us, but to glorify God."[15] The Eucharist, according to Jungmann, "is primarily designed for those who have already been purified in Christ's blood and enjoy his new life."[16] "The Mass," in his mind, "is designed as the church's sacrifice of praise and thanksgiving."[17] Although Christ's sacrifice of atonement is present at every Eucharistic celebration, it is not the primary focus of the Mass: "The sacrifice of praise and the sacrifice of atonement are not on the same plane."[18]

Jungmann sought to integrate the Eucharistic sacrifice with the notions of Communion and Eucharistic adoration: "If we are to advance in the spiritual life we must see clearly that permanent union with Christ can and must be strengthened in many different ways, and that the *opus operatum* of Holy Communion must not in any event be allowed to stand in isolation, as though in itself providing an infallible, more or less magically effective means of spiritual progress. For this reason one should maintain a certain detachment even towards daily communion."[19] Rather than seeing them as three separate acts, they should be understood as an integral part of the Church's "sacrifice of praise and thanksgiving." The Eucharist, "should once again be seen chiefly in its primary and true function, from which all else is derived. It is not primarily an object for our adoration, nor yet for the nourishment of the soul, but is, as its name indicates, a sacrifice of thanksgiving, a sacrifice within the assembled congregation. It is only this basic view that gathers all of the aspects into a unity."[20]

---

[15] Ibid., 115.
[16] Ibid., 116.
[17] Ibid., 117.
[18] Ibid.
[19] Ibid. , 119.
[20] Ibid., 110.

Jungmann also highlights the Eucharist's important relationship to the other sacraments: "We are accustomed to list the Eucharist as the third of the sacraments. This corresponds to its role within the scheme of initiation sacraments at the beginning of the Christian life: baptism, confirmation, Eucharist."[21] According to this view, the other four sacraments, coming after the Eucharist, are seen as "a kind of supplement, a second line of pious practices in which the generic concept of a sacrament is likewise realized."[22] Jungmann challenges this position by orienting all of the sacraments toward the Eucharist: "In reality, like baptism and confirmation, although in a different way, they form the foundation for the possibility of the Eucharist: they purify the people of God from sin; they extend the priestly powers; they bless the exit from Christian life; and sanctify the door through which new generations press into the Church to become the host who glorify God in the Eucharist."[23] When seen in this light, the Eucharist is the sacrament toward which all the others tend and find their fulfillment.

Some Further Insights

Although the above remarks barely scratch the surface of Jungmann's teaching on the Eucharist, they highlight the main contours of his thought and demonstrate how he tried to shape Catholic thinking on the sacrament in a number of areas. The following observations, while in no way exhaustive, seek to draw out some of the implications of Jungmann's thought for today's believers.

To begin with, Jungmann acknowledges Christ's presence in the Sacrament, the reception of Holy Communion, and the

---

[21] Ibid., 124.

[22] Ibid., 124-25.

[23] Ibid., 125.

sacrifice of the Mass as three important dimensions of the mystery of the Eucharist. He believes that they should not be separated in the devotions and common piety of the Catholic faithful, but closely integrated. Christ's presence in the consecrated species, the nourishment he gives us through them, and the atonement for our sins are all integral parts of the Eucharistic celebration. Rather than separating them, however, in Catholic spirituality, efforts should be made to show their intimate relation to one another. Otherwise, the Eucharist is in danger of becoming both theologically and spiritually fragmented in the hearts and minds of the faithful.

Jungmann maintains, moreover, that another, often neglected, dimension underlies these three dimensions in the Church's explanation of the Eucharist. The sacrament is, first and foremost, a sacrifice of praise and thanksgiving on the part of the Church. He makes this claim based on his study of the development of the Mass and by identifying its foundational elements supplied by Christ. The Eucharist's primary purpose, in other words, is not to give nourishment or to be an object of adoration, but to be a sacrifice of praise and thanksgiving to God for the work of redemption accomplished in Christ. This sacrifice is an offering of the Church made to God in union with Christ and his paschal mystery.

Connected with the notion of the Eucharistic celebration as a sacrifice of praise and thanksgiving is the added dimension of it being a memorial. Jesus told his disciples to break bread and pass the cup in memory of him. This memorial action celebrates the Christ's redeeming passion and death and is intimately connected to it. Jesus celebrated his Last Supper on the evening before his crucifixion. The action of Holy Thursday anticipated the action of Good Friday and looked beyond it to the empty tomb of Easter Sunday morning. In this way, the entire paschal mystery is represented in the Eucharistic action, which at one and the same time is both in time and out of time.

Jungmann points out the intimate connection between the Eucharist and Sunday. As the day of the Lord's resurrection, Sunday is the "eighth day" when God completes his work of Creation though the redeeming action of Christ. The Sunday Eucharist, from this perspective, is the culmination of the week and points to the fullness of Creation made possible by Christ's salvific action. It also points beyond the pale of death to life in the Risen and Glorious Christ. Jungmann calls for a rediscovery of the true meaning of Sunday as a day of thanksgiving and as a time when the Church, the body of Christ, offers itself with Christ in a sacrifice of praise to glorify God and the New Creation wrought by Christ.

At Eucharist, Jungmann claims, the Church's sacrifice of praise and thanksgiving and Christ's sacrifice of atonement are not on the same plane. Although, he recognizes that Christ's sacrifice on the cross and the consequent forgiveness of sins are present at every Mass, he says that the celebration of the Eucharist presupposes this redemptive action and exists primarily as a means by which the entire body of the faithful offers itself with the Risen Lord in a sacrifice of praise and thanksgiving to God the Father. Here, Jungmann emphasizes the multidimensional nature of the Eucharist and wishes to bring to the fore one aspect that, until the Second Vatican Council, had been largely overlooked.

For Jungmann, the sacrifice of the Church is distinct but not separate from Christ's sacrifice on the cross. Christ's Mystical Body can do nothing apart from its Head. The Church's sacrifice is possible only because of the sacrifice of Calvary. The Last Supper anticipated this sacrifice of atonement and looked beyond it to the empty tomb of Easter Sunday morning. The celebration of the Eucharist makes it possible for the entire body of believers to participate in Christ's paschal mystery. The sacramental realism of the Eucharist makes it possible for the community of the faithful to share in Christ's passion, death, and resurrection. In doing so, the community glorifies God by its offering of praise and thanksgiving.

Finally, Jungmann gives the Eucharist a central place in its relationship to the other sacraments. While he recognizes that it is one of the sacraments of initiation and often listed as the third of the sacraments, he says that all of the other sacraments in their own way "form the foundation for the possibility of the Eucharist." The Eucharist stands apart from the other sacraments, because it represents the summit of Christian worship and is the primary means by which the Church renders praise and thanksgiving to the Father. He draws a distinction between the order in which the sacraments are received and the role they play in the ongoing life of the Church. In this respect, the Eucharist stands apart from the other sacraments and can be considered as the "sacrament of sacraments."

Conclusion

Josef A. Jungmann was one of the principal architects of the liturgical reforms of the Second Vatican Council. His writings on catechesis and the liturgy in the decades leading up to the Second Vatican Council garnered him much respect in the Catholic theological word and led to his being selected as a Council *peritus* and a member of the redaction committee of *Sacrosanctum concilium*, the Council's document on the Liturgy. His knowledge of the origins and historical development of the Roman Catholic Mass was unparalleled in his day and his writings remain to this day an important resource for an understanding of the historical context of Catholic worship.

The Eucharist, for Jungmann, is the Church's sacrificial offering of praise and thanksgiving to God for the work of Christ's redemption. Although this sacrament embodies many facets—the sacrifice of Christ's atonement, the nourishment received from Holy Communion, the adoration of Christ's presence in the Blessed Sacrament—its primary function is the sacrifice of praise and thanksgiving offered to God for the work of Christ's passion, death, and resurrection. From the beginning, this memorial celebration was closely associated with Sunday. If, as Jungmann suggests, Sunday is the "eighth day," the day God completed in Christ the work of Creation, then the Eucharist, by all counts, is the sacrament par excellence of the New Creation.

Jungmann reminds us of the roots of Catholic worship and the role the Eucharist plays in our Catholic identity. The Eucharist, for him, is the primary means by which the Church participates in Christ's paschal mystery and offers herself to God in a sacrificial prayer of thanksgiving. At a critical time in the Church's history, he reminds believers of the Mass' corporate nature and the manner in which it enables the entire body of the faithful to glorify God by its grateful celebration of the sacramental memorial of Christ's redemptive activity.

Reflection Questions

- Jungmann maintains that the Eucharist is primarily a memorial. What does the sacrament memorialize? How is it similar and different from other memorials? How does this memorial action, this action of remembering, make Jesus present in his sacrificial self-offering and in the consecrated bread and wine? What role does "remembering" play in your own spiritual life?

- Jungmann also claims that the Eucharist is a sacrifice of praise and thanksgiving. How is our offering of praise and thanksgiving connected to Jesus's sacrificial self-offering on the cross? Why are they not on the same plane? Who are we praising and why? How has Jesus made our sacrifice of praise and thanksgiving possible?

- Jungmann gives the Eucharist a primary place in its relationship to the other sacraments. Why does it have such a prominent place? How are the other sacraments oriented toward it? How do they form the foundation for the possibility of the Eucharist? Do you view the Eucharist in this way?

Voice Eight

Dietrich von Hildebrand: Forming the Supernatural Personality

Our next voice was another of the great Catholic philosophers and theologians of the twentieth century. Born in Florence of German parents, Dietrich von Hildebrand (1889-1977) studied philosophy at the University of Munich from 1906-1909, where he was influenced by the phenomenology of Max Scheler, and from 1909-1911 at the University of Göttingen, where he pursued his interest in phenomenology under Edmund Husserl and Adolf Reinach. He converted to Catholicism in 1914, became a lecturer at the University of Munich in 1918 and an associate professor in 1924. A vocal opponent of Hitler and Nazi Germany, he escaped capture and almost certain death by fleeing with his family first to Austria, and then to Switzerland, France, Spain, Portugal, and Brazil, before arriving in New York in 1940, where he taught at Fordham University in the Bronx until his retirement in 1960. A prolific author, Hildebrand wrote more than 30 books and numerous articles on various philosophical and theological subjects. Pope Pius XII, who knew Hildebrand from his time as papal nuncio to Germany, once referred to him informally as "the 20th-century Doctor of the Church."[1]

Hildebrand's Philosophical and Theological Outlook

The notion of "value" holds a central place in Hildebrand's aesthetics, ethics, and theology. A phenomenologist in training and outlook, he describes it as what in itself is excellent and to be admired. Value, for him, has an objective foundation in reality and, unlike the proponents of value clarification, is not subject to the vagaries of subjective interpretation. By its very nature, a value points beyond the subject to something that shapes (and even transforms) human life into its deepest and fullest expression of itself.

For Hildebrand, all values radiate from God and return to him. Our purpose in life is to cooperate with God's grace and conform ourselves to these fundamental values so that the image and likeness of God might shine forth in us. Jesus Christ, the Word-of-God-made-flesh, entered this world to show us how to live a life that is purpose- and value-full. He came to us to show us the way to the Father and to transform us into living members of his body, the Church. He suffered, died, and rose for us to move us out of our self-centeredness and bring us to God-centeredness, to free us from our egoism and so become our deepest, truest selves.

In his greatest work, *Transformation in Christ* (*Die Umgestaltung in Christus*, 1940; English translation, 1948), Hildebrand outlines this process of transformation that takes place in the human person in great detail. He points out that our

---

[1] This biographical information comes from Dietrich von Hildebrand, *Liturgy and Personality: The Healing Power of Formal Prayer* (Manchester, N.H.: Sophia Institute Press, 1993), 163-65. See also "Dietrich von Hildebrand (1889-1977)," Catholic Authors, http://www.catholicauthors.com/vonhildebrand.html.

primary response to values is a longing to be united with them so that our true personality might become alive in Christ. Such longing evokes from us a deep sense of reverence for God and for all the beauty, truth, and goodness in the created world that comes from him. Such a personality conforms to this hierarchical world of values not only in action, but also in one's attitude toward the creation. It recognizes God as the highest of all values and understands that it must pursue lesser values in relation to their place in the natural order created by him. The Liturgy, for Hildebrand, is the primary context of humanity's transformation and the place where it unfolds.[2]

Hildebrand on the Eucharist

Although Hildebrand touches upon the Eucharist at various times in his writings, his most extensive treatment appears in *Liturgy and Personality* (*Liturgie und Persönlichkeit*, 1932; English translation, 1943).[3] In this work, he presents the Eucharist as the highest expression of the Liturgy, the Church's public and formal worship, which also includes the other sacraments and the recitation of the Divine Office.

The Liturgy, in his mind, has two purposes. Its primary one is to give praise and glory to God, and its secondary one is to ask for graces.[4] Transformation of one's personality in Christ is a gratuitous effect of the Liturgy and comes about not by our seeking it directly, but as God's response to the love we express for Him during worship. The Liturgy is the place where the Church, being at home with God and most herself, teaches us to

---

[2] Summaries and resources for Hildebrand's philosophical and theological outlook may be found on "Dietrich von Hildebrand Legacy Project," http://www.hildebrandlegacy.org.

[3] See Hildebrand, *Liturgy and Personality*, iv.

[4] Ibid, 4-6.

adore God properly.[5]

Hildebrand maintains that the Liturgy is God's chosen instrument for bringing about our transformation in Christ, without whom we cannot become a full personality. "A personality," in his mind, is someone "who rises above the average only because he fully realizes the classical *human attitudes*, because he knows more deeply and originally than the average man, loves more profoundly and authentically, wills more clearly and correctly than the others, and makes full use of his freedom; in a word, he is the complete, the profound, and the true man."[6]

In this respect, a full or true personality is the normal person and is distinct from someone who is average, abnormal, or pathological. A normal personality is not necessarily someone with great talents, but a person whose capacities for loving and knowing have reached their full potential. Such a person has a deep link with values and is able to live in unity with the deepest truths of existence. This unity expresses itself in a harmony between one's inner and outer being, where a person's "speech, expression, movements, and external style of life are organically molded by their inner attitudes."[7] Because of Christ, every person has the opportunity to become a full personality and a true individual. We look to the saints as models of what is possible for each and every one of us.[8]

God, for Hildebrand, is the ontological foundation for the development of the personality and enables us through the action, meaning, and structure of Liturgy to come to a conscious awareness of the world of value. As the highest expression of the Liturgy, the Mass awakens us to the value of God's kingdom and actualizes communion—the true mark of personality—with

---

[5] Ibid., 3-9.

[6] Ibid., 20.

[7] Ibid., 23.

[8] Ibid., 19-27.

God, self, and others. It makes us rich in values, especially those of communion, reverence, wakefulness, discretion, and continuity. That is to say, it makes us one with the ground of our existence, gives us a deep reverence for the supernatural and the created world, makes us spiritually adept, morally discerning, and at peace with our temporal experience. What is more, it links us to the divine order and enables us to respond to life in an organic manner. It balances the Christocentric and theocentric in our lives, embodies for us both the ascetical and mystical dimensions of human experience, and instills in us a classical spirit that acknowledges the reality of sin and our need for salvation.[9]

Hildebrand maintains that the Eucharist is the fullest expression of the Church's liturgical worship and perfects the transformation in Christ begun in us at Baptism. As "the eternal loving sacrifice of Christ," it creates the spiritual climate and provides the structural context for "the formation of the supernatural personality in us, the formation of Christ in us, as it takes place in every saint—not in his words and teachings, not in the form of asceticism he has chosen, but in his saintliness— in a St. Augustine as well as a St. Thérèse of the Child Jesus, in a St. Benedict as well as in a St. Francis, in a St. Bernard as well as in a St. Vincent de Paul."[10] For Hildebrand, the Eucharist glorifies God and mediates grace to those who partake in it. It renders worship to the Father, forms us into saintly, Christ-like personalities, and heralds the coming of the new creation through the transforming action of the Holy Spirit.

_____

[9] Ibid., 29, 33, 155-61.
[10] Ibid., 32-33.

Some Further Insights

This brief exposition of Hildebrand's teaching on the Eucharist highlights the central role it plays in his understanding of a person's transformation in Christ and the formation of a full (and what he calls "normal") personality. What follows are some concise summaries and observations on the values the Eucharist radiates and the response it seeks to elicit from us.

To begin with, Hildebrand sees the Liturgy as the place where we can become "normal" personalities. He views it as the place where through our praise and worship of the Father we can overcome the effects and influence of sin in our lives and become the people God originally envisioned us to be. The "normal" personality, for Hildebrand, is the saintly personality, someone whose life has been thoroughly transformed by Christ. The Liturgy effects this transformation by putting us in touch with the Christ event and allowing true (as opposed to apparent) values shine forth in our lives. The Eucharist does so in a special way because it embodies the eternal, sacrificial love of Christ himself and invites us to be partakers of that mystery. As members of his Mystical Body, Christ promises to transform our lives so that his values might be instilled in our souls and take root in our hearts.[11]

Hildebrand also emphasizes the communion-forming power of the Liturgy. He sees this value as something that radiates from the communion of the Triune Godhead itself and that pours itself into the liturgical prayer of Christ and his Mystical Body, the Church. The bonds of communion are forged and strengthened at the table of the Lord, where the action of Christ's paschal mystery enters our midst and brings about its salvific purpose. The spirit of communion in the Liturgy reveals

---

[11] Ibid., 19-33.

the spirit of Christ, gives glory to God the Father, and preserves our unique individuality as believers. This power of communion comes to the fore especially when we receive the Body and Blood of Christ, which nourishes us and deepens our hope of one day sharing in the fullness of a close, intimate friendship with the Triune God of Father, Son, and Holy Spirit. In this respect, the Eucharist actualizes communion, deepens it, and points to its final perfection that takes place and is made possible only through the Christ event and the action of his Spirit.[12]

Hildebrand calls reverence the "mother of all virtues" and the basis for "a relationship with the Absolute, the supernatural, and the divine."[13] As a value it flows from God through the Liturgy, and is particularly present in the Eucharist, where Christ offers his reverential sacrificial worship to the Father. Those who participate in the Eucharist respond to this value with an attitude of reverence toward God, others, self, and all creation. Irreverence, the opposite of reverence, is the result of pride, which fills a person with arrogance, and concupiscence, which blunts a person's sensitivities in the search for earthly pleasure. Hildebrand looks to reverence as the basis of all true personality and says that the Liturgy is imbued with the spirit of reverence and instills it in those who participate in it. When seen in this light, Christ's reverence for the Father permeates the Eucharist and elicits a similar response from those who join him in his act of sacrificial worship.[14]

Hildebrand also states that the Liturgy embodies "in a unique fashion the spirit of true response-to-value that is so necessary for the formation of personality and a person's transformation in Christ."[15] It enables us to offer a proper

---

[12] Ibid., 35-45.

[13] Ibid., 47.

[14] Ibid., 47-58.

[15] Ibid., 64.

response to true values, for it overcomes egocentricity and is permeated with a spirit of praise. Those formed by the Liturgy delight in all values and long to be in union with them. Because these values come from God, they also long to be one with him. This longing for God is the proper response due to him and is a primary theme of the Eucharistic celebration. It reaches its summit at Holy Communion when Christ gives us his Body and Blood to eat and drink. Being united with God in this way makes us conscious of the bestowal of God's gift of himself and our unworthiness to receive it. It reminds us that God himself is the highest of all values and that all else is secondary. It also reminds us that we have nothing to offer God on our own and that everything we do must be done through, with, and in Jesus Christ, the Word-made-flesh, and only-begotten Son of the Father.[16]

Hildebrand also says that the Liturgy heightens our spiritual wakefulness, thus making us more conscious of the values in our midst. Such wakefulness deepens our spiritual receptiveness, gives us a truer consciousness of our metaphysical situation, and makes us more open to God. The spirit of wakefulness permeates the Liturgy. When we celebrate the Eucharist, we humbly stand before God as his creatures and affirm his great bounty. The Eucharist forms us in wakefulness by bringing us out of our narrowness and small mindedness and drawing us toward the divine reality. In doing so, it enables us to be mindful of our brothers and sisters created in God's image and likeness and deepens our awareness of his vestigial presence in all creation. The Eucharist makes us more conscious of the influence of evil in our lives and careful to guard against its hold over us. It also opens our eyes to the divine reality in our midst and encourages us to open our hearts to its transforming

---

[16] Ibid., 59-82.

grace.[17]

Hildebrand also emphasizes the Liturgy's role in fostering a spirit of discretio *(discretion) in our lives.* This "sense of distinguishing" deepens our sense of "the dramatic rhythm of being: preparation, ascension, fulfillment, and decline" and puts us in touch with the "inner rhythm of development" that forms the basis of all true communion.[18] *Discretio* is important for the formation of true personality. It gives us a sense of depth in our lives and an appreciation for the different gradations in our relations. The Liturgy fosters discretion by helping us distinguish true values from false. The spirit of *discretio* permeates its structure and atmosphere. The Mass, in particular, reveals this dramatic rhythm in its various parts and allows it to unfold organically in humanity's confrontation with the ineffable mystery of Christ's paschal mystery. It unveils the primal image of God's redemptive love for humanity by putting us in touch with the dramatic rhythm of existence manifest in Christ's passion, death, and resurrection.[19]

Hildebrand also emphasizes the importance of continuity in the Liturgy and the way it helps us interpret our experience of time in a dignified, Christ-like manner. "Continuity," he holds, "is necessary in a fully developed person."[20] It enables us to construct a meaningful narrative of our past experience, present duties, and future hopes. For Christians, this narrative is rooted in Christ's paschal mystery and enables us to embrace the proper values and give them the right response. "Continuity," he believes, "is the mother of contrition."[21] Without it, we would not able to confront the wrongs we have committed in

---

[17] Ibid., 83-103.
[18] Ibid., 105-6.
[19] Ibid., 105-25.
[20] Ibid., 127.
[21] Ibid., 130-31.

the past, respond appropriately to the exigencies of the present moment, or anticipate the role we will play in eternity. This inner unity of past, present, and future is necessary for our transformation in Christ and is the basis for true communion. It uses frequent ritual repetitions to pervade our celebration of the Eucharist, form us in true simplicity, and highlight our need to offer praise and thanksgiving to God at all times.[22]

The Liturgy, for Hildebrand, also has an organic quality about it that roots a person in what is authentic and true as opposed to what is artificial and arbitrary. It offers a comprehensive interpretation of the meaning of existence, one that is rooted in the paschal mystery of Christ. The Liturgy fosters our spiritual lives and gives us a deep appreciation of this organic quality and the values it sustains. Participating in it transforms us and gives shape to our true personality in Christ. It helps us remain conscious of God in our daily response to life and enables us to live the Gospel on a deep level of awareness. In doing so, the Liturgy offers us a link with the supernatural and helps us to respond to suffering as an organic part of life. It also offers us to situate all goods in their proper place and provides us with a context where Christ can transform our suffering. At Eucharist, this organic quality of the Liturgy shines through in a special way, since those who celebrate it are members of his Mystical Body and participate organically in Christ's sacrificial passing from death to life.[23]

Finally, for Hildebrand, the Liturgy breathes the classical spirit by enabling us to stand in full primal relation to the various spheres of life and to know the world in its true dimensions. In his mind, the classical spirit "sees the world in its dimension of depth and its luminous plenitude of value as a

---

[22] Ibid., 127-35.
[23] Ibid., 137-46.

manifestation of God."[24] It is that which deepens our spirit of true communion and reverence in us and opens our eyes to the hierarchy of values. The Eucharist manifests the classical spirit because it conforms us to the order of being, reflects the totality of truth, balances the theocentric with the Christocentric, and emphasizes both Christ's humanity and his divinity. These classical values shape us into spiritually healthy individuals with knowledge of our creaturely status, a consciousness of our sinfulness, a healthy outlook toward sexuality, and a balanced appreciation of the ascetical and mystical dimensions of Christian spirituality. They also make us more aware of our participation in the Mystical Body and how we are immersed in the depths of Christ's paschal mystery.[25]

Although these observations do not exhaust Hildebrand's teaching on the Eucharist, they convey its major contours and demonstrate the important role it plays in our transformation in Christ and the formation of true personality. Most of what has been said in the preceding pages applies to the Liturgy as a whole, but has special relevance for the celebration of the Eucharist.

Conclusion

Dietrich von Hildebrand was a prolific and seminal thinker in Catholic thought, who wrote on a wide variety of philosophical and theological topics. Having studied under some of the great phenomenological thinkers of his day, he used his interest in values and the attitudes they impart to break new ground in Catholic spirituality, especially as it relates to the formation of personality and the transformation of the person in Christ. His teaching on the Eucharist is embedded in his

---

[24] Ibid., 148.
[25] Ibid., 147-61.

writings on the Liturgy, especially in *Liturgy and Personality.*

In this book, Hildebrand, calls the Eucharist the fullest expression of the Church's liturgical worship, which perfects the transformation in Christ begun in us at Baptism. As the central act of Catholic worship, it immerses us in Christ's paschal mystery and plays an essential role in the formation of a saintly personality. It also radiates a vast array of values—communion, reverence, response, wakefulness, discretion, continuity, the organic, and the classical—and mediates them to all who participate in and who seek to give glory and praise to God through it.

Hildebrand focused on essential and necessary truths of the faith and did not concern himself with passing fads or fashions. For this reason, what he wrote about the Liturgy was valid for both its pre-Vatican II expression in the Tridentine Mass and in the liturgical reforms of the Council. Although he was a vocal critic of the changes in the Liturgy brought about by the Council, it was more out of a concern that Catholic worship was losing some of the values that had been instilled in it and which it communicated to worshipers for centuries. His thinking on the Liturgy has great relevance today, for it draws a clear and certain relationship between the way we celebrate and the kind of people God wants us to become.

Reflection Questions

- Hildebrand says the purpose of the Liturgy is to give praise and glory to God, and to ask for graces. Why do you go to Mass? Do you consider it the primary way in which you give praise and glory to God? Do you go there to ask him for grace? What do you ask for?
- Hildebrand maintains that the Mass awakens us to the value of God's kingdom and actualizes communion with God, self, and others. Has your experience of the Eucha-

rist deepened your communion with God and others? Has it deepened your communion with yourself? How has it shaped your personality and perception of yourself?

- Hildebrand says the Eucharist perfects the transformation in Christ begun in us at Baptism. Do you think of the Eucharist in this way? Can you point to areas in your own life where you have experienced such growth? Have you become more Christ-like as a result of your sharing in the Eucharist?

Voice Nine

Fulton Sheen:
Spiritual Plasma

Fulton J. Sheen (1895-1979) was an American bishop, theologian, author, radio broadcaster, and Emmy Award winning television personality. He was born in El Paso, Illinois and was ordained a priest for the Diocese of Peoria in 1919. He received a Ph.D. in philosophy from the Catholic University of Louvain in 1923 and a S.T.D. in theology from the Angelicum in 1924. He served the Church as a parish priest, taught theology and philosophy at the Catholic University of America for 23 years, was the national director of the Society for the Propagation of the faith from 1950-66, and became an auxiliary bishop for the Archdiocese of New York in 1951. From 1930-50, he hosted *The Catholic Hour* on the radio. Then from 1951-57 and 1961-68, he hosted respectively *Life is Worth Living* and *The Fulton Sheen Program* for television. In 1966, he was made Bishop of Rochester, New York, and resigned from that post in 1969 when he became the Titular Archbishop of Newport Wales. The author of more than 34 books and numerous articles, he was highly regarded for his clarity of thought in both philosophical and theological concerns. In 2002, his cause for canonization was officially opened. In 2012, the Vatican recognized his life as one of "heroic virtue" and declared him "Venerable." In 2014, miracle for his cause of canonization was recognize by a panel of medical experts and another comprised of theologians. He considered the Eucharist a central element of his life, the sacred pole around which all else revolved.[1]

Sheen's Spiritual Outlook

Sheen was one of the leading Churchmen of his day and had that rare combination of being a Catholic bishop, intellectual, and TV personality that few, if any, have been able to emulate since. He held two doctorates, was a prolific author, and hailed as a great communicator. Although he addressed a largely Catholic audience, he appealed to many outside the fold, who were lured to the faith by his personal charisma and skills in public speaking. He had a talent for probing the deepest truths of the faith and presenting them in a way that everyone could understand. He was a man of God, a man of the Church, and a man of the people.

Sheen's spiritual outlook was rooted in his notion of the three phases of whole-Christ: "first, His Earthly Life; second, His Glorified Life; third, His Mystical Life."[2] He believed that each of these must be taken into account in our understanding of Christ's identity and purpose. "Those who consider His (Christ's) physical Life alone," he claimed, "either develop a sentimental spirituality or else end by regarding Him merely as a good man and a teacher of humanitarian ethics; those who consider Him only in His heavenly Life of glory, regard Him as an absentee landlord, disregarding both His promise to send His Spirit, and His abiding interest in the souls which He came

---

[1] For a biographical profile of Archbishop Fulton J. Sheen, see http://fulton-sheen.cua.edu/bio/index.cfm.

[2] Fulton J. Sheen, *The Mystical Body of Christ* (New York: Sheed and Ward, 1935), 19.

to save."[3] Sheen believed that Christ was presently living his Mystical Life in the members of his body, the Church: "He is not past; He has not left us orphans; He is with us and more intimately than we are with ourselves. He is still living in the world, moving amongst its poor, instructing the ignorant, comforting the doubtful, and healing the souls of men."[4] In his mind, Christ's mystical life represents the culmination of his earthly and glorified existences and stands in marked continuity with them.

This continuity, however, does not mean homogeneity, but radical transformation. The historical Jesus, Sheen believed, was one with the glorified Christ. His resurrection and ascension, however, elevated him to another dimension. The glorified Christ, in turn, continues to exist mystically in the members of his body, the Church. This continued existence happens as a result of the outpouring of his Spirit upon the Church and the graces it makes available to the community of believers through the sacraments and its manifold gifts and fruits. Sheen puts it this way: "It is within the power of man to prolong himself through space and time by doctrine and example. It is within Christ's power to prolong Himself, not only by doctrine and example, but also by His Life."[5] Christ, in other words, continues to live his paschal mystery by extending his life in and through the community of the faithful. He does so in a very real and palpable way that remains continuous with his earthy and glorified existences. He is united to his body, the Church, in the same way that the soul is united to the body. If the two are separated, the living organism ceases to exist. The Eucharist, for Sheen, was the spiritual food of the Mystical Christ, the unifying force within the body of believers and the

---

[3] Ibid., 25-26.
[4] Ibid., 26.
[5] Ibid., 27.

means by which the body remains united to its head.

Sheen's Teaching on the Eucharist

One place where Sheen develops his views on the Eucharist is in his book, *The Mystical Body of Christ*. The Eucharist, he states, "is the efficient cause of all the other sacraments" and thus "the source of the unity of the Mystical Body."[6] This unity is twofold: "(a) the unity of Christ and His Mystical Body; (b) the unity of the members of the Mystical Body with one another."[7] These two unities, he believes, are intimately related.

Sheen employs a number of analogies to describe the Eucharist's role in maintaining the unity of Christ and his Mystical Body. He refers to the Church as "the great Tree of Life" and says that the source of its energy lies not in its external structures but in something invisible and spiritual.[8] He likens the Eucharist to the energy of the sun: "What the solar energy is to the tree, that the Eucharist is to the Mystical Body; what the leaf is to the tree, that each individual Catholic is to the Church. As each leaf draws force from the great invisible solar energy, so does each Catholic draw life through Communion with Divinity in the Eucharist. Without the sun, the tree could not live; without the Eucharist, the Church could not live. The more Catholic leaves there are on the tree of Life or the Church, the greater her strength and her unity; and as the tree is one though made up of a multiplicity of leaves because all nourished by the same sun, so the Mystical Body is one though made up of many Catholics because all nourished by the same Eucharist. Such is the secret of Catholic unity—the communion of man with God."[9]

---

[6] Ibid., 357.

[7] Ibid., 357-58.

[8] Ibid., 359.

[9] Ibid.

The Eucharist, for Sheen, is indispensable to the life and well-being of the Church. Without it, there would be no Church, no community of believers, no communion with Christ.

Sheen also likens the Eucharist to the plasma in our blood: "Now, the Eucharist is to the Mystical Body what the blood plasma is to the human body, though in a far superior way. This great Spiritual Plasma, the Eucharist, flows and streams through the Mystical Body in every part of the world wherever a Mass is celebrated. It offers itself first to this Catholic and then to that; dips the Chalice of Life to one, for the increase of its Divine Life; breaks its Bread of Life to another, for the remission of sin and its punishment, and in general strengthening every soul with its Christ-Love. And just as the human body is one, though composed of many cells, because nourished by the same plasma, so the Mystical Body is one, though composed of many Catholics, because nourished by the same Eucharist."[10] The plasma that runs through the veins of the Church is the blood of Christ himself. Without this Precious Blood, the Church would be devoid of all life and vitality.

Sheen also says that the Eucharist represents the perfection of a law that runs through all of nature: minerals are subsumed into a higher world of vegetation; plants enter the animal world by surrendering their lives to them; animals become more than animals when they are consumed by humans. In a similar way, we are taken up into the Divine Life whenever we receive the Eucharist.[11] What is more, just as natural life has catabolic and anabolic processes, the Supernatural life involves the tearing down of the old Adam (the catabolic) and the building up of the Christ-pattern (the anabolic).[12] Sheen maintains that both of these processes are at work in the Eucharist: "The amount of

---

[10] Ibid., 360.

[11] Ibid, 361-62.

[12] Ibid., 363.

Divine Love we receive depends upon our capacity. The fuller we are of ourselves, the less room there is for Christ; the more empty we are of ourselves by crucifying our flesh, the more He can pour forth the torrents of His Love."[13]

In addition to maintaining the unity of Christ and his Church, Sheen also states that the Eucharist also "concorporates us to one another as brothers in Christ."[14] The Church, he says, considers religion not only as "a personal relation between man and God, but also a social relation."[15] It guarantees the social character of religion and reminds us that we cannot love God without loving our neighbor—and vice versa.[16] It fosters this "holy fellowship" not through external structures, but by nourishing the interior life. It unites people not on the basis of economics or social status, but on the basis of their being children of God.[17] According to Sheen, this common brotherhood crosses all ethnic, racial, and cultural boundaries and has concrete implications for the political, economic, and social order. "This brotherhood through the Eucharist, he states, was intended by our Lord to be the basis of all international agreements as well as relations between Capital and Labor."[18]

The Eucharist, for Sheen, is "the end and perfection of all the others" and "intrinsically bound up with sacrifice."[19] It also reveals the extent of God's love for us: "Now by a wonderful paradox of God's love, the human race which crucified Christ is the same race which has been nourished by the very life they slew. He might have ended His Life by Sacrifice, but to let us

---

[13] Ibid., 365.
[14] Ibid.
[15] Ibid., 366.
[16] Ibid.
[17] Ibid., 367.
[18] Ibid., 369.
[19] Ibid., 374.

take His Life away, and then to take it up again from the grave, in order to give it to us, as *our* LIFE—that is a love which is beyond a human comprehension. To be willing to die for us, was much; but to be willing to live for us all over again, was everything."[20] "Sacrifice," for Sheen, "leads to Sacrament."[21] Jesus' Eucharistic Presence is possible only because he poured himself into simple bread and wine in anticipation of his kenotic self-emptying on the hill of Golgotha.

Some Further Insights

The purpose the above description was to paint in broad strokes a picture of Sheen's views on the Eucharist against the background of his overall spiritual outlook. The following remarks develop these insights in more detail to provide a better sense of the place of the sacrament in his life and thought.

To begin with, Sheen presents the Eucharist as the lifeblood of Christ's Mystical Body. It is therefore primarily concerned with the third phase of the whole-Christ, that of the Mystical. That is not to say that it has nothing to do with the historical Jesus or the glorified Christ. Such a conclusion would run totally against many of Sheen's underlying presuppositions of there being an intrinsic unity and continuity among all three phases. Sheen's concern, however, is not so much with the Eucharist as an historical event or as a heavenly banquet, but as the graced energy uniting the Church to Christ and her members to one another. This energy sustains the Church and keeps it in existence. The Church cannot exist without the daily bread of the Eucharist.

The Eucharist, for Sheen, unites the Church with the sacred humanity of Christ. When the faithful receive Holy

---

[20] Ibid., 375.
[21] Ibid.

Communion, they are united with the body and blood, soul, and divinity of the Risen Lord. This mystical union takes place on the level of being and action. Christ has become one with the community of the faithful, who now join in his redemptive mission. As a result, Christ lives out his paschal mystery in and through the members of his body. He unites himself to the community of the faithful in much the same way that the soul is united to the body. The two can be separated only in death. Since the Risen Lord has conquered death, however, death has no lasting power over his Mystical Body. Its reign is dwindling, short-lived and doomed to fail. Just as the historical Jesus rose from the dead to become the Risen Lord, so will his Mystical Body overcome the darkness of the grave and rise to new heights. The communion of saints, for Sheen, is a vivid reminder of the Church's mystical destiny.

The Eucharist, for Sheen, does more than unite the Church to Christ. It also unites the members of Christ's Mystical Body to one another. This fellowship among the members flows from Christ's union with the Church. As Sheen points out, we cannot say we love God, but hate our neighbor. Jesus took the Golden Rule seriously and expects his followers to do the same. As Sheen points out, Christ has identified himself with the community of believers so closely that to hate one member is the equivalent of hating Christ himself. This insight has many implications for Christian action in the world. If Christ has united himself so closely to the members of his body, then the actions of the members must reflect the spirit and mind of Christ. Doing otherwise gives scandal to Christ and his Church. Doing otherwise weakens the Church's credibility and lessens the impact of its apostolic witness in the world.

The Eucharist, for Sheen, is the cause of the Church's unity. It constitutes this unity, both with Christ and among its members, not through external structures, but by providing spiritual nourishment for the soul. This nourishment sustains the Church's interior life and enables her members to take an active part in Christ's ongoing redemptive mission. Action, in other words, flows from being and reveals a person's deepest values. The Eucharistic action flows from Christ's being and reveals his deepest values in and through the members of his Mystical Body. It mediates the power of Christ's love to the Church and enables her members to live as Christ lived and to serve as Christ served. For Sheen, it is the sacrament of love that binds the members of the Church to one another and to Christ. It tears down the Old Adam and builds up the Christ-pattern in the lives of the faithful.

Sheen has a gift for explaining theological concepts by engaging the imagination. To explain the Eucharist, he uses images from nature (e.g., a tree, blood plasma, nature itself) to give us a sense of what the Eucharist is, for whom it is for, and what it purports to achieve. In doing so, he stands in marked continuity with many before him, who used simple images and common everyday experiences as a way of explaining the things of God. Jesus' parables, the preaching of the Apostle Paul, and the writings of Church fathers such as Augustine and Gregory the Great immediately come to mind. His training in scholastic philosophy and theology, moreover, gave him an appreciation of the principle, "Grace builds on Nature," and the insight that the "Book of Creation" is itself revelatory of the divine. His talent for making divine things accessible to his audience also stems from his years of experience as a radio broadcaster and television personality where he honed his communication skills to bring the Good News to a general audience.

For Sheen, the Eucharist involves both Sacrifice and Presence. The relationship between these two is clear: Sacrifice comes first and leads to Presence. This order reflects the catabolic (breaking down) and anabolic (building up) processes at work in the supernatural order of Christ's redemptive mission. When seen in this light, Christ's sacrificial offering on the cross represents the breaking down of the Old Self which makes possible the building up of the New. The Old Man must be put to death before the New Man can bless the world with his transforming Presence. Christ's kenotic self-emptying is a prerequisite for his unifying Presence in the Church. Each of these processes, moreover, is at work in the Eucharist. The same self-emptying love that Christ displays on Calvary enables him to pour himself into simple bread and wine to become a transforming nourishment for us. These processes, moreover, are at work in everyone who receives the Eucharist: the Sacrifice it embodies breaks down the Old Man in us, while the Presence it engenders builds up the New.

Finally, Sheen points out that the Eucharist not only makes Christ's sacrificial death on Calvary present to us in an unbloody manner, but is also an even fuller expression of God's love for us. It was not enough for Christ simply to die for us on the cross. Rather than ending his life in Sacrifice, he took up Life again in order to give it to us. In the Eucharist, Christ's Life becomes our Life. Out of love for us, he emptied himself through death on the cross, poured himself into the bread and wine of the Last Supper, and gives himself to us in Holy Communion to dwell there by the power of his Spirit. Sheen would identify closely with the words of the Apostle Paul, "I have been crucified with Christ; and it is no longer I who live, bit it is Christ who lives in me" (Gal 2:19-20). The Eucharist, for him, makes it possible for us to live in Christ and for Christ to live in us.

Conclusion

In his day, Archbishop Fulton Sheen was a charismatic figure and larger than life personality. He used his intellectual talents and skill as a communicator to preach the Gospel message through his teaching, books, radio broadcasts, and television programs. He did so for decades and came across not only as someone who could understand and explain the faith in simple down-to-earth terms, but also as someone who lived it. He has been declared, "Venerable" in the eyes of the Church, and his cause for beatification and eventual canonization holds much promise.

The Eucharist was central to Sheen's life and thought. As a priest and bishop, he celebrated it daily and reflected often on its significance for the life of the Church. He understood very well the role it played in unifying the Church to Christ and the faithful to one another. He saw it as the lifeblood of Christ's Mystical Body, the vital energy that enabled the Church to preach the Good News of Jesus Christ down through the ages. The Eucharist, he believed, was Christ's gift of himself to the Church. Through it, he would be a nourishing presence to his disciples until the end of time (cf. Mt 28:20),

The Eucharist, for Sheen, was the end and purpose of all the other sacraments. The others all presuppose it and either lead up to it or flow from it. Sheen's love for the Eucharist reflects his deep love for Christ and his Church. He saw the social implications of the sacrament and understood that receiving Holy Communion meant fellowship not only with Christ, but also with one another. The Eucharist, he believed, held the secret to international peace and world brotherhood. It represented the hope of a redeemed humanity baptized in the blood of Christ and nourished by his quiet, sustaining Presence in their midst.

Reflection Questions

- According to Sheen, the Eucharist is the efficient cause of all the other sacraments, the agent that brings them into being. How is this so? What sets the Eucharist apart from the other sacraments? What is it about this sacrament that allows the other to flow from it?

- For Sheen, the Eucharist is the source of unity between Christ and his Mystical Body, and among the members of his body. What kind of unity is this? Does it mean uniformity? Does it imply unity in diversity? Can this unity be broken? Does it touch the very heart of Church's identity?

- Sheen uses a number of images to convey his teaching on the Eucharist: the tree of life, the energy of the sun, spiritual plasma, a spiritual version of the catabolic and anabolic processes found in nature—to name but a few. Which of these carry his thought best? Which of them speaks to you the most? Are any of these images new to you? Why does he use so many?

Voice Ten

Henri de Lubac:
Making Church

Our next voice was one of the great proponents of the Nouvelle Théologie. Henri de Lubac, S.J. (1896-1991) was born in Cambrai, in northern France, and spent his childhood in Bourg-en-Bresse and Lyons. He received his early education in Catholic schools and sought entrance into the Society of Jesus in October of 1913. He was drafted into the French army in 1914 and discharged in 1917 after receiving a serious head injury at Verdun. After his release from the army, he continued his religious and priestly formation with the Jesuits, was ordained to the priesthood in 1927, began lecturing at the Catholic University of Lyon in 1929, and professed solemn vows as in 1931.

De Lubac was appointed professor of fundamental theology at Lyon in 1938 and professor of the history of religion in 1939. From 1940-44, he worked on a French underground journal for the French resistance against the Nazi-controlled Vichy regime. In 1941, he founded with Jean Danielou the French series, *Sources chrétiennes*, a collection of bilingual, critical editions of early Christian texts. He resumed his teaching responsibilities after the war but was relieved of his post in 1952, transferred to the Jesuit house in Paris, and effectively "silenced" by his Jesuit superiors due to pressure emanating from suspicions in the

Vatican concerning his involvement with the *Nouvelle Théologie*. He became a member of the French Academy of Moral and Political Sciences in 1958 and was permitted to resume his teaching and publishing soon afterward.

In 1960, De Lubac was invited to serve on the theological preparatory commission of the Second Vatican Council and was a theological expert (*peritus*) at the Council from 1962-65. A prolific author, his major works include: *Catholicism* (1938), *Corpus Mysticum* (1944), *The Drama of Atheist Humanism* (1944), *Surnaturel* (1946), *The Splendor of the Church* (1953), Exégèse *médiévale* (1956-64), *Man in the Presence of* God (1963), *The Mystery of the Supernatural* (1967), De *Lubac: A Theologian Speaks* (1985), and *Theology in History* (1988). He was a member of the International Commission from 1969-74, a founding member of the theological journal *Communio* in 1972, and made a cardinal by Pope John Paul II in 1983. The Eucharist, for him, lies at the very heart of the Church, is preeminently social, and contains within itself the source of ecclesial unity.[1]

De Lubac's Theological Outlook

De Lubac reacted against the lack of historical awareness in the Catholic theology of his day by rooting his writings in the sources of Christian antiquity. One author describes his work as a theology of the Easter Vigil: "It situates itself in the resurrection event, but at the first moment of it, when the only

---

[1] For a detailed chronology of de Lubac's life, see Rudolf Voderholzer, *Meet Henri de Lubac: His Life and Work*, trans. Michael J. Miller (San Francisco: Ignatius Press, 2008), 11-13. For the biographical context of his scholarly writings, see Henri de Lubac, *At the Service of the Church: Henri de Lubac Reflects on the Circumstances that Occasioned His Writings*, trans. Anne Elizabeth Englund (San Francisco: Ignatius Press, 1989).

light visible is the flame of the *lumen Christi* shining in the Darkness of Holy Saturday night."[2] When seen in this light, "the Church's mission is to carry the *lumen Christi*, while singing the Easter proclamation, into the darkness of a world waiting for Christ."[3]

De Lubac's theology ponders the Word of God in silence and leads all who are open to the Word of God into the heart of the Christian mystery.[4] It immerses them in the baptismal womb of the Church and divinizes them in the Spirit by making them anew in Christ.[5] From there, his theology gathers the community of believers around the paschal table where, "...as 'the Church produces the Eucharist ... the Eucharist produces the Church,' forming it into one Catholic communion, the Body of Christ, the '*vir perfectus*' and the '*totus Christus*.'"[6]

In his approach to theology, de Lubac makes four principal contributions. In the first place, he retrieves a richer and more balanced pre-Tridentine Catholicism. He does this by his emphasis on *Ressourcement*, that is, putting Roman Catholic theology back in touch with the primary sources of the tradition. He founded the series *Sources chrétiennes* with this specific goal in mind and roots his own theological research as much as possible in Scripture and the teaching of the Church fathers.[7]

Secondly, de Lubac brings the Eucharist back into the center

---

[2] Christopher Walsh, "Henri de Lubac and the Ecclesiology of the Postconciliar Church: An analysis of His Later Writings (1995-1991)" (Ph.D. diss.: The Catholic University of America, 1993), 4.

[3] Ibid.

[4] Ibid.

[5] Ibid., 5.

[6] Ibid.

[7] Fergus Kerr, "French Theology: Yves Congar and Henri de Lubac," in *The Modern Theologians: an Introduction to Christian Theology in the Twentieth Century*, ed. David F. Ford (Cambridge, MA: Blackwell Publishers, 1997), 111.

of the Church's self-understanding. In his historical research, he documents in clear and no uncertain terms a marked shift in the Church's self-identity that began in the second half of the twelfth century and was marked by a new Eucharistic piety that had become more private and devotional. As a result of his research, he sought to bring the Eucharist back to the center of the study of ecclesiology.[8]

Thirdly, de Lubac defends the biblical exegesis of the premodern period at a time when the historical critical method had displaced it as a primary approach to studying the sacred texts of Scripture. His *Exégèse médiévale* has become a classic work in explaining the approach of medieval exegesis and the deep spiritual meanings it sought to uncover.[9]

Finally, de Lubac criticizes the strict nature/grace distinction of the post-Tridentine Church, which he claims sought to safeguard nature against the Lutheran emphasis on *sola gratia* and grace against the onslaught on Enlightenment humanism, and which he further claims was itself the cause of deism and atheism.[10] His book *Surnaturel* argues that the state of pure nature does not exist and that prior to the sixteenth century humanity was generally understood in terms of the image of God. From a historical perspective, in other words, there is no such thing as a "graceless nature" or a world where the movement of God grace is not in some way operative.[11]

Because many of these insights were met with suspicion and perceived as destructive to the Church's authority and theological integrity, de Lubac in 1950 was silenced by the Church, removed from his teaching responsibilities, and forbidden to publish. His central and most controversial

---

[8] Ibid.
[9] Ibid.
[10] Ibid., 109
[11] Ibid., 111, 113.

theological insight is that, although the vision of God (*visio Dei*) is a gratuitous gift, a yearning for it lies at the root of every human soul. All of his theology flows from this fundamental thesis, including his views on the Eucharist and its central place at the heart of the Church.[12]

De Lubac on the Eucharist

The quotation most closely associated with de Lubac is: "The Church makes the Eucharist and the Eucharist makes the Church."[13] For him, this key idea is not a new, ground-breaking insight, but merely a retrieval of an earlier patristic notion. The two realities—Eucharist and Church—are intimately related and should not be considered separately. Flowing from this key insight is de Lubac's understanding of the essential social character of each. In much of his writing he emphasizes the communal character of the Church and her sacraments to counteract an exaggerated individualism, which in his mind represents a departure from the intuitions of the early Church.[14]

Beginning with *Catholicism*, and then with such works as *Corpus Mysticum* and *The Splendor of the Church*, de Lubac explores the Eucharistic teaching of the patristic and medieval periods and notes an important shift in language and emphasis. Until the middle of the eleventh century, he says, the phrase

---

[12] Ibid., 108.

[13] Henri de Lubac, *Corpus Mysticum* (Paris: Aubier, 1949), 104. For an critical study of de Lubac's views on the Eucharist, see Paul McPartlan, *The Eucharist Makes the Church: Henri de Lubac and John Zizioulas in* Dialogue Edinburgh: T&T Clark, 1993), 3-120. See also Lam T. Le, "The Eucharist and the Church in the Thought of Henri de Lubac," *Irish Theological Quarterly* 71 (nos. 3-4, 2006): 339; Kerr, "French Theology," 110.

[14] Lee, "The Eucharist and the Church," 340-46; Ferr, "French Theology," 110-11.

corpus mysticum (mystical body) was used to describe both the Eucharist and the Church. After that time, the term *mysticum* (mystical) was dropped in reference to the Eucharist to counteract, at least in part, Berengar's heretical denial of the real presence. From the middle of the twelfth century onward, he asserts, the term *mysticum* was increasingly associated with the Church alone and the term itself shifted in meaning from "sacramental" or "pertaining to the mystery" to "mysterious" or "mystical" in a more modern sense. De Lubac points out that this shift in language had the unfortunate consequence of moving the Eucharist from the center of the Church's self-understanding to its periphery. This shift in emphasis also brought about an individualistic (as opposed to communal) Eucharistic piety that focused on the real presence of Christ in the consecrated host, when the real purpose of the sacrament was to bring the fullness of Christ's presence to the body of believers.[15]

The locus of the true body of Christ *(verum corpus)*, in other words, was transferred from the Church to the Eucharist. What is more, one could now speak of the Church without referring to the Eucharist when, as de Lubac discovered from his study of the sources, "the Eucharist is related to the Church as the cause to the effect, as the means to the end, at the same time as the sign to the reality."[16] The intimate relationship between the Eucharist and the Church, in his mind, preserves the latter's true identity and prevents it from being treated as a mere juridical entity. The Eucharist, in other words, roots the Church in its founding sacramental mystery and enables it to embrace

---

[15] Henri de Lubac, *Catholicism* (London: Burns & Oates, 1962), 48. See also Lee, "The Eucharist and the Church," 342; Ferr, "French Theology," 110.

[16] De Lubac, *Corpus Mysticum*, 23. See also, Lee, "The Eucharist and the Church," 344.

that mystery and proclaim it in its apostolic *missio.*

For de Lubac, the Eucharist conveys the fullness of Christ and is the effective sign that both makes the Church and is made by it: "Thus everything points to a study of the relation between the Church and the Eucharist, which we may describe as standing as cause to each other. Each has been entrusted to the other, so to speak, by Christ; the Church produces the Eucharist, but the Eucharist also produces the Church."[17] This line of thinking represents a retrieval of the patristic understanding of the "symbolic inclusion" as opposed to the scholastic emphasis on "dialectical antitheses."[18] It also means that the Eucharist lies at the very heart of the Church's self-identity as the "sacrament of sacraments" and the "sacrament of Church unity".[19]

Some Further Insights

This brief presentation of de Lubac's teaching on the Eucharist demonstrates how the Church's self-understanding has evolved over time and how the Eucharist, while always present to it, has moved first from the center, then to the periphery, and finally back to the center of its ecclesiological identity. It also shows how de Lubac's persistent examination of the sources of the Church's living tradition enabled him to bring such insights to the fore and challenge many of the theological presuppositions of his day. He attempts to present the doctrine of the real presence in a way that is faithful to the tradition, yet also takes into account our present-day sensitivities and

---

[17] See Ferr, French Theology," 110.

[18] Henri de Lubac, *The Splendour of the Church* (San Francisco: Ignatius Press, 1999), 133. See also Lee, "The Eucharist and the Church," 340.

[19] De Lubac, *Catholicism*, 88-89. See also Lee, "The Eucharist and the Church," 340.

patterns of thought. The following remarks show de Lubac's teaching on the Eucharist more deeply, with special emphasis on its relevance for today.

To begin with, de Lubac does not purport to add anything new to the Church's understanding of its relationship to the Eucharist, but only to retrieve something that had been relegated to the sidelines of its theological awareness and bring it back into focus. He does so through a critical examination of the texts of the tradition pertaining to Church and Eucharist, with particular emphasis on the teachings of the Church fathers and their commentaries on Scripture. His careful reading of ancient Christian sources enables him to see the question of the Church's relationship to the Eucharist from an entirely different vantage point, one that leads him to question the highly individualistic Eucharistic piety of his day and nudge it in a different direction. In this respect, de Lubac's contribution is his strong emphasis on recuperating a deeper sense of the Church's theological tradition and using this *ressourcement* as the basis for further theological reflection and development. Through his study of the texts of the Church's theological tradition, he conveys a deep historical awareness of the changing contours of the Church's self-understanding and places the insights gained from such study at the service of the Church.

De Lubac emphasizes the fundamentally social character of the Eucharist and places it at the very heart of the Church's identity. He does so, while also recognizing the dignity and worth of each human individual by virtue of him or her being created in the image and likeness of God. The social dimension of the Eucharist, in his mind, does not suppress the dignity of the individual, but elicits his or her true worth. When seen in this light, the individual believer and the community of the faithful need and cannot do without each other. The Church's unity preserves the identity of its members and enables them to live in harmony. He reacts against the individualistic Eucharist piety of his day because it had become detached from the deeper awareness of the Church's communal and social identity. In this respect, he seeks not to suppress individual Eucharistic piety but redirect it to its true source. When seen in this light, private Eucharistic piety should flow from the Church's communal self-understanding and flow back to it.

The connection between de Lubac's retrieval of the central role of the Eucharist in the Church's self-identity should also be seen in relation to his defense of the various senses of Scripture in the Church's pre-modern hermeneutics.[20] To see the close relationship between the Eucharist and the Church requires the same interpretative stance of "symbolic inclusion" required for uncovering the various spiritual senses of Scripture. Rather than focusing on a single meaning of a text, the interpreter recognizes that the text of Scripture possesses various dimensions of meaning conveyed to the text ultimately by God himself. As Scripture reveals the face of God, so the Eucharist reveals the face of the Church. De Lubac's analysis of a subtle linguistic shift in Eucharistic language leads him to uncover the theological shift in the location of Christ's real presence from the Church to the consecrated species. It is not an accident that this shift in meaning coincides historically with a similar shift in theological method that moves away from the patristic and monastic sensitivity to symbolism to a scholastic emphasis on dialectics.

De Lubac was criticized by some for introducing a misplaced naturalism into the Church's self-understanding when, in point of fact, his was merely pointing out that the real

---

[20] For the categories and principles of the spiritual senses of Scripture as the key to understanding de Lubac's theology, see Susan K. Wood, *Spiritual Exegesis and the Church in the Theology of Henri de Lubac* (Grand Rapids, MI/Edinburgh: William B. Eerdmans/T&T Clark, 1998), 140-54.

presence and the ecclesial body of believers are constituted together. While it is true that the Eucharist and the Church are not the body of Christ in precisely the same sense, it is also true that they are intimately related to and cannot exist without each other. In this sense, the real presence exists for the ecclesial body of believers—and vice versa. For precisely this reason, de Lubac affirms that the Church makes the Eucharist, but the Eucharist also makes the Church. So deeply intertwined are these two realities that they cannot be separated without doing damage to a proper understanding and appreciation of each. This insight lies behind the Church's self-understanding as presented in the document of the Second Vatican Council, especially in the first chapter of *Lumen gentium*, "The Church as Mystery" and in its affirmation that the Eucharist represents the "source and summit of the Christian life."[21]

Finally, de Lubac sees the Eucharist not only as the "sacrament of sacraments," but also as the "sacrament of Church unity." It is the first, because it brings the fullness of Christ (*totus Christus*) into our midst in consecrated host, as well as in the ecclesial body of the faithful. In this respect, all other sacraments point to it and, in some very real sense, flow from it. It is the second, because of the intimate connection between the sacrament and the body of believers, both of which are authentic manifestations of the *corpus mysticum*. De Lubac's theology has been described as a "theology of the Easter Vigil" precisely because it is rooted in the resurrection event and calls the Church to carry forth the *lumen Christi* on its mission to cast out darkness from the world. For de Lubac, the Risen Christ himself constitutes the Eucharistic and ecclesial body of believers, holds them together, and preserves their unity. The Eucharist mediates the Risen Christ to the body of believers, and the Risen Christ in the body of believers constitutes the

---

[21] Second Vatican Council, *Lumen gentium*, no. 11.

sacrament. The two, while not identical, are so closely united, that it would be a serious distortion of their meaning and purpose to separate them.

Although these observations do not exhaust de Lubac's teaching on the Eucharist, they cover its main contours and show how a single, persistent, probing theological voice can effect a change the Church's historical self-awareness with the hope of deepening its understanding of the mysteries of the faith and pushing the tradition forward.

Conclusion

Henri de Lubac was one of the major proponents of the twentieth-century Roman Catholic movement known as the *Nouvelle théologie*, the purpose of which was to reform Catholic theology from within by means of a *ressourcement* or return to the sources of the tradition. De Lubac excelled at combing through some of the overlooked and, in many cases, forgotten patristic and medieval sources in order to retrieve and bring them to light for the Church. To promote that end, he founded *Sources chrétiennes*, a bilingual series of critical patristic and medieval texts and published a number of his own ground-breaking studies on a variety of topics relevant to the Church of his day.

De Lubac's interest in the renewal of Catholic theology did not come without a price. It is widely believed that Pius XII directed his encyclical *Humani generis* (1950), at least in part, against some of the views expressed in *Surnaturel* (1946). With instructions from Rome, he was transferred by his Jesuit superiors from Lyon to Paris and from 1952-58 was forbidden to teach or publish. He was viewed with suspicion by Catholic conservatives and even by some of his fellow Jesuits. In the end, de Lubac's reputation was rehabilitated and his views vindicated, especially at the Second Vatican Council, where he served on the theological preparatory commission, was invited as a theological expert (*peritus*), played a significant role in shaping the theological outcome of the Council, and was eventually made a cardinal in recognition for his contribution to the Church. What is more, along with Hans Urs von Balthasar and Joseph Ratzinger his founding of the theological *Communio* guaranteed that the voices of *ressourcement* would continue to play an important role in interpreting the meaning of the Council.

De Lubac's teaching on the Eucharist highlights the social character of the sacrament and moves it from the periphery to the center of the Church's theological self-awareness. This shift had important ramifications for ecclesiology, many of which are enshrined in the documents of Vatican II, especially *Lumen gentium* (1963). The Eucharist, for de Lubac, is intimately related to the Church and must be considered together with it. In his mind, this sacrament both makes the Church and is itself made by it. If this insight seems obvious to today's believers, it is only because of the tireless research and dogged persistence of theologians, like de Lubac, who placed their theological acumen at the service of the Church and suffered silently until the time was ripe for their views to be heard and ultimately embraced as part of the Church's rich theological tradition.

Reflection Questions

- De Lubac points out that a shift in language from the middle of the twelfth century onwards moved the Eucharist from the center of the Church's self-understanding to its periphery. Has the way we speak about the Eucharist today given rise any other shifts in the Church's Eucharistic spirituality? If so, how would you describe any of these shifts? To what extent do we think of the Eucharist today as the "sacrament of sacraments" and the "sacrament of Church unity?

- According to de Lubac "the Church makes the Eucharist and the Eucharist makes the Church." What does this intimate relationship between the Church and the Eucharist say about the relationships among her many members? What does it say about the relationship between the individual believer and Christ? As a member of the Church, to what extent do you share in the making of the Eucharist? To what extent does the Eucharist make you?

- According to de Lubac the real purpose of the Eucharist is to bring the fullness of Christ's presence to the body of believers. Is your reverence for the Eucharist primarily communal or individualistic? Is there a place for both in an authentic Eucharistic piety? How would you describe the elements of a well-balanced Eucharistic spirituality?

Voice Eleven

Dorothy Day:
Serving the Poor

Our next voice was a prominent twentieth-century Catholic social activist and a co-founder of the Catholic Worker Movement. Dorothy Day (1897-1980) was born in Brooklyn, New York, to John Day, a sports journalist, and Grace Satterlee Day, a homemaker. The family moved to Berkeley, California in 1904, and later to Chicago, where she spent the remainder of her youth. Even though her family was not very religious, she had a distinct memory of holding a Bible at an early age and having a sense of the sacred while reading it. Although baptized an Episcopalian as a child, her early interest in organized religion waned as she came to believe that she could honor God without having to go Church.[1]

---

[1] This biographical information comes from Woodeene Koenig-Bricker, *Meet Dorothy Day: Champion of the Poor* (Ann Arbor, MI: Servant Publications, 2002), 13-16. For other biographies of Day, see Robert Coles, *Dorothy Day: A Radical Devotion* (Reading, MA: Addison-Wesley Publishing Co., 1987; Jim Forest, *All Is Grace: A Biography of Dorothy Day* (Maryknoll, NY: Orbis Books, 2011). For her autobiography, see Dorothy Day, *The Long Loneliness* (New York: Harper & Row, 1952; reprint, Chicago, IL: The Thomas More Press, 1989), 1ff. (page references to *The Long Loneliness* are from the reprint edition).

Day graduated high school 1914 and attended the University of Illinois for a few years before leaving school and traveling to New York City in 1916, where she became involved in the literary scene of Greenwich Village and befriended the playwright Eugene O'Neill. During that time, she wrote for several socialist and progressive publications and got involved in radical politics. She was jailed several times for taking part in social protests, was romantically involved with the writer, Lionel Moise, with whom she conceived a child and at whose insistence she terminated the pregnancy. She later became involved with activist and biologist, Forster Batterham, with whom she had a child, Tamar Therese, in 1924. Neither relationship was long-lived.[2]

While immersed in the literary and art world of Greenwich Village and imbued with a growing sense of social activism, Day was quietly undergoing a religious conversion that would eventually lead her to a radical change of heart. Citing the famous poem by Francis Thompson, she said she was haunted by "The Hound of Heaven" and eventually found her spiritual home in the Catholic faith. She had her infant daughter baptized in a local Catholic Church, and finally converted to Catholicism herself in 1927. In 1932, she founded *The Catholic Worker* newspaper with Peter Maurin, a French immigrant and former Christian Brother. The success of this paper spawned The Catholic Worker Movement, a community dedicated to service, prayer, and refection, and which set Day on a course of social activism that was deeply rooted in her love for the Church and visibly expressed in her service to the poor. Her teaching on the Eucharist flows from this dedicated spirit of faithful giving.[3]

---

[2] Koenig-Bricker, *Meet Dorothy Day*, 17-54.

[3] Ibid., 55-75.

Day's Spiritual Outlook

Day's spirituality was marked by "a love of Scripture... solidarity with the poor... personalism... prophetic witness... peacemaking... a sacramental sense... and gratitude."[4] She describes her journey to Catholicism in her autobiography, *The Long Loneliness* (1952), the title of which she received, at least in part, from her daughter, who once spoke to her of the loneliness of the human situation.[5] In time, Day came to see only one constructive way of dealing with such isolation: "The only answer in this life, to the loneliness we are all bound to feel, is community. The living together, working together, sharing together, loving God and loving our brother, and living close to him in community so we can show our love for Him."[6] Life in community was one of the underlying themes of The Catholic Worker Movement, the movement Day founded with Peter Maurin: "Community—that was the social answer to the long loneliness. That was one of the attractions of religious life and why couldn't lay people share in it? Not just the basic community of the family, but also a community of families, with a combination of private and communal property."[7] She dedicated the rest of her life to building community as a way of healing the loneliness of the human heart.

Day came to this vision by way of a long journey involving a continual search to fill the hole in her soul left by the loneliness of life and the dreariness of existence. Her childhood was mired in a dysfunctional family life, with a demanding father who paid

---

[4] James Allaire and Rosemary Broughton, *Praying with Dorothy Day* (Winona, MN: Saint Mary's Press, 1995), 31-32.

[5] Ibid., 111.

[6] Day, *The Long Loneliness*, 280; Allaire and Broughton, *Praying with Dorothy Day*, 111.

[7] Day, *The Long Loneliness, 261.*

little attention to his children and a mother who put on a cheerful face for her children, but was living in denial about the lack of love present in her marriage and family life. Although a bright, promising young student, she left college before finishing her degree in order to experience for herself the intellectual and cultural melting pot of New York City, earn her keep as a journalist, and lose herself in social causes. Her search for identity led to a rejection of organized religion, a generally loose (even bohemian) lifestyle, and a dedication to the plight of the impoverished masses. At the same time, it deepened her sensitivity to her deep spiritual wounds, her love for life, and her continuing personal quest for God.[8]

Day's conversion to Catholicism enabled her to see the connection between her deep spiritual yearnings and her desire to serve the poor and marginalized in society. She saw in her newfound faith's emphasis on the communion of the faithful and Christ's mystical body, a vision that offered a remedy to "the long loneliness," one that offered a balance between the individual and the collective and which pointed out the inconsistencies of her intensely individualistic bohemian ways and her deep social consciousness. With her identity firmly rooted in the person of Christ and his Body, the Church, she began to see his presence in the lives of the people she served. She found in The Catholic Worker Movement a way of giving concrete expression to the unity of the community of the faithful and Christ's love for the poor. The members of this movement did so by creating houses of hospitality and working farms where everyone was welcome and where the Eucharist provided

---

[8] See Catherine Faver, "Identity, Community, and Crisis: The Conversion Narratives of Dorothy Day," in *Dorothy Day and the Catholic Worker Movement: Centenary Essays*, Marquette Studies in Theology No. 32, eds. William Thorn, Phillip Runkel, and Susan Mountin (Milwaukee, WI: Marquette University Press, 2001), 351-69.

food for the soul and the body of believers met the material needs those want. Christ's presence in the sacrament enabled Catholic workers to sense his presence in the ordinary affairs of daily life, especially life in community, and in the lives of the poor and marginalized.[9]

Day's Teaching on the Eucharist

Day believed the Gospel was for all Christians, not a spiritual elite or a select few. She was very fond of quoting a saying of St. John of the Cross: "Love is the measure by which we shall be judged."[10] She saw a close connection between the presence of Jesus in the Blessed Sacrament and his presence in the faces of the poor. Through the Eucharist the material word spoke to her of the love of God.[11] It was the "sacrament of love," which sought to bring about a revolution of the heart. "The greatest challenge of the day," she once wrote, was "how to bring about a revolution of the heart, a revolution which has to start with each one of us? When we begin to take the lowest place, to wash the feet of others, to love our brothers with that burning love, that passion , which led to the Cross , then we can truly say, 'Now I have begun.'"[12] To this end, she tried to start her day with Mass or at least some time before the Blessed Sacrament so that this revolution of heart might take root in her.

Day also drew a connection between the Eucharist and the meals she shared with others: "Meals are so important," she once wrote. "The disciples knew Christ in the breaking of bread.

---

[9] Ibid., 360-61.

[10] Forest, *All Is Grace*, 174.

[11] Forest, *Love Is the Measure*, 187.

[12] Dorothy Day, *Loaves and Fishes: The Inspiring Story of the Catholic Worker Movement* (New York: Harper & Row, 1963; reprint, Maryknoll, NY: Orbis Books, 1997), 215 (page refences are from the reprint edition).

We know Christ in each other in the breaking of bread. It is the closest we can ever come to each other, sitting down and eating together. It is unbelievably, poignantly intimate."[13] The Eucharist, for her, was also a reminder of the importance of ritual in our lives: "Ritual, how could we do without it! ...And just as a husband may embrace his wife casually as he leaves for work in the morning, and kiss her absent-mindedly in his comings and goings, still that kiss on occasion turns to rapture, a burning fire of tenderness and love....We have too little ritual in our lives."[14] The Eucharist, for her, was a celebration of the rituals of everyday life. It heightened our awareness of the sacred in the ordinary events of life: farming the land, watching a sunrise, sharing a meal with friends. It was a reminder to her of the presence of the sacred in the rituals of everyday life.

In addition to sustaining a sense of ritual, the Eucharist, for Day, also had a strong penitential aspect to it. At the Eucharistic Congress in Philadelphia in 1976, she spoke of her love for the Church and the need to do penance and to make reparation for the sins of humanity. The Church, she says, "taught me the crowning love of the life of the Spirit. But she also taught me that before we bring our gifts of service, of gratitude, to the altar--- if our brother have [sic] anything against us, we must hesitate to approach the altar to receive the Eucharist."[15] The Eucharist, for her, presupposed acts of penitence: "Otherwise we partake of the Sacrament unworthily."[16] In true prophetic vein, she sought to challenge people in their complacency and console them in their times of grief and sadness. Her love for God, the

---

[13] Dorothy Day, *Writings from Commonweal*, ed. Patrick Jordan (Collegeville, MN: The Liturgical Press, 2002), 81.

[14] Koenig-Bricker, *Meet Dorothy Day*, 127-28.

[15] Dorothy Day, "Bread for the Hungry," *The Catholic Worker* (September, 1976), 1.5, https://www.catholicworker.org/dorothyday/articles/258.html.

[16] Ibid.

community of the faithful, and for all humanity moved her at that same Eucharistic Congress to speak out against the sin of nuclear holocaust, calling on everyone to ask the Lord for forgiveness in reparation for the lives that were needlessly lost at Hiroshima on August 6, 1945. She was not afraid to identify the hidden prejudices woven into the fabric of our lives, (even those lodged deep in the heart of the Church), especially if she perceived that they were terribly off-base and rooted in ill-conceived stereotypes and misunderstandings.[17]

Day's love for the Eucharist was also very Marian. One of her daily rituals was to pray to Mary after receiving her Son in the sacrament: "I always say to the Blessed Mother after Communion—'Here He is in my heart; I believe, help thou mine unbelief; Adore Him, thank Him and love Him for me. He is your Son; His honor is in your hands. Do not let me dishonor Him."[18] She looked to Mary, the Mother of the Christ and the Mother of the Church, for the courage and strength to give birth to Christ in and through her love for the poor. She fostered a Marian approach both to the sacrament and to service of Christ in the world's poor and marginalized, one rooted in humility, truth, and the love of God and neighbor.

Some Further Insights

Although this brief presentation of Day's approach to the Eucharist does not do justice to her love for the sacrament and the central role it played in her life, it highlights some of the major characteristics of her Eucharistic outlook on life and points to the deep connection she saw between Jesus' presence in the Blessed Sacrament and in the lives of the poor. The following remarks seek to tease out some of the implications of

---

[17] Ibid.

[18] Koenig-Bricker, *Meet Dorothy Day*, 135.

her teaching and point out their relevance for today's believers.

To begin with, Day saw a close connection between the Eucharist and ordinary, daily life. The sacrament, for her, was not an escape of life, but a free and open embrace of it, especially of the poor and marginalized of society. She attended Mass not only to render God glory, and honor, and praise, but also to be nourished by the Bread of Life so that she could serve those in need by seeking to meet their material and spiritual wants. The Eucharist, in this respect, is the sacrament of the love of both God *and* neighbor. These two loves, while distinct, are also intimately related. We cannot say we love God, if we ignore our brothers and sisters and fail to reach to them in compassionate and loving ways. The presence of Christ in the Eucharist enabled Day to see his face more clearly in the ordinary events of life, especially in the faces of the poor. Believers today should heed her example and look upon the sacrament as a means of experiencing life on a deeper level of awareness. When the priest says at the end of the celebration, "Go forth, the Mass has ended," the liturgy of daily life is continues.

Day's approach to the sacrament also heightens our awareness of the central role of ritual in daily life. We are creatures of habit and navigate our way through life by means of a constant repetition of structured ways of acting: prayers, meals, learning, work, recreation. Our lives are dotted with activities that are repeated day after day in very similar (if not identical) ways. "Ritual. How could we do without it!" says Day. The Eucharist, for her, was the central ritual of life. It is the "ritual of rituals," for it places all the other rituals of life in their proper perspective and enables us to focus on the one thing that matters: our relationship with God. This relationship affects the way we relate to others. It shapes our character by conforming us more and more unto the heart and mind of Christ. As members of his body, we become Christ's eyes and ears, arms and hands, in the particular corner of space and time in which we find ourselves. The Eucharist reminds us that the rituals of daily life have a sacred character and that they should reveal Christ's presence in our midst.

The Eucharist, for Day, also reminds us of the importance of community. She believed deeply in the community of the faithful and saw a close, intimate connection between the body of Christ and the body of believers. The Eucharist, for her, was not a private affair between the believer and God, but a communal celebration of the power of love over hatred and of life over death. For Day, life in community was the only remedy for the long loneliness that everyone experienced deep within their hearts. The Eucharist, moreover, was the remedy that heals our hearts and teaches us to relate to each other in compassionate and loving ways. As a sacred meal, the sacrament draws us together and unites us in bonds of faith and fellowship rooted in Christ and his relationship to the Father. The Holy Spirit, the bond between the Father and the Son, is the bond that holds together the Christian community and, ultimately, the entire human family. The Eucharist turns loneliness into solitude and solitude into life in the Spirit, the fruits of which are "love, joy, peace, patience, kindness, generosity, faithfulness, gentleness, and self-control."[19]

Because the Eucharist is a means for building community, Day also saw it as a catalyst for addressing the needs of society. As the sacrament of love, it challenges the community of the faithful to identify the various social ills that plague human society and to find constructive ways of healing them. Day was an outspoken critic of the attitudes behind the vicious cycle of hunger, poverty, prejudice, and violence endemic to so many areas of modern society, and she was not afraid to speak out against those who either knowingly or unknowingly per-

---

[19] Galatians 5:22-23.

petuated such ills. The Eucharist, in this respect, enables us to hear the Word of God within our hearts and move us to challenge those who ignore or are simply numb to or unaware of the social evils existing in their very midst. By nourishing our own relationship with God, it gives us the strength and courage to speak out in a prophetic way on behalf of society's poor, marginalized, and voiceless.

According to Day, "Love is the measure by which we shall be judged." As the sacrament of Christ's love, the Eucharist represents the measure of God's love for us, the standard by which we are called to live, and by which we shall be judged. The breaking of bread at Eucharist is more than the sharing of a meal. It also points to the breaking of Jesus' body and the spilling of his blood on Calvary. Day was very much aware that the Eucharist was a sacrificial offering of Christ for the sins of humanity. She also knew that, as members of his body, believers were called to embody the mystery of his passion, death, and resurrection in their daily lives. The Eucharist, for Day, embodied every aspect of Christ's paschal mystery and was the means by which it lived on in the lives of the faithful. The sacrament allows the mystery of redemptive self-offering to take root in our hearts and empowers us to love as Christ loved through the presence of his Spirit living within us. We shall be judged according to the extent to which we allow the love of Christ to fill our lives and overflow to those in need.

The Eucharist, for Day, also represented a call to penitence. To receive the sacrament worthily, we must make sure that we have asked God's pardon for our sins and sought to make appropriate reparations for them. The sacrament calls us to live in right relationship with both God and neighbor. Day was very much aware of our human tendency toward sin and saw the sacrament as a call to examine or consciences, take a good look at our willing participation in evil (be it personal, societal, or universal), seek God's forgiveness, and be resolved to make things right. In her mind, penance and love were two sides of the same sacramental coin. We cannot love others, if we do not know how to seek forgiveness. Saying we are sorry is the best (perhaps the only) way of making broken relationships right. When extended to the societal ills in which we all participate, we express our sorrow by committing ourselves to making things right. For this reason, the Eucharist calls us to work for justice on every level of human experience. The sacrament of love, in other words, calls us to live for justice by giving everyone their due on both the personal and societal levels.

Finally, Day's love for Mary overflowed into her love for Christ in the Eucharist. Aware of the Blessed Mother's intimate relationship with her Son, she turned to her frequently to seek her help in remaining faithful to him and not dishonoring him in any way. Mary, for her, was not only the Mother of Christ, but also the Mother of the Church and, as such, someone who looked upon every believer (and every potential believer) with deep motherly affection. Day turned to Mary as a loving mother and sought her help in remaining faithful to her son. She also saw her as a faithful disciple who followed Jesus from his birth in Bethlehem, to his death on Calvary, to the birth of the Church in the Upper Room and the birth of the Christian community on Pentecost. Day's love for Mary deepened her love for the Eucharist—and vice versa. She prayed to her always after receiving Holy Communion, because she wished to remain in communion with her Son and be faithful to him to the very end. Mary was a source of hope for Day and for all the members of The Catholic Worker Movement. She was the mother of the Church, the mother of all disciples, the mother of the poor.

Conclusion

Dorothy Day was one of the most outspoken Catholic social activists of the twentieth century. A convert to Catholicism in her early thirties, she experienced in her heart a fundamental conversion that led her to leave a conflicted life of practical atheism and social activism to embrace a life of deeply spiritual longings and a capacity to see the face of Christ in the lives of the poor and marginalized. Her Catholic spirit and desire led her to serve the poor of society and to found the Catholic Worker Movement with her colleague and close friend, Peter Maurin.

Day saw in this Movement the possibility of building authentic Christian communities throughout the world. Community, for her, was the human and spiritual remedy to "the long loneliness" which has plagued the human from time eternal. She lived in community and sought to build community in all her actions, be it feeding the poor on bread lines, sharing supper with them in her Catholic Worker Home on the Lower East Side of Manhattan, or working with them on their Catholic Worker Farm in Upstate New York. The Eucharist, for her, was a fundamentally communal action, one that gave her the strength to reach out to others and to find Christ in their broken, enfeebled lives.

The Eucharist, for Dorothy Day, embodied three things that formed the basis of the Catholic community of faith: a sacred meal, a sacrificial offering, and a Divine Presence. She understood that the awareness of these aspects of authentic community varied from believer to believer, and she sought to remedy that situation by dedicating herself to The Catholic Worker Movement, a community that would embrace all of these Eucharistic elements in a life of faith dedicated to service to the poor. The Body of Christ, for Day, was physically and spiritually present in the Blessed Sacrament *and* in the faces of the masses. She dedicated her life to serving God at the altar of the poor. Like him, she emptied herself out of love for God and out of love for humanity. Like him, she gave herself to others without counting the cost. Like him, she put the needs of others before her own. She dedicated her life to living in Holy

Communion with the Lord and with the poor and marginalized. She sought to become eucharist for others, as Christ became Eucharist for her.

Reflection Questions

- Day believed the Gospel was for all Christians, not a spiritual elite or a select few. Do you consider yourself a member of a Gospel elite? Do you belong to a group that excludes others rather than welcomes them? How do you reach out to strangers? How do you reach out to the poor and the marginalized?
- Day drew a connection between the Eucharist and the meals she shared with others. Are you present for meals? Do you look at them as a way of drawing closer to others and building community? Do you turn off the television and put aside your cell phone? What could you do to make your meals with others more conducive to the living out of Gospel values?
- Day saw the Eucharist as a catalyst for addressing the needs of society. Why does it challenge us to be positive agents for change in the world? How does it do so? What social needs does your local parish need to address? How would you go about identifying them? How would you prioritize them and seek to respond to them?

Voice Twelve

Frank Sheed:
Heart of the Church

F. J. Sheed (1897-1981) was a popular twentieth-century Catholic lay theologian, public speaker, publisher, translator and apologist. He was born in Sydney, Australia, graduated with First Class Honors from the University of Sydney, and went on to study law. He moved to England with his wife, Maisie Ward, and worked for more than forty years as a street corner evangelist for the Catholic Evidence Guild. In 1926, he and his wife founded the publishing house Sheed & Ward in London and the American house in 1933. The author of more than twenty books, he was a central figure in what he called the "Catholic Intellectual Revival" and instrumental in renewing and promulgating Catholic thought throughout the English-speaking world. In recognition of his many achievements, Rome's Sacred Congregation of Seminaries and Universities awarded him an honorary doctorate in theology, which was bestowed at the Catholic University of Lille, France in 1957. His teaching on the Eucharist was central to his life and thought.[1]

---

[1] This biographical information comes from Shawn G. Kennedy, "Frank J. Sheed, 84, Lay Theologian *New York Times* (November, 21, 1981), http://www.nytimes.com/1981/11/21/obituaries/frank-j-

Sheed's Spiritual Outlook

Sheed was very much aware of being a member of a minority religion in a country (England) that had persecuted Catholics for centuries, and where its people were in many ways still suspicious of and, in some cases, even hostile toward them. For this reason, he placed a great deal of emphasis on the intellectual defense of the faith and the need to confront the world with the truth. His street preaching for the Catholic Evidence Guild, his publishing house, Sheed & Ward, and his own writing were manifestations of this fundamental spiritual outlook.

The best place to see Sheed's spiritual outlook at work is in his most popular work, *Theology and Sanity*.[2] In this book, he seeks to provide "the indispensable minimum that every man needs in order that he may be living mentally in the real world—which is what the word Sanity means in my title."[3] The concern of the book, he says, "is not with the Will but with the Intellect, not with sanctity but with sanity."[4] He does not mean to imply that the intellect matters more than the will, only that the intellect is often neglected and now needs some attention.

Sheed's spiritual outlook may be summarized thus: "For the soul's full functioning, we need a Catholic intellect as well as a Catholic will. We have a Catholic will when we love God and obey God, love the Church and obey the Church. We have a Catholic intellect when we live consciously in the presence of the realities that God through his Church has revealed. A good working test of a Catholic will is that we should do what the Church says. But for a Catholic intellect, we must also see what

---

sheed-84-a-lay-theologian.html.

[2] F. J. Sheed, *Theology and Sanity* (New York: Sheed & Ward, 1946).

[3] Ibid., v.

[4] Ibid., 3.

the Church sees. This means that when we look out upon the Universe we see the same Universe that the Church sees; and the enormous advantage of this is that the Universe the Church sees is the real Universe, because She is the Church of God. Seeing what She sees means seeing what is there. And just as loving what is good is sanctity, or the health of the will, so seeing what is there is sanity, or the health of the intellect."[5] Sheed spends the rest of *Theology and Sanity* covering the essential elements of Catholicism's view of the universe, focusing primarily on related topics related to God and his Creation.

With respect to God, Sheed says that He is both Infinite Existence and Personal, both changeless and infinitely active, transcending both time and space. He also is Triune: the First Person generates the Second; the Third Person proceeds from the First and Second. This generation and this procession go on for all eternity. The Persons, moreover, are equal by nature, yet distinct by virtue of their relations to one another. Although they always act as one, each one appropriates a certain role in God's outward activity: The Father appropriates to himself the act of creation; the Son, the act of redemption; the Spirit, the act of sanctification.

With respect to Creation, Sheed ponders why God created at all, what it means to be created, and how it is indeed the work of the Trinity. He goes on to cover the created universe, the existence of angels and men, the fall of man, and the whole of salvation history. He writes of how God chose the Jews as his people and how in the fullness of time he would send his Son to enter the world in the mystery of the Incarnation. He treats the mission of Christ, his Divine Personhood, his full humanity, the nature of his redeeming sacrifice, the gift of the Spirit, the birth of the Church, the role of the twelve apostles, and the role of Peter. He writes of the coming of God's kingdom, the dispensing

---

[5] Ibid., 3-4.

of God's sacramental gifts, and the nature of Christ's Mystical Body. He describes what life in the Mystical Body is like both during life and after death. He writes of the end of the world and of the importance of all people to habituate themselves to this reality, taking into account their extraordinary place in God's creation, their insufficiencies, their need for grace, and their ability to find what they need in the Church. He writes about all these things—and so much more—including the Eucharist, which for him holds a central place in the Church's vision of reality.[6]

Sheed's Teaching on the Eucharist

Sheed discusses the Eucharist at various places in *Theology and Sanity*. In the chapter entitled, "The Redeeming Sacrifice," he recounts what the Gospel writers say about its institution by Christ at the Last Supper: "He ate the paschal meal prescribed by Jewish law with His Apostles and then went on to make them the priests of the Eucharistic meal whereby until the end of the world men would receive His own Body and Blood."[7] The Eucharist, for him, is the supernatural food that sustains our supernatural life in Christ. It nourishes the Church and her members and enables them to live through Christ, with Christ, and in Christ.

In the chapter entitled, "Dispensing the Gifts," Sheed says: "The Blessed Eucharist obviously differs from the others in this—that whereas by the others we receive the life of Christ, by the Blessed Eucharist we receive Christ Himself."[8] For him, all the other sacraments presuppose this sacrament and look to it: "The others all lead to increase of life, but the Blessed Eucharist

---

[6] Ibid., vii-x.

[7] Ibid., 218.

[8] Ibid., 257-58.

is the basis of them all, for it is the very food of the soul and without food there can be no continuance of life."[9] Sheed summarizes the Church's teaching on the Eucharist in this way: "It is, of course, the living Christ whom we receive. The bread ceases to be bread and becomes His body. But because death has no more dominion over Him, where His body is, there He wholly is, body and blood and soul and divinity. The wine ceases to be wine and becomes His blood: but where His blood is, there He wholly is body and blood and soul and divinity. Therefore if we receive either, we are receiving the whole Christ. And receive Him we must, for He is the food of our life."[10] Sheed embraces the Church's sacramental realism and relishes it. He takes the words of institution at their face value and does not attempt to water down or modify in any way there obvious meaning.

In the chapter entitled, "Life in the Body," Sheed identifies the Eucharist as the food of the supernatural life: "By Baptism we enter into the life of the Body: or, to put it another way, the life of the Body enters into us. Either way, we become alive supernaturally. But a living thing needs food, and without food will almost certainly perish. But all life must be fed by food like in nature to itself. Our bodily life is fed by bodies, of animal or vegetable. Our mental life is fed by minds, the minds of those who instruct us. But this new life of sanctifying grace is Christ Himself living in us: the only food that could feed a life which is Christ must itself be Christ. And what we receive in the Eucharist *is* Christ."[11] What is more, the Eucharist, for him, not only nourishes the members of Christ's Mystical Body, but is also a source of unity: "Receiving Christ Our Lord thus, we are in the profoundest sense one with Him, and this is the great thing; but also we are one with all, in all ages, who by receiving

---

[9] Ibid.
[10] Ibid., 258.
[11] Ibid., 282-83.

Him have become likewise one with Him. And this is no small thing. The blessed Eucharist serves the growth of each member of the Body in holiness; but it serves also the unity of the Body as a whole, drawing the whole more profoundly into oneness with Christ"[12] The Eucharist, in this sense, "is the life principle of the Church even more than of the individual soul."[13] Sheed goes on to draw a close connection between the Eucharist and Christ's eternal self-offering to the Father. The Mass, he says, "is the breaking through to earth of the offering of Himself that Christ makes continuously in Heaven simply by His presence there."[14] There is only one difference: "Christ makes His offering in Heaven in His own sacred humanity; Christ makes His offering on earth through His Mystical Body."[15]

Some Further Insights

While this brief description of Sheed's understanding of the Eucharist does not exhaust his views on the sacrament, it gives us a sense of his general concerns and helps us find its place in his overall spiritual outlook. The following remarks expand on this description with the hope of providing deeper insights into the place of the Eucharist in his life and thought.

To begin with, Sheed views on the Eucharist must be seen in the larger context of his understanding of the Mystical Body of Christ. This Body, for him, is not a simple metaphor used to describe the unity of the fellowship believers, but a living mystical entity that continues Jesus' historical presence in the world through those who believe in him. The Risen Lord is truly present in this mystical communion, and the Eucharist is the

---

[12] Ibid., 283.
[13] Ibid.
[14] Ibid., 285-86.
[15] Ibid., 286.

means by which this Mystical Body is sustained in time. His point that all life must be nourished by food similar in nature to itself underscores the reality of this supernatural organism. Only the Body and Blood of the Risen Lord himself can feed those whom he has incorporated into his risen life. The doctrine of the Mystical Body of Christ underlies the entire sacramental system of the Church. The grace of the sacraments comes through, with, and in the person of the Risen Lord. Unlike the other sacraments, which give us life in Christ, the Eucharist gives us Christ himself.

Sheed professes a hearty sacramental realism that lies at the heart of the Church's teaching on the Eucharist. "The bread," he says, "ceases to be bread and becomes His body...The wine ceases to be wine and becomes his blood."[16] This realism takes Jesus' words of institution seriously by asserting that the elements of bread and wine are more than mere signs or symbols of Christ's body and blood, but that they actually become Christ's body and blood. His experience as a street preacher enabled him to explain the Church's teaching on transubstantiation in a way that ordinary people could under-stand. He shied away from using philosophical terms and categories and sought instead to translate Church teaching in a way that was accessible to the masses. Sheed was a theologian for everyman. His teaching on the Eucharist displays his talent for translating difficult concepts into the ordinary language used by the common man.

The Eucharist, for Sheed, stands apart from all the other sacraments. It does so in a way that accentuates the intrinsic worth of each. All the other sacraments presuppose it and refer to it. The Eucharist, in turn, justifies their existence. Without the Eucharist the community of believers could not exist and there would be no further need for the other sacraments. The

---

[16] Ibid., 258.

Eucharist, in this respect, gives believers the supernatural sustenance of Christ's body and blood. This food brings those who receive it into close personal communion with the Risen Lord. Sheed points out that the Eucharist, for this reason, is both the life principle of the Church and the primary means through which individual believers grow in holiness. Without it, there would be no Church and without the Church there would be no individual believers. The gift of the Eucharist is Christ's promise to all believers that he would always be with them and share with them the riches of his Risen life.

The connection that Sheed draws between the Eucharist and Christ's eternal self-offering before the Father in heaven reveals the deep sacramental bond between Christ and his Church. The Risen Christ who offers himself in his sacred humanity to the Father in heaven and who intercedes for us on our behalf is the same Christ who acts in the sacraments of the Church and continues to spread his Gospel message through the members of his Body. The Eucharist, in other words, perpetuates Christ's presence in time by bringing Christ's eternal self-emptying into our midst. When seen in this light, Christ's sacrificial offering on Calvary is both eternally present to the Father and present in time in the Eucharistic celebration. Through the Eucharist, Jesus lives his paschal mystery through the community of believers. In the words of St. Paul, "In him we live and move and have our being" (Acts 17:28).

Sheed also recognizes the Eucharist is the source of unity within the Church. When a person receives Holy Communion he or she receives the body and blood, soul and divinity of Jesus Christ. Receiving Eucharist thus puts the believer in a close, intimate communion with Christ himself and with all who receive the sacrament and who profess their faith in the Risen Lord. This unity is not superficial or cosmetic, but real, intimate, and life sustaining. By receiving the body and blood of Christ, the members of Christ's body are united both to Christ and to each other. Since not every member of the body has the same function within the body, there must be a certain degree of unity in the midst of diversity: "As it is, there are many members but one body" (1Cor 12:20). To use Sheed's terminology, such unity requires that "we see what the Church sees" and "will what the Church wills." It presupposes the sharing of a common vision of reality and professing it in our words and actions.

The Eucharist, for Sheed, sustains the supernatural life of the community of believers, conveys the real presence of Christ's body and blood, and is the a redeeming sacrifice of Calvary made present in the sacrament in a real but bloodless manner. He sees the Eucharist as a mysterious blend of banquet, presence, and sacrifice, affirming the traditional teaching of the Church, yet doing so in a way that translates difficult theological realities into common everyday language. He does not emphasize any one of these dimensions over the others, but balances them (even holding them in tension with one another) to convey a sense of the unfathomable mystery that Christ has revealed in this great sacrament. The Eucharist, for him, is the central act of Catholic worship and brings together the many aspects of Christ's redemptive mission into a single action of liturgical worship. At one and the same time, it nourishes us, gives us a taste of the messianic banquet, immerses us in the redemptive action of Christ's sacrificial offering on Calvary, and brings into our midst the presence of the Risen Lord.

Finally, Sheed draws a strong analogy between Christ's hidden presence in the Church and his mysterious presence in the Eucharist under the appearances of bread and wine. Christ's presence in the Eucharist can be seen only with the eyes of faith. For many, it is hard to believe that the Lord of the universe would humble himself to such an extent and become the very food that we eat and drink. It stretches and strains the imagination to think that God would empty himself in such a way and hide himself in what, by all measurements, seems to be nothing more than ordinary bread and wine. In a similar way, it is difficult to imagine that Christ is truly present in his Church, which so often seems marred by sin and human frailty. His presence there is hidden and we need to view this mystery through the eyes of faith. Christ's hidden Eucharistic presence sustains his hidden presence in the Church, even as it sustains us as we seek to understand his hidden presence in our own lives and in the lives of those we love.

Conclusion

F. J. Sheed accomplished many things in his life, and it is difficult to select any one as the most important or memorable. He was not afraid to bring the truth of the Catholic faith to the world and did so through his many years of street corner preaching for the Catholic Evidence Guild. He started a successful Catholic publishing house that promoted some of the most prominent Catholic voices of his day: G.K. Chesterton, Evelyn Waugh, Ronald Knox, Fulton Sheen—to name just a few. He was a respected lay theologian at a time in the Church when the field was largely the domain of priests and religious. His own writings were widely popular, although he did not receive the same degree of recognition as some of the authors whose writings he published. He viewed himself as a servant of the truth and strove to impress upon those whose lives he touched the importance of seeing what the Church sees and willing it.

The Eucharist, for Sheed, was the supernatural food that sustained the supernatural life of the Church. It was Christ's gift of himself to the community of believers: the gift of his presence, the gift of redemptive action, and the gift of his own nourishing body and blood. For him, it was also the source of the Church's unity with Christ and with one another. Christ's presence in the sacrament, hidden beneath the appearances of bread and wine, could be seen only through the eyes of faith. He took the words of the Apostle Paul to heart, "...we walk by faith, not by sight" (2Cor 5:7). That hidden presence nourishes our life of faith and enables us to sense Christ's presence in the life of the Church, as well as in our own lives. The Eucharist, for him, was a sacrament of life, but not just any life. It was the sacrament of the life of Christ in his Mystical Body and its many members.

Sheed did not treat the Eucharist in isolation, but placed it at the heart of the Church's life and teaching. He knew that the Church's very existence depended on it, because it represented not merely the life of Christ, but the very person of Christ himself. For this reason, he encouraged all Catholics to embrace the Church's Eucharistic faith, take it to heart, and embody in their lives the act of self-offering and sacrifice it represented.

Reflection Questions

- Sheed does not treat the Eucharist in isolation, but places it at the very heart of the Church's life and teaching. It differs from the other sacraments because it gives us not merely the life of Christ, but Christ himself. Can the Church exist without the Eucharist? Can it exist without the sacraments? In what sense do the other sacraments presuppose the Eucharist?
- Sheed says that the Eucharist is supernatural food that sustains our supernatural life in Christ and unites the members of his body, the Church. Why is it important to receive this sacrament? Do you agree with his insight that our souls must be fed with the grace that comes from receiving the Body and Blood of Christ in the Eucharist? How does this sacrament unite us? How does it unite us with Christ?
- Sheed considered himself a theologian for everyman. His teaching on the Eucharist displays a talent for translating

difficult concepts into the ordinary language used by the common man. Is his teaching on the Eucharist clear? Is there anything in it that you do not understand? Is it faithful to Church teaching? Is it watered down in any way? What strikes you most about it? What aspects of it would you like to see further developed?

Voice Thirteen

Adrienne von Speyr:
Means and Sign

Our next voice was a married Catholic laywoman, medical doctor, spiritual writer, and Christian mystic. Born in Switzerland and raised in the Reformed Protestant tradition, Adrienne von Speyr (1902-1967) converted to Catholicism in 1940 through the influence of the Swiss theologian, Hans Urs von Balthasar. Together, the two founded the secular institute known as *The Community of St. John*. She composed more than sixty-five works, many of which were dictated to von Balthasar while in the throes of contemplative prayer. Her writings on the Eucharist reflect her deep love for the Holy Mass and Jesus' presence in the Blessed Sacrament.[1]

Speyr's Call to Mysticism

Speyr was born in La Chaux-de-Fonds, a city in Switzerland's Jura mountains. She was the second of four children of Theodor von Speyr and Laure Girard. Although her mother was emotionally distant, her father loved her dearly until his

---

[1] For a complete listing of Speyr's works, see Hans Urs von Balthasar, *First Glance at Adrienne von Speyr*, trans. Antje Lawry and Sr. Sergia Englund (San Francisco: Ignatius Press, 1981),102-111.

premature death in 1918. She also had a close, loving relationship with her grandmother and developed a deep trust in God at an early age.

Although a bright student, Speyr suffered from asthma and intense back pains and was forced to discontinue her studies for a time. Shortly after her father's death, she contracted tuberculosis in both lungs and her doctors thought she would die within a year. She was sent to Leysin, a village near Lake Geneva known for its sanitariums for those with consumption, and was slowly nursed back to health. After a relapse and yet a second recovery, Speyr returned to secondary school where she excelled and, upon graduation, decided to follow in the footsteps of her father by becoming a physician. She pursued medical studies and an internship, paying her way by giving private lessons, and eventually became the first woman medical doctor in Switzerland. Despite her poor health and periods of intense suffering, she practiced medicine successfully for some twenty years, seeing at times as many as eighty patients a day.

Speyr's first husband, Emil Dürr, was a professor of history at the University of Basel and died in 1934. In 1936, she married Werner Kaegi (1901-79), an associate of her husband's at the university. Her attraction to Catholicism started early in life and increased with her attempt to cope with her own suffering and close encounters with death. She developed a close spiritual friendship with von Balthasar, who brought her into the Catholic faith and gave her valuable help in interpreting her mystical experiences. During her lifetime she became friends with many other leading Catholic intellectuals of the day.

After her conversion in 1940 at the age of thirty-eight, Speyr would experience in her life a series of lifelong sufferings that would culminate in a very real experience of Christ's experience on Golgotha. Christ's suffering and death was his final act of obedience toward "Abba," his Father in heaven. In dying, he descended into hell and encountered the pain of humanity's separation from God. In her mystical visions, she experienced the reality of what it would mean to lose God for all eternity. Her experiences were so vivid that they could easily seem unreal to the ordinary believer.[2]

Speyr's Spiritual Outlook

Speyr's spirituality involved being completely transparent before God. By forgetting oneself, she believed a person acquired in time an attitude of obedient listening that would allow him or her to understand God's will and receive it with open arms. The quest for holiness involved a constant movement away from self so that one would be ready to receive God's Word and carry it out. This gradual movement away from self-centeredness to God-centeredness resulted in living a life of spiritual childhood where she could be both "in God and for God." For her, the quest for perfection consisted in always being available for God in order to listen to his Word and to give glory to the Father by carrying it out.

Speyr also had a deep devotion to Mary and, like her, pondered the mysteries of the Incarnate Word deep within her heart. This Marian dimension to her spiritual outlook enabled her to share herself with God on every level of her being: the physical, emotional, intellectual, spiritual, and social. For such transparency, she was rewarded with deep mystical insights and

---

[2] All historical information in this section comes from Adrienne von Speyr, *My Early Years*, ed. Hans Urs von Balthasar, trans. Mary Emily Hamilton and Dennis D. Martin (San Francisco: Ignatius Press, 1995), 17-427; Balthasar, *First Glance at Adrienne von Speyr*, 17-49; *Doctor, Convert, and Mystic: The Life and Work of Adrienne von Speyr*, http://www.ignatiusinsight.com/authors/adrienne_ von_ speyr.asp (accessed October 5, 2016); Regis Martin, "Von Speyr's Life of Grace," http://www.christendom-awake.org/pages/balthasa/ vonspeye.htm.

intuitions that could only come from someone with a deep, personal knowledge of the divine. Although she was too sickly to climb the mountains and hike the valleys of her native Switzerland, she experienced in her soul the heights of mystical ecstasy, as well as the horror of complete spiritual abandonment.

Like Mary, Speyr was also a woman of joy, courage, and childlike simplicity, qualities which shone through her even in the midst of illness and excruciating spiritual darkness. She radiated these qualities because of a life of prayer that gave her that deep sense of God's providential care for her and an assurance that in the end all would be well. All that was necessary was to open one's heart to God and keep nothing back from him. Her openness before God allowed her to enter into the depths of God's love and look upon life and death through the eyes of faith. In her later years, she faced her sickness, blindness, and approaching death with complete resignation to God's will. Shortly before her death, she is known to have said that it would be a beautiful thing to die, because Christ was waiting for her on the other side. The Eucharist, for Speyr, pointed to Christ and to his promise of resurrection. It was a visible sign given to believers of the life waiting for them beyond the pale of death.[3]

---

[3] See Hans Urs von Balthasar, *First Glance at Adrienne von Speyr*, 47-111, 115-92; *Doctor, Convert, and Mystic: The Life and Work of Adrienne von Speyr*, http://www.ignatiusinsight.com/ authors/adrienne _von_speyr.asp; Regis Martin, "Von Speyr's Life of Grace," http://www.christendomawake.org/pages/balthasa/ vonspeye.htm. For more on Speyr's spirituality, see Jacques Servais, "The Ressourcement of Contemporary Spirituality under the Guidance of Adrienne von Speyr and Hans Urs von Balthasar," trans. David L. Schindler, *Communio* 23(1996): 300-321;

Speyr on the Eucharist

Speyr's writings on the Eucharist occur a number of times in her literary corpus, and it would be impossible in this brief chapter to do justice to the depth of her insights in a short article of this kind. To convey a sense of her teaching, two works in particular come to mind: her little book, *The Holy Mass* (1950)[4] and her meditation on Jesus' words in the John 14:19: "In a little while the world will no longer see me, but you will see me; because I live, you also will live."[5]

In *The Holy Mass*, Speyr provides a commentary on the different parts of the celebration of the Eucharist. She opens her book with these words: "The Holy Mass is both the means and sign through which the Lord bequeaths us his love. His whole life was a Eucharist to the Father, and it is in this, his Eucharist, that he wants to include all his people."[6] She believes that, as the official worship of the Church, Jesus' thanksgiving to the Father in the Eucharist unites believers of all ages around a single altar: "Each celebration of Holy Mass is a unique introduction to the love of the Lord. No single Holy Mass is to be considered in itself, but rather it stands in relation to all other Holy Masses, which together stand for the indivisible sign of the whole and indivisible love of the Lord for his Church."[7] This love, for Speyr, is present in Holy Mass in both active and contemplative forms and comes to fruition when receiving Holy Communion.

---

[4] Adrienne von Speyr, *The Holy Mass*, trans. Helena M. Saward (San Francisco: Ignatius Press, 1999.

[5] Idem, *The Farewell Discourses*, trans. E. A. Nelson (San Francisco: Ignatius Press, 1987), 124-27. Cited in Michael L. Gaudoin-Parker, ed., *The Real Presence through the Ages* (Staten Island, NY: Alba House, 179-81.

[6] Speyr, *The Holy Mass*, 11.

[7] Ibid.

For Speyr, Holy Mass is first and foremost a sacrifice of Jesus to God the Father. This sacrifice consists "in his allowing himself to become man anew, in his return to the situation and mood of the Last Supper with all the bitterness of his earthly life and its ending."[8] Through the Eucharist, Jesus finds a new opportunity for shedding his blood: "For him the Eucharist is rather like a reliving, a reenactment of his Incarnation and Cross. His eternally steadfast willingness to sacrifice himself for humanity is again put to the test."[9] This sacrifice has both vertical and horizontal dimensions for he is being sacrificed "in relation to the Father and to humanity."[10]

Speyr also likens the Mass to someone asking Jesus to describe his suffering and death in more detail: "A person, having experienced something dreadful about which he would rather not think, is asked by someone else: 'Tell me more precisely what happened.' He is thus once again drawn wholly into the experience. He experiences it anew in order to make it clear for others."[11] When seen in this light, the celebration of the Eucharist is Jesus' clear and definitive word about his paschal mystery. It is a word that reminds us of God's compassion for us as we undergo our own suffering and walk our own path to Golgotha. God's care for us, in her mind, knows no bounds: "It is not true that the citizens of heaven are indifferent to what happens on earth. They are in fact deeply concerned, unable to say: 'I no longer know what suffering is.'"[12]

Jesus' compassion for us manifests itself in his hidden presence in the bread and wine, and in the Tabernacle. In her meditation on John 14:19, Speyr writes of this hidden presence

---

[8] Ibid., 97.

[9] Ibid.

[10] Ibid., 97-98.

[11] Ibid., 98.

[12] Ibid.

which can be recognized only by the eyes of faith: "In the Eucharist...there is the space of time in which one sees the Lord, and the space of time in which one does not see him."[13] She maintains that one can tell a great deal about a person's faith by the way he or she reacts to Jesus' presence in the Blessed Sacrament: "For the person whose faith is not really alive, the time in which one does not see him is that during which he is hidden in the Tabernacle....But those who truly believe will see him even then."[14] For Speyr, Jesus' hidden presence in the Tabernacle is a call to view the mystery it embodies with the eyes of faith.

Speyr also views the relationship between Jesus' hidden and visible presence in the Eucharist as another way of talking about the relationship between contemplation and action: "For not only hiddenness is contemplation, and not only exposition is action."[15] For her, contemplation and action are like two sides of the same coin: "The Eucharist is at work also in the Tabernacle; there is also vision in Exposition."[16] She employs a Physics metaphor to make her point: "For contemplation and action are, so to speak, different isotopes of a single and tran-scending reality of the life of the Lord and our life in him, which can appear under different aspects."[17] The two represent different dimensions of the same reality: "there is no division between action and contemplation, no equipoise to be esta-blished between them."[18] She saw an intimate bond between contemplation and action and saw it reflected in Jesus' hidden

---

[13] Speyr, *The Farewell Discourses*, 125-26; Gaudoin-Parker, ed., *The Real Presence*, 180.

[14] Ibid.

[15] Ibid., 127, 181.

[16] Ibid.

[17] Ibid.

[18] Ibid.

presence in the Tabernacle and the actions of the Mass and Exposition of the Blessed Sacrament.

Some Further Insights

The above presentation provides only the main contours of Speyr's teaching on the Eucharist and does not pretend to exhaust the quality and depth of its insights. The following remarks seek to probe her teaching still further and to emphasize their relevance for believers today.

To begin with, Speyr says that Jesus' entire life was "a Eucharist to the Father"[19] *and wanted her own life to be the same.* Her transparency before God, her courageous embrace of suffering, and her childlike simplicity in her relationships were all a reflection of this one underlying desire, the deepest of her life. She believed that the Eucharist was "a fundamental element of the Church"[20] and that, without it, it would be next to impossible to find our way to the Father. The Eucharist was central to her life, because Jesus was central to it and the sacrament he instituted was both the "means and sign"[21] by which he manifested his love to us. This love was a divine love and also a human love. As such, Speyr also recognized it was also an "ecclesial love."[22] Just as the many parts of Holy Mass come together to form an integral unity, so does the Eucharist bind the many members of Christ's body, the Church, to one another.

For Speyr, contemplation and action were two intimately related facets of divine love and thus inseparable. What is more, she strove to integrate these two dimensions of love in her

---

[19] Speyr, *The Holy Mass*, 11.
[20] Ibid.
[21] Ibid.
[22] Ibid., 12.

own life by means of her medical profession and intense prayer life. She saw that the Eucharist reflected these same two facets of love and recognized them, on the one hand, in Jesus' transforming action of bread and wine into his body and blood (action) and, on the other hand, in his divine hiddenness beneath the Eucharistic species and in the Tabernacle (contemplation). She was also able to recognize that Jesus was both active in his hiddenness and hidden in his activity. She understood, in other words, that there was a contemplative dimension to action and an active dimension to contemplation. This multifaceted understanding of the sacrament demonstrated for her how Jesus strives in the Eucharist to meet people every day where they are. A person, she believed, "can...give his life in the Eucharist differently every day, so that each day's work is defined and colored by the particular character of the Communion that one has received."[23]

The Marian dimension of Speyr's spiritual outlook also comes to play in her understanding of the Eucharist. The Eucharist, for her, was "a reenactment of the Incarnation and Cross."[24] While these actions were primarily actions of Christ, Mary's role in each was, without question, central to the divine plan for humanity's redemption. Without her holy fiat, that her transparent and open acceptance of God's will in her life, the Word of God would never have been able to become flesh and thus take on the human condition. Her words to the Angel Gabriel, "Let it be with me according to your word" (Lk 1:38), closely resemble Jesus' words in the Garden of Gethsemane, "My Father, if this cannot pass unless I drink it, your will be done" (Mt 26:42). When Mary stood at the foot of the cross, her heart was also pierced; she shared in the sufferings of her son in

---

[23] Speyr, *The Farewell Discourses*, 125; Gaudoin-Parker, ed., *The Real Presence*, 180.

[24] Speyr, *The Holy Mass*, 97.

a terrible, heart-rending manner. Speyr reminds us that authentic devotion to Mary will always lead us to a deep reverence and love for her son and hence to the Eucharist. By receiving the Eucharist, she saw that the Incarnation and Cross could become a reality in our lives, as it was for Mary, our mother and the Mother of God.

When Speyr describes the Eucharist as Jesus' attempt to describe for us his suffering and death in more detail, she places the sacrament in the overall movement of Jesus' kenotic self-emptying. God's Word, the Logos, entered our world by taking on our human condition (in the Incarnation), gave himself to us completely to the point of dying for us (in his ministry and in his passion and death), and became our nourishment (in the transformation of bread and wine into his body and blood) and source of hope (in his Resurrection and Ascension). The Eucharist is the visible sign of all of these facets of Christ's kenotic self-emptying, as well as Jesus' desire to leave behind a visible sign of his paschal mystery that would express it in all its fullness and in the clearest way possible. His desire to communicate with us in this way reveals his desire to reveal himself not to a select few in an arcane and esoteric manner, but through table fellowship and the simple act of eating accessible to everyone. Jesus, in other words, intended the Eucharist to be an easily recognizable communication of himself to all his people, regardless of their circumstances and level of sophistication.

Finally, Speyr recognized that the Eucharist was Jesus' sacrifice to the Father on our behalf and that we are included in his offering by virtue of our being members of his body, the Church. Because Jesus was both God and man, his sacrifice on the cross had both vertical and horizontal dimensions to it. These dimensions are present in the Eucharist, the sacrament of love, and expressed in a vital way through the mediation of the priest, who offers prayers of thanksgiving to the Father on our behalf as another Christ. "The priest mediates," Speyr liked to say, "and the people celebrate with him in the one, ecclesial love."[25] This ecclesial love lies at the very heart of the Church's mission to proclaim the good news to the world. It lies at the heart of every Christian vocation and requires the total transparency and childlike simplicity that permeated Speyr's entire spiritual outlook. When seen in this light, the joy, courage, and childlike simplicity that marked her life are qualities of this ecclesial love and should be evidenced in the lives of all Christians, regardless of time, place, or circumstances.

Conclusion

Adrienne von Speyr plumbed the depths of Christ's paschal mystery and understood the desolating effects of spending eternity without God. Although she suffered greatly in her own life from both physical ailments and deep spiritual torments, she looked at the world around her through the eyes of faith. This posture of belief enabled her to be completely transparent before God and to experience the gift of life, of suffering, and even death with a sense of wonder and awe.

Speyr's spiritual outlook involved a movement away from self-centeredness to living in God and for God. Her life of "contemplation in action" and "action in contemplation" was a direct result of her intimacy with her Lord and her deep veneration of Mary his mother. In her many writings, many of which were written through dictation while in contemplative prayer, she emphasized again and again the glory to which God has called us and the cross everyone must bear in order to share in it. For Speyr, Mary's sharing in the cross of her Son marks a path that all disciples must follow if they wish to one day make

---

[25] Ibid., 12.

their way to the empty tomb. The Eucharist gives us the strength to follow that path and embrace it with all our hearts.

Holy Mass, for Speyr, was the visible sign that connected the cross with the empty tomb. As such, it represents the fullness of Christ's love for humanity and a clear, detailed expression of the meaning of his paschal mystery. As a sacrificial offering of Christ to the Father on our behalf, it continues the work of the Incarnation and Cross in the lives of God's people, the members of his Mystical Body, the Church. As seen in Christ's hidden presence in the Tabernacle and in the transforming action of the words of consecration, it also displays the contemplative and active dimensions of Christ's love for the Father and for all humanity. For Speyr, the Church could not exist without the sacrament that is "the sign of love that exists between heaven and earth."[26] The Eucharist, for her, was fundamental to the Church and central to the message it proclaims.

Reflection Questions

- Speyr says the Eucharist is both the means and sign through which the Lord extends his love to us. Of all the ways available to him, why did the Lord choose to manifest his love in the setting of a meal? What does the idea of a Eucharistic banquet say about God's love for us? How has the Eucharist affected the way you break bread with others?
- Speyr claims that Jesus' hidden presence in the Eucharist can be recognized only through the eyes of faith. What does this say about the role of faith in the spiritual life? Do you consider yourself a person of faith? Have you ever sensed this hidden presence? What does Jesus' presence in the Blessed Sacrament say about the humility of God?

---

[26] Ibid.

- Speyr maintains that contemplation and action represent different dimensions of the same reality. How do you experience contemplation in your own life? Is one more difficult than the other? Which dimension challenges you the most? How are they manifested in the celebration of the Eucharist?

Voice Fourteen

Dom M. Eugene Boylan:
Our Food and Our Life

Our next voice was an Irish Trappist monk, spiritual writer, confessor, and retreat master. Dom M. Eugene Boylan, O.C.R. (1904-64), born Richard Kevin Boylan, was born in Dublin, he studied for some time at the local diocesan seminary and completed his studies at University College Dublin. He entered St. Joseph's Cistercian Abbey in 1931, professed solemn vows in 1936, and was ordained a priest in 1937. In 1953, he was sent to Australia to establish Notre Dame monastery (Tarrawara Abbey) and was later made acting superior of a Trappist monastery on Caldey Island off the Welsh coast. In 1959, he returned to Roscrea and was elected abbot in 1962. He died in an automobile accident in 1964 as the Second Vatican Council was nearing its end. His writings include *Difficulties in Mental Prayer* (1943), *This Tremendous Lover* (1946), *The Spiritual Life of the Priest* (1949), and the posthumous, *The Priest's Way to God* (1963). His teaching on the Eucharist lies at the very heart of his spiritual vision.[1]

---

[1] This biographical information comes from Lawrence S. Cunningham, "Foreword" in M. Eugene Boylan, *This Tremendous Lover* (Notre Dame, IN: Christian Classics, 2009), xiii-xvi.

Boylan's Spiritual Outlook

The Church's doctrine of the Mystical Body, what the Apostle Paul called the "Body of Christ" and what St. Augustine referred to as the "Whole Christ," lies at the heart of Boylan's spiritual vision. Christ, he believed, came to this earth not only to redeem us, but to create a New Man from the Old. Jesus was the New Adam and, Mary, his Mother, was the New Eve. Together, they worked to bring about humanity's redemption and recreation, making it possible once again for each human being to enter into and enjoy an intimate friendship with God.[2]

Boylan makes it clear that being a member of Christ's Mystical Body needs to be understood in its proper sense: "The Mystical Body of Christ, while being one mystical person, endowed with life coming from within, is not one physical person."[3] Just as there are two natures united in the person of Christ and three persons united in the mystery of the Blessed Trinity, so also in the Christ's Mystical Body "there are millions of persons, sharing in the divine nature, but each preserving his own human nature."[4] The Mystical Body is thus a "four-dimensional entity" that extends beyond the boundaries of time and space.[5] The doctrine in no way means that a person who is member of the body loses his personal identity. On the contrary, a person's identity is elevated (transformed, if you will) to become the person that he was meant to become in the plan of Divine Providence. At the same time, this person lives in Christ—and Christ lives in him. For this reason he calls Christ, "Our Tremendous Lover," since through him an intimate union with God becomes possible that far exceeds any other intimacy

---

[2] See M. Eugene Boylan, *This Tremendous Lover*, 305-20.

[3] Ibid., 38.

[4] Ibid.

[5] Ibid., 41

known to man.[6] He goes on to say that we can picture this union in three ways: "as the life of Christ in us; as our life in Christ; or as what we might call a 'shoulder to shoulder' partnership with Jesus, a constant companionship of two lovers sharing every thought and every deed."[7] "Each of these pictures," he adds, "corresponds to a true aspect of the reality, the intimacy of which is so extraordinary that it defies description."[8] Christ, in other words, not only walks with us, but also lives in us, as we live in him. In the words of St. Paul, "it is no longer I who live, but it is Christ who lives in me (Gal 2:20)."

For Boylan, living in Christ allows us to pray in union with him and requires a fourfold purity upon which the health of our spiritual life depends: "purity of conscience, purity of heart, purity of mind, purity of action."[9] Each of these address a different aspect of our relationship with God:

"Purity of conscience results from our avoidance of sin and from our general conformity with God's will. Purity of heart is achieved by keeping our heart for God and avoiding or suppressing all *inordinate* attachments, that is, attachments that are not according to His will. Purity of mind arises from a continual control over one's thoughts and memories, and from a frequent but gentle effort at recollection. Purity of action requires that we watch carefully the motives and intentions in our work towards God so that we may act only for His love and according to His will."[10]

---

[6] Ibid., 321-34.

[7] Ibid., 321.

[8] Ibid.

[9] Boylan, *This Tremendous Lover*, 259.

[10] Ibid.

These four dimensions of the spiritual life embody the goal of a healthy spiritual life. Boylan recognizes, however, that many of us are on a long spiritual journey and suffer from a variety of deadly spiritual ills. A deep disruption of soul, a product of humanity's primeval fall from grace, prevents us from achieving these goals and can even discourage us from even reaching out for them. For this very reason, we must turn to Christ and rely on him for healing our wounds and bringing us back to health. What Jesus says in the Gospel of Mark is true: "for God all things are possible" (Mk 10:27). Only he can restore us to health and make us whole.

Boylan identifies five ways of getting in touch with Jesus and the power of his transforming grace: prayer, the sacraments, spiritual reading, doing his will, and going to him through his mother, Mary.[11] He points out, moreover, that these ways are not independent, but are meant to work in concert with one another. Those who sincerely and honestly seek to incorporate them into their lives will be able to open every dimension of their lives to Jesus, and he will gradually draw them more and more deeply into his mind and heart. The power of his Spirit will root out whatever keeps them from turning their lives over to him and it will empower them to put on his mind and heart. They will come to see that holiness of life is not something beyond their grasp, but a gift from God offered to all who humbly turn to God in search of his compassion, mercy, and love.

Holiness, for Boylan, means "to live in union with Him [Christ] by faith, by hope, by love, by humility, and by complete abandonment to His will."[12] It involves trusting in God, looking forward to the fulfillment of his promises, and loving him with all our hearts and minds. It also has to do with recognizing the

---

[11] Ibid., 87.

[12] Ibid., 190.

truth about ourselves before him and letting go of our self-centeredness and selfish desires so that his will can be accomplished in our lives. Sanctity means becoming so close to Jesus that, in the words of St. Augustine, "there shall be one Christ loving Himself."[13] Christ loving himself in us and in our neighbor is its ultimate manifestation and can be achieved in any state of Christian life. The Eucharist, he claims, is "Our Food and Our Life"[14] and is the primary means by which Christ brings about this intimate union with the members of his body.

Boylan's Teaching on the Eucharist

The Eucharist, for Boylan, is "the sacrament of union *par excellence* to which baptism is, as it were only the gateway."[15] In creating the New Man, this Mystical Body of Christ, the Whole Christ, "our Lord insisted that its food must be His own Flesh and Blood; and He warns the Christian that unless he eat of this Flesh and drink of this Blood, he shall not have life everlasting"[16]

What happens in Holy Communion is almost beyond description: "Our Lord, so to speak, 'folds up' His whole life and death and sacrifice into the Sacrament of the Eucharist, re-enacts His sacrifice sacramentally on the altar, and comes to us in Holy Communion with His whole self and all His riches as God and Man."[17] Boylan continues, "Jesus Christ...is really, truly, and substantially present in the sacramental species of bread, and also in the species of wine."[18] However, there is one important difference between the priest's presence at the altar

---

[13] M. Eugene Boylan, *The Spiritual Life of the Priest* (Eugene, OR: Wipf & Stock, 2013), 161.

[14] Boylan, *This Tremendous Lover,* 147.

[15] Ibid., 45.

[16] Ibid.

[17] Ibid., 47.

[18] Ibid., 147.

and Christ's: "The priest makes contact with the ground by the surface and size and weight of his *own* body; our Lord makes contact with the altar, by the surface and size and weight of the *bread*. The priest is localized by his own accidents; our Lord is localized by the accidents of the bread. These indicate and reveal His presence, but He Himself is invisible."[19] Boylan also points out that, in the Eucharist, Christ becomes our very food and drink. Unlike normal bread and wine, however, which when digested, becomes a part of our own body, whenever we eat and drink of the flesh and blood of the Son of Man, we are assumed (digested, if you will) and incorporated more deeply into Christ's Mystical Body.[20] This "sacrament of union," in other words, makes us one with Christ and the members of his Body, the Church.

The reception of Holy Communion, for Boylan, constitutes only one aspect of the Eucharist. Christ is contained and received in Holy Communion, which is a partaking of the fruits of the sacrificial offering of the Mass, "the central act of the Catholic Church. Everything else is centered on it."[21] For Boylan, "It is the Mass that matters."[22] Boylan summarizes his teaching on the Eucharist in twenty-four points:

1. On Calvary, our Lord offered Himself in Sacrifice to God.
2. This sacrifice gave God full and perfect worship.
3. It was a complete satisfaction for our sins.
4. It merited every grace that we might need.
5. Our Lord instituted the sacramental and sensible rite of the Mass,
6. In which He offered Himself to God the Father,

---

[19] Ibid., 149.
[20] Ibid., 154.
[21] Ibid., 161.
[22] Ibid.

7. And ordered His apostles and priests to repeat the same offering;
8. That the salvific power of the sacrifice of the Cross might be applied to our needs.
9. In the Mass the victim is the same Christ.
10. And the offerer is also the same Christ, who once offered Himself on Calvary;
11. Who now offers by the ministry of His priests.
12. The Mass, therefore, is truly propitiatory,
13. And, if we are rightly disposed, can be a source of grace and timely aid for us.
14. The Mass appeases God and obtains the forgiveness of even the most enormous sins.
15. The fruits of the cross are received most plentifully through Mass.
16. In the Mass the minister represents not only Christ,
17. But also the whole Mystical Body and each one of us, its members.
18. Through the priest we offer to God, Christ the victim,
19. In praise and propitiation for the needs of the whole Church.
20. As on the cross, Christ offered Himself as the Head of the whole human race,
21. So in the Mass He offers Himself not only as Head of the Church,
22. But in Himself He encloses each of us His members.
23. For He encloses us all—even the weakest of us—
24. Most lovingly in His Heart.[23]

Boylan then summarizes his summary in these words: "In the Mass, then, each of us can say: Christ is offering Himself as a perfect sacrifice to God; I, too, am offering Him; He is offering

---

[23] Ibid., 167-68.

me in Himself; *am I also offering myself with Him?*"[24] To clarify this point he turns to the words of St. Thomas Aquinas: "The sacrament [the Blessed Eucharist] is both a sacrifice and a sacrament. It is a sacrifice inasmuch as it is offered to God; it is a sacrament in so far as it is received by men."[25]

Boylan also points to the special relationship between the Holy Sacrifice of Christ in the Mass and the priesthood: "The priest 'takes over' this sacrifice in the Mass and makes it his own. He therefore has to endeavor to make his interior sacrifice correspond with the exterior sacrifice sacramentally renewed in the Mass, and then he has to make his whole life correspond to that interior sacrifice!"[26] The transformation that takes place is similar to what takes place in the sacred species: "Just as God changes the bread and wine offered up at Mass into the Body and Blood of Christ, so too, He will by His paternal providence and the sequence of events, effect our 'consecration,' our incorporation, our transformation into Christ."[27] He goes on to point out that priests are called to be "partners and partakers not only with Christ as Priest, but also with Christ as Victim."[28] A priest offers himself with Christ every time he celebrates the Eucharist; for this reason, he must endeavor to *mean* the Mass.[29] To be sure, "if he accepts the priesthood of Christ as it really is—a participation in the priesthood of Christ with the *de congruo* obligation of self-sacrifice with Christ—he can and should integrate all his experience into his spiritual life. His

---

[24] Ibid., 168.

[25] Thomas Aquinas, *Summa theologiae*, III, q. 83, a. 5, ad 2m.; Boylan, *This Tremendous Lover*, 172.

[26] Boylan, *The Spiritual Life of the Priest*, 55.

[27] Ibid., 56-57.

[28] Ibid., 59. See also Dom Eugene Boylan, *The Priest's Way to God* (Maryland, US: The Newman Press, 1962; republished, London: Catholic Way Publishing, 2014), 40.

[29] Boylan, *The Priest's Way to God,* 40.

efforts for souls are to be made as part of his work—as fulfillment of the offering he makes of himself at Mass."[30] This offering of self along with Christ the High Priest in accordance with the Father's will lies at the very heart of the priestly identity: "It is by doing the will of God that we truly live up to the title of 'Father.'"[31] Catholics, Boyle maintains, are called to follow suit: "The external sacrifice on Calvary was the perfect expression of that interior sacrifice that was our Lord's whole life of submission to the will of God. That external sacrifice is given to us in the Mass, and we have to make our life one similar interior sacrifice, if the Mass is to have that full and perfect meaning for us and from us to God, which it should have. There is the plan of the whole Christian life—to live up to what we say in the action of the Mass.[32]

Some Further Insights

The above presentation, while not exhaustive, touches on many of the key points of Boylan's teaching on the Eucharist, and, when seen against the backdrop of his overall spiritual outlook, provides an opportunity to make a number of observations regarding the role the sacrament plays in the everyday lives of Catholics.

To begin with, Boylan maintains that in the Eucharist Christ has given his own body and blood as the necessary food for Christ's Mystical Body. Without it, the health of the members of Christ's body weakens and becomes spiritually enfeebled. His teaching reminds believers of the necessity of receiving Holy Communion for their own well-being and for that of the Mystical Body. Without the Eucharist, the Church

[30] Boylan, *This Tremendous Lover*, 60.
[31] Ibid., 62.
[32] Boylan, *This Tremendous Lover*, 169.

will starve for lack of food and nourishment, and will eventually become starved and emaciated. With it, she will remain mystically united to Christ as her head and her members will continue to have access to his transforming grace.

Just as Christ's Mystical Body transcends the dimensions of time and space, so does its food. The Eucharist comes from the earth, but is made a part of the new creation through the power of Christ's Spirit. As such, it goes beyond the present boundaries of time and space. The sacrament, like Christ himself, is in the world, but not of it. As long as they are properly disposed, believers who receive this food are also mystically incorporated into the Body of the Risen Lord. When they receive Holy Communion, believers, when properly disposed, become more deeply united to Christ and are empowered to live in faith, hope, charity, humility, and, like Jesus himself, complete abandonment to God's will.

The Eucharist, according to Boylan, works as a kind of digestion in reverse. When normal food is digested, it is broken down and becomes a part of our own bodies. When the Eucharist is consumed, it breaks us down and assimilates us into Christ's Mystical Body, but without compromising our individual identities and personalities. This process of mystical assimilation is the means chosen by God to bring about the New Man and the New Creation. When seen in this light, the Christian life truly is "Life in Christ." Christ lives in us, and we live in Christ. To be a disciple means more than merely following Christ and walking in his footsteps. It asks us to offer ourselves in faith through Christ as Eucharist for others so that we might become food and nourishment for them and enable them to live in and through his Spirit.

Boylan calls the Eucharist the "sacrament of union par excellence." The union it effects, moreover, is multidimensional. Receiving Holy Communion, in other words, does much more than merely feed each person spiritually. It unites us not only personally to Christ, but also to the Body. It incorporates the individual into the community of believers and helps it to find its special place in the Mystic Christ. When seen in this light, the sanctity of the human person is intimately bound up with the sanctity of the whole. There is no doubt that God views us as individuals and actively seeks our own personal well-being. Our individual good, however, cannot be separated from the good of the whole. Holy Communion, therefore, celebrates the unity of Christ's Mystical Body and the union of each member of that Body with Christ through the vivifying presence of the Holy Spirit.

In the early Church, the saints were known as the "friends of God."[33] The union believers celebrate when receiving the Eucharist is their unique participation in an intimate community of friends. This friendship with Christ is both personal and communal. It celebrates the intimate love that the Triune God celebrates in its interior life and pours out freely onto all who would accept it willingly with open hearts. This friendship far exceeds the limits of earthly friendship and ultimately points to the transformation, union, and assimilation of all human loves through their participation in the Divine. When seen in this light, everyone is called to be a "friend of God"—and so very much more.

Boylan maintains that priests share not only in Christ's priesthood, but also in his victimhood. This insight has enormous implications for priestly spirituality. When they celebrate Mass, priests stand in the place of Christ as an *alter Christus*. In doing so, they not only offer the sacrifice of Christ in a visible, sacramental manner, but by virtue of their close identity with Christ are also offering themselves as victims. Priests live out this victimhood in their service to the Church in

---

[33] See Peter Brown, *The Making of Late Antiquity* (Cambridge. MA: Harvard University Press, 1978), 54-80.

their daily ministry. It means closely identifying with the people they serve and consciously placing the needs of the community of believers before their own.

Finally, while Christ is the New Adam, Boylan also emphasizes Mary's subordinate yet nonetheless all-important role as the New Eve in the mystery of Redemption. Mary is the Mother of God, Mother of the Church, the Mother of Christ's Mystical Body, the Mother of all believers. She gave her own flesh and blood to bring her Son into the world. She suckled him as an infant, and prepared his food for him throughout his hidden life in Nazareth. She followed him throughout his public ministry, stood beneath the cross as he died, and was present in the upper room when the Church was born on the day of Pentecost. She fed Christ because she loved him, but also so that he could feed us in the Eucharist. She offered herself to God so that her Son could offer himself to God for us. She has a special place in the heart of the Church, in the heart of every priest, and in the celebration of every Mass.

These remarks represent just a few of the implications of Boylan's overall spiritual outlook and teaching on the Eucharist for today's believers. They remind us to lift our eyes beyond our present circumstances and to ponder the meaning of this sacrament through the eyes of Christ, the New Adam, and through those of the Mystical Body of believers incorporated into his Mystic Personality. Most of all, they remind us that the Eucharist is a precious gift, one not to be take for granted, but celebrated with grateful hearts and lovingly poured out into our daily activities as a humble offering to God and to the world.

Conclusion

Dom M. Eugene Boylan roots his Eucharistic spirituality in the doctrine of the Mystical Body of Christ. In doing so, he identifies the "sacrament of union," the primary means by which Christ incorporates people into his Mystic Personality. Just as the human body needs food to nourish its various parts, the community of believers—the Church, purgative, militant, and triumphant—needs spiritual sustenance in order to maintain its identity as a supernatural organism.

The Eucharist, for Boylan, has a threefold function in the life of the Mystical Body. It is offered, contained, and received. Because Christ offers himself in the Mass for the sins of humanity, it is a sacrifice. Because he is substantially present in sacred species, it is a sacrament. Because he is received and consumed in Holy Communion, it is a banquet. The Mass is the central action of the Church, because it extends Christ's salvific activity through time so that the community of believers can gain access to and be incorporated more deeply into his Mystical Body. In this respect, it is first and foremost an action of Christ himself.

Boylan's teaching on the Eucharist has great relevance for today's believers: It emphasizes the transcendental character of the sacrament and roots it firmly in the present dimensions of time and space. The sacrament, we might say, is *in* time and space, yet goes *far beyond* them. His teaching reminds us that, in the end, the present world will not simply devolve into chaos or nothingness, but be transformed (lifted up, if you will) into something far greater. The Eucharist represents the first fruits of this New Creation. Given to us by Christ, the New Adam, it is the food that nourishes and sustains his Mystical Body, the community of believers called the Church. It is the "sacrament of union" that incorporates us into Christ and thus enables us to offer ourselves with him to the Father.

Reflection Questions

- Boylan believes that, when we receive the Eucharist, we are incorporated more deeply into Christ Mystical Body. In what sense is the Eucharist a "sacrament of union?" Do you look upon the sacrament as food that deepens your union with Christ and his body? How does the Eucharist accomplish this? What dispositions are necessary on our part for this to occur?

- According to Boylan, the Eucharist works as a kind of digestion in reverse. When we eat the Body and drink the Blood of Christ, we are broken down (digested, if you will) to become a part of Christ's body. Is this image more than a mere metaphor? Do you believe that when you receive the Eucharist you are actually becoming a part of Christ, the New Adam? If so, do you retain your personal identity all the while?

- Boylan holds that the Eucharist has a threefold function in the life of Christ's Mystical Body: It is offered, contained, and received. How are these three functions related? In what sense does the sacrifice offered require Christ's presence in the sacrament and establish a union with the body of believers? When you receive the sacrament how are these three functions manifested in your life?

Voice Fifteen

Yves Congar:
Begetting Christ

Our next voice was a Dominican friar, priest, and one of the most influential Catholic theologians of the twentieth century. Yves Congar, O.P. (1904-1995) was born in Sedan in northeastern France, entered the Dominicans at Amiens in 1925, studied at the Dominican house of studies at Saulchoir in Belgium, and was ordained a priest in 1930. He was a chaplain in the French army during the Second World War and a German prisoner of war for much of that time. After the war, he continued his teaching and writing apostolates and eventually became famous for his involvement in the French worker-priest movement and for his works on the Holy Spirit, the Church, ecumenism, and the role of the laity. His writings in these areas laid much of the theological groundwork for the Second Vatican Council. In 1994, Pope John Paul II recognized his groundbreaking contribution to Catholic theology by naming him a cardinal.[1]

---

[1] For more on Congar's life, see Aidan Nichols, *Yves Congar* (Wilton, CT: Morehouse Publishing, 1989), 1-13; *The New Catholic Encyclopedia*, 2d ed., (Thomas Gale/The Catholic University of America: Detroit/Washington, D.C., 2003), s.v. "Congar, Yves Marie-Joseph," by J. A. Komonchak.

Congar's Spirituality

Congar's life was rooted in the spirituality of St. Dominic and the theology of St. Thomas Aquinas, especially as interpreted by such early twentieth-century Catholic thinkers as the philosopher Jacques Maritain (1882-1973) and the Dominican theologian, Reginald Garrigou-Lagrange (1877-1964). As a Dominican friar, he placed a high premium on the life of prayer, study, and community life. These fundamental values permeated his life as a friar and his entire spiritual and theological outlook.[2]

In his book, *I Believe in the Holy Spirit*, Congar examined the place of the Holy Spirit in the history of the Church and showed how it is the life-giving, vivifying force of the Christian life. It is the Spirit who gives birth to the Church, sanctifies its members, and empowers them to preach the Word of God to the world. The Spirit calls all men and women to the following of Christ and the life of discipleship. It is the principle of unity within the faith and the binding force of all vocations within the Church. Congar saw the Spirit at work not only within the Church, but also outside of it and, in many ways, anticipated many of the findings of the Second Vatican Council. Although he recognized the importance of the Church's hierarchical structure for preserving unity of belief and practice, he placed a

---

[2] For the philosophical, theological, and spiritual influences on Congar, see Jean-Pierre Jossua, *Yves Congar: Theologian in the Service of God's People* (Chicago: The Priory Press, 1968, 11-37; Nichols, *Yves Congar*, 1-13; *The New Catholic Encyclopedia*, 2d ed., (Thomas Gale/The Catholic University of America: Detroit/Washington, D.C., 2003), s.v. "Congar, Yves Marie-Joseph," by J. A. Komonchak; Fergus Kerr, "Yves Congar and Thomism," in *Yves Congar: Theologian of the Church*, ed., Gabriel Flynn, Louvain Theological and Pastoral Monographs 32 (Louvain: Peeters, 2005), 67-97.

great emphasis on the role of the laity in the life of the Church and, through their participation in the priesthood of believers, their important role of bringing Gospel values and life of the Spirit to the marketplace. He also saw the Spirit at work in the Ecumenical Movement and played a major role in getting the Catholic Church involved in repairing its relations with other Christian churches and ecclesial communities. The Holy Spirit, he believed, was also at work in the hearts of non-Christians and even non-believers in their search for truth and their desires to dedicate themselves to an authentic search for truth.[3]

For Congar, the Holy Spirit was the soul of the Church at work in every aspect of its life, the internal as well as the external. These two converged in the Church's celebration of the Liturgy, especially in the Eucharist when during the epiclesis the Spirit is asked to descend upon the gifts of bread and wine which the priest offers to God on behalf of the community of believers. The transformation of the bread and wine into the body and blood of Christ is a work of the Spirit that takes place through, with, and in Christ in order to render glory and praise to the Father. This transformative action of the Spirit sanctifies the faithful by empowering them to live the Gospel and share it through lives of authentic discipleship. For Congar, life in the Spirit is intimately related to the celebration of the Eucharist. His spirituality was rooted in the Holy Spirit and the mystery of the Church and its sacraments, with special emphasis on the Eucharistic banquet, sacrifice, and presence.[4]

---

[3] See Yves Congar, *I Believe in the Holy Spirit* trans. David Smith, 3 vols. (New York: Crossroad, 1997), 1:167-73; 3:267-72.

[4] Ibid., 3:258-66.

Congar's Teaching on the Eucharist

Congar roots the Eucharist in the mystery of Christ's passion and death and calls it the source of Church unity. For him, "the real meaning and function of the sacraments is this, that by them Christians are placed in contact with the Lord himself, their Redeemer, the one and same Lord who, at a particular time, suffered and was raised up; that they receive the same life-giving sap that proceeds from the tree of the cross; in short, that life by which they are to live is the very life *of Christ*."[5] "The Eucharist," in his mind, "imparts [Christ's] fellowship and life."[6] This fellowship and life is a work of the Spirit and manifests itself in unity. Congar maintains that "theologians, both ancient and modern, are at one accord in seeing the unity of the Mystical Body as the effect proper to the sacrament of the Eucharist."[7]

Congar is quick to point out that the Eucharist "does not begin anew Christ's sacrifice nor is it, strictly speaking, a supplement to the cross."[8] On the contrary, "it makes Christ present again as victim offered so that his sacrifice ever recurs without ceasing to be unique and becomes, wherever Christians are gathered together, their own sacrifice and that of the Church, and the accomplishment by them of what was accomplished for them, once and for all by Christ."[9] He maintains that the Eucharist is a work of the Spirit mediated through the Church. As such, it reflects the Church's apostolic, sacramental, and social nature, as well as all the spiritual realities of life in

---

[5] Yves Congar, *The Mystery of the Church*, 2d ed. (Baltimore/Dublin: Helicon Press, 1965), 33.

[6] Ibid., 32.

[7] Ibid.

[8] Ibid., 33

[9] Ibid.

Christ.[10] Congar places a great emphasis on the role of the Holy Spirit in constituting the Church, effecting the sacraments, sanctifying its members and carrying out its missionary activity. In his mind, "[t]he moving force, the animating principle, of everything Christian, everything holy, since Christ, is the Holy Spirit. He it is who leads us back to the God of holiness, and unites us to him."[11]

In his magisterial work, *I believe in the Holy Spirit*, Congar asserts that in the Western Church "the part played by the Holy Spirit in the Eucharist—not only in the change of the bread and wine into the body and blood of the Lord, but also in our communion—has hardly been developed."[12] He goes on to say that "[t]he Eucharist is seen and experienced in an essentially Christological perspective."[13] To counteract this tendency, he spends a great deal of time dealing with the Spirit's role in the Eucharistic epiclesis and provides exhaustive evidence to show that "the Latin West has always been convinced not only of the consecratory function of the words, 'This is my body' and 'This is my blood,' but also equally of the part played by the Holy Spirit."[14] In pointing this out, Congar offsets the tendency of some theologians to focus too heavily on the words of consecration and to downplay the important role of the invocation of the Holy Spirit. He points out that the epiclesis cannot be separated from the whole of the Eucharistic Prayer and that the role of the Spirit in the Eucharist is similar to its role in the Incarnation: "The Eucharist... is like a begetting every day of Christ, body and blood. Just as the incarnation came about through the action of the Holy Spirit, so too should the

---

[10] Ibid., 34

[11] Ibid.,151-52.

[12] Congar, *I Believe in the Holy Spirit*, 1:162.

[13] Ibid.

[14] Ibid., 3:250.

consecration and sanctification of the gifts sanctify believers and incorporate them into Christ."[15] Congar also points out that "[t]he same Spirit is at work in the three realities that bear the name of the body of Christ and are dynamically linked to each other through the dynamism of the Spirit: Jesus, who was born of Mary and who suffered, died and was raised from the dead and glorified; the bread and wine that are 'eucharisted;' the communion or Body of which we are members."[16] In this respect, the life of the Church may be likened to one long invocation of the Holy Spirit.[17]

Some Further Insights

This brief exposition of Congar's teaching on the Eucharist underscores its close connection to his theology of the Holy Spirit and its vivifying role in the life of the Church. The following observations highlight some of the spiritual and theological underpinnings of his view of the sacrament and their relevance for today's Catholics.

To begin with, Congar is correct in pointing out the underdeveloped aspect of the Holy Spirit in the Western Church's theological tradition. He is also justified in pointing out the unifying role played by the Spirit in the sacramental life of the Church and underscoring this significance for the Eucharist. This sacrament, in his mind, is not a substitute for the Holy Spirit (as some authors have wrongly held),[18] but the fullest expression of God's love for humanity. It is the Spirit who immerses the community of believers in Christ's paschal mystery and who empowers them to proclaim its redemptive

---

[15] Ibid., 3:228, 230
[16] Ibid., 3:264.
[17] Ibid., 3:267-72.
[18] Ibid., 160-62.

message. By highlighting the role of the Holy Spirit in the mystery of God's salvific plan, he underscores the unity of God's inner Trinitarian life and external Trinitarian activities (creation, redemption, sanctification) and how they are reflected in the internal life and missionary activity of the Church.

Congar accentuates the centrality of the Holy Spirit in the life of the Church with respect to its apostolic, sacramental, communal, and missionary dimensions, all of which are deeply intertwined. The Church, in his mind, finds its origin in the gift of the Spirit to the community of disciples on Pentecost. Their experience of the Spirit on that day propelled them to proclaim the Gospel boldly and without fear of reprisals. This same Spirit guides the Church and its members through time through its hierarchical structures, the sacraments, its life in community, and the proclamation of the kerygma. For Congar, all of these dimensions come together in the celebration of the Eucharist, which constitutes the Church, affirms its unity, and immerses the believing community in the redemptive mystery of the cross. The Church, in his mind, cannot exist without the sacrament--- and vice versa.

Congar emphasizes the Eucharist's role in imparting the life and fellowship of Christ to the Church. It not only immerses us in the life of his Spirit, but it also creates in us a bond of unity rooted in the mystery of the Divine Love. Along with Baptism, the Eucharist is the greatest of the sacraments. If the former makes us members of Christ's Body, the Church, the latter nourishes and sustains us in the life of the Spirit. In this respect, the Eucharist is "the perfect sacrament of our incorporation with Christ."[19] That is to say, "it incorporates us in Christ precisely by catching us all into the supreme act of love by which

---

[19] Congar, *The Mystery of the Church*, 91.

he offered himself for us on the cross."[20] The simple act of breaking bread together affirms our participation in the mystery of Christ's Mystical Body. To receive the sacrament is to proclaim our dying and rising with Christ and to affirm the moving force of his Spirit in our lives.

Congar emphasizes the role of the Holy Spirit in the Eucharistic epiclesis, when the priest asks God to send forth his Spirit upon the gifts of bread and wine that he is offering on behalf of the believing community. He insists that this invocation of the Holy Spirit is an integral part of the Mass and should not be separated from the Eucharistic Prayer. To do so would be to isolate something that lies at the very heart of the Liturgy and to take away from its mystery and the sacrifice of glory and praise offered to God the Father through Christ and in the unity of the Holy Spirit. This invocation of the Spirit over the bread and wine of the New Creation is an echo of the wind of the Spirit which blows over the waters at the beginning of the First Creation (Gn 1:2). When seen in this light, the epiclesis highlights the Spirit's role in bringing about the New Creation and the divinizing and sanctifying role it plays in God's plan for the world.

The Eucharist, for Congar, is an action of Christ and his Mystical Body, the Church. As such, it is an action of all of the members of the body, bishops, priests, deacons, religious, and the laity. He is keen to point out that all of the members of Christ's Body are called to participate in the Church's life and mission. He is fond of recalling St. Pauls' words to the Corinthians, "the body is one and has many members, but all the members, many though they are, are one body; and so it is with Christ" (1Cor 12:12). However, since some members might not understand their role in the Body, he emphasized the importance of authorities within the Church to guide, nourish,

---

20 Ibid.

and care for it. Congar was a man, a priest, and a religious of the Church, who sought, at one and the same time, both to challenge it and think with it as it faced the challenges of the future. In his mind, the Church needed to remain in touch with its roots in the Spirit—or face the consequences.

Congar devotes much of his writing to the role of the laity in the Church and their apostolate of bringing the Gospel to the marketplace. He rightly points out that, if they are to assume their rightful place in the Church, they need to actively participate in the Eucharistic liturgy and not consider themselves mere passive onlookers. By emphasizing the believing community's active role in the Church's life, he is able to give the laity a more visible role in the Eucharistic worship of Christ's Mystical Body. Although he always maintains the importance of the Church's hierarchical priesthood, he insists that the threefold order of bishop, priest, and deacon is at the service of the priesthood of the laity—and not vice versa. His insights into the vocation of the laity contributed to the Second Vatican Council's emphasis on their active role in all levels of Church life and their call to promote Gospel values especially in society and in the secular sphere of daily life.

Finally, as a Dominican, Congar has a deep and lasting devotion to the Blessed Virgin Mary, the Theotokos, Mother of God. While he recognizes the apprehensions some may have regarding the highlighted emphasis Catholics give to the Blessed Mother, he is quick to point out that "[t]he part played by Mary is situated within that played by the Holy Spirit, who made her the mother of the incarnate Word and who is the principle of all holiness and of the communion of the saints."[21] Mary, in other words, is not a substitute for the Holy Spirit, but the fullest expression of what it means to be a human being fully open to and imbued by its sanctifying and redemptive presence.

---

[21] Congar, *I Believe in the Holy Spirit*, 1:164.

She is the Mother of the Church only because she is fully alive with the Spirit of God. Congar spoke often of the Holy Spirit as being the "soul of the Church" and looked to Mary as being the fullest expression of its presence in redeemed humanity.

Although these observations do not exhaust Congar's teaching on the Eucharist, they cover its main contours and reflect its centrality to his understanding of the mystery of the Church and the work of the Spirit in the lives of the faithful. The Eucharist, for Congar, was central to the life and message of Christ and his body, the Church. Without it, the faithful would be without food and nourishment for their pilgrim and missionary journey through time.

Conclusion

Yves Congar brought a renewed emphasis on the Holy Spirit to Roman Catholic life, thought, and worship. The Spirit, he believed, was the soul of the Church and the vivifying force of its institutional structure, doctrinal teachings, and sacramental worship, especially as they relate to the Eucharist. No twentieth-century Catholic theologian did more than he to place the Spirit at the very center of the Church's self-understanding and mission.

The Eucharist, for Congar, both constituted the Church and was constituted by it. It gathered the community of believers around the table of the messianic banquet and placed them in direct contact with the saving mysteries of Christ's passion, death, and resurrection. Through the power of the Spirit, it brought the Risen Lord into the midst of the body of the faithful and enabled them to recognize his presence in the breaking of the bread. If believers became members of Christ's body through baptism, they were nourished, sustained, and united in that body through the Eucharist. His writings on ecumenism and the laity, as well as his participation in the worker-priest movement, are a reflection of his belief in the unifying role the Spirit played in the life of the Church, its teachings, sacramental worship—and beyond.

Congar's insights laid the groundwork for the Second Vatican Council's emphasis on the mystery of the Church, and its understanding of it as the pilgrim People of God. They also helped the fathers of the Council appreciate the importance of reaching out to other Christian churches and ecclesial communities in a Spirit of dialogue and respect. He saw the Eucharist as the "sacrament of unity" and believed it should inspire the members of Christ's body to work to overcome their divisions and find common ground in doctrine, life, and worship. The Spirit, he believed, was at the heart of this movement toward unity. Through his writings, he exhorted the community of believers not to stand in its way.

Reflection Questions

- The Eucharist, for Congar, imparts Christ's fellowship and life. Does this sacrament impart these to the body as a whole or to each individual member? To what extent is this fellowship and life shared by each of the members? In what ways have you experienced this fellowship and life?
- Congar maintains that the Eucharist is a work of the Spirit mediated through the Church. Do you consider the Eucharist a work of Christ or the Spirit. In what sense is it a work of both? Has the Spirit's role in the celebration of the sacrament been emphasized enough in our theology of the Eucharist?
- Congar maintains that the Holy Spirit is at work in the three realities that bear the name the body of Christ: Jesus, the Eucharist, and the Church. How are these three realities related? Does anyone have priority over

the others? Has the Eucharist increased your love for Christ and his Church?

Voice Sixteen

Josef Pieper:
Festive Celebration

Our next voice was another of the twentieth century's great Catholic philosophers. Josef Pieper (1904-97) was born in Elte, Germany, moved to Münster with his family in 1912, graduated from the gymnasium there in 1923, studied philosophy, law, and sociology at the universities of Münster and Berlin from1926-27, and received his Ph.D. from Münster in 1928. From 1928-32 he was a professorial assistant at Münster and did freelance literary work from 1932-40. He served in the psychology section of the German army during World War II and later as a civilian helper at the central welfare office of Westphalia, during which time he examined the aptitude of soldiers with severe battlefield injuries. Conscripted into the German air force in 1944, he served in a military hospital, was imprisoned for a few months at the war's end, and afterwards returned to his work at the central welfare office.

Pieper began his post-doctoral habilitation in 1945 with the Faculty of Philosophy at the University of Münster, was appointed lecturer of philosophy at the Pedagogical Academy of Essen in 1946, and gave his inaugural lecture at the Faculty of Philosophy of the University of Münster the same year. He became a member of the German Academy for Language and Literature in 1949, was promoted to extraordinary (associate) professor at Münster in 1950, then to ordinary (full) professor in 1959, and finally emeritus professor in 1972. He continued lecturing and writing after his retirement and gave his last lecture a year before his death in 1996. The author of numerous books and monographs, he is probably most remembered for his works on leisure, festivity, and the virtues. His teaching on the Eucharist flows from his deep Catholic faith, his love of the philosophy and theology of St. Thomas Aquinas.[1]

Pieper's Philosophical and Theological Outlook

Pieper was deeply rooted in the philosophical and theological outlook of St. Thomas Aquinas (1224/25-74). When he was in his late teens, a teacher of his, who was also a priest, convinced him to delve into the writings of Thomas Aquinas. This early encounter led to a lifetime dedicated to exploring the writings of the Angelic Doctor, one that would make his thought more accessible to the sensitivities of a twentieth-century audience without sacrificing any of its substance or accuracy. Pieper's *Guide to Thomas Aquinas* (1962) remains to this day one of the best (and most readable) introductions to the life and work of this seminal Catholic thinker available. His treatises on the moral virtues, *The Four Cardinal Virtues* (1966), and the theological virtues, *Faith, Hope, and Love* (1986) touch the heart of Aquinas's theological and spiritual outlook and are widely used in Catholic colleges and seminaries even today.

More than a mere popularizer of Aquinas's thought, Pieper was a probing thinker in his own right and used Thomistic philosophy to delve deeply into some of the most fascinating,

---

[1] This information on Pieper's life and work comes from "Josef Pieper Arbeitstelle," https://josef-pieper-arbeitsstelle.de/?id=33&L =1 (Accessed October 5, 2016); Josef Pieper: Philosopher of Virtue, http://www.ignatiusinsight.com/authors/ josefpieper.asp.

yet elusive and seldom discussed elements of Western culture. In *Leisure: The Basis of Culture* (1948), he shows that leisure forms the very foundation of Western culture, since it gives man the energy and time to turn away from matters relating to mere survival and to explore the deeper questions of human existence. In it, he asserts that philosophy begins in wonder and that man's fascination with the world leads him to construe innovative ways of explaining his place in the universe and means of interacting with it. His book, *In Tune with the World: A Theory of Festivity* (1963), explores the relationship between work and play, shows how festivity involves the whole of existence, and sees affirmation at the very heart of all Christian worship. His book, *In Search of the Sacred: Contributions to an Answer* (1988), looks into the meaning of the sacred as it relates to time and space, Christian worship, Church architecture, and the meaning of the priesthood. In it, he affirms that, while God alone is "holy," the term "sacred" is typically used to refer to more tangible earthly realities (time, space, people, actions) in their orientation toward the holy and the threshold of the divine.[2]

Pieper's Catholic faith permeates his writings, and for this reason, they are remarkably cohesive in their philosophical and theological outlook. He is a "Catholic philosopher" in the best sense of the term, someone who understands the depths of human reason (and its limitations), yet is not afraid to explore its interface with the realm of faith. His deep love for the thought of Aquinas opened up for him a way of philosophizing about some of the most fundamental questions of human existence. He did so in a manner that was respectful of his Catholic

---

[2] The publication dates are those of the English translations. For a complete bibliography of Pieper's original works in German, see "Josef Pieper Arbeitstelle," http://josef-pieper-arbeitsstelle.de/index.php?id=49&L=1.

heritage, open to human experience, and appreciative of the dialogue between faith and reason. His teaching on the Eucharist appears in a number of his works, but shines through most clearly in *In Search of the Sacred.*

Pieper's Teaching on the Eucharist

Perhaps the best way of introducing Pieper's teaching on the Eucharist is to examine a passage from his work on festivity: "The inner structure of real festivity has been stated in the clearest and tersest possible fashion by Chrysostom" *'ubi caritas gaudet, ibi est festivitas,'* 'Where love rejoices, there is festivity.'"[3] Pieper published this work at the time of the Second Vatican Council and recognized its reaffirmation of the Eucharist as "'the summit' of the Church's activity and the 'fount from which all her powers flow.'"[4] He saw the Eucharist, first and foremost, as a time for rejoicing in the love of Christ and thus a festive celebration. Catholics attend Mass on Sunday, their day of rest and a time when they cease from the ordinary demands of life, in order to place their lives in perspective and thank God for the many gifts he has bestowed on them. According to Pieper, "The Mass is called and is *eucharistia*. Whatever the specific content of this thanksgiving may be, the 'occasion' for which it is performed and which it comports with is nothing other than the salvation of the world and of life as a whole."[5] While he recognizes that everything depends on whether we believe Christ can transform us and the world

---

[3] Josef Pieper, *In Tune with the World: A Theory of Festivity*, trans. Richard and Clara Winston (South Bend, IN: St. Augustine's Press, 1999), 23.

[4] Pieper, *In Search of the* Sacred, 46; Second Vatican Council, *Sacrosanctum concilium* ("*The Constitution on the Sacred Liturgy*"), no. 10.

[5] Pieper, *In Tune with the World*, 38.

around us, Pieper sees Christian worship "as an act of affirmation that expresses itself in praise, glorification, thanksgiving for the whole of reality and existence."[6]

Pieper further points out that, when a priest celebrates Mass, he acts *"in persona Christi."* He considers the priesthood tied to the Eucharist—and vice versa. At his ordination, the Church bestows upon the priest *potestas sacra* (sacred power) to celebrate the Eucharist in the person of Christ for the universal Church. He is given authority in the service of the Church "to make God's incarnate Logos, in sacramental signs, present among men."[7] For Pieper, the social and sociological context of the priesthood does not obscure this fundamental reality, for it operates on an entirely different level. During the Eucharistic Prayer, when the priest says, "This is my Body" and "This is my Blood," he is not merely quoting Christ's words, but speaking and acting as Christ Himself. When he says them, these words are not merely recited as a professor might quote them at a lecture, or as a group gathered in a room might recite them for Bible study, or even a lector or the priest himself might proclaim them during the Liturgy of the Word. When the priest says them at the appropriate time during the Eucharistic Prayer, Christ himself speaks. For Pieper, "[i]t is rather Christ himself who effects this identity, he who 'in the sacrifice of the Mass...is present in the person of the priest.'"[8]

As might be expected, Pieper's teaching on the Eucharist is deeply rooted in the thought of St. Thomas, who understood the sacraments as "the means by which the Incarnation of the divine

---

6 Ibid.

7 Josef Pieper, *In Search of the Sacred: Contributions to an Answer*, trans. Lothar Krauth (San Francisco: Ignatius Press, 1991), 64.

8 Ibid., 68; Second Vatican Council, *Dei Verbum* ("The Dogmatic Constitution on Divine Revelation"), no. 7.

Logos is sustained and perpetuated throughout history."[9] St. Thomas, Pieper points out, considers the Eucharist "the most prominent of all the sacraments, comparable to bread, the most prominent of all foods."[10] For this reason, it constitutes and perfects all the other sacraments. Pieper also points out that, except for the Eucharist, the priest speaks for himself when he presides at all the other sacraments and says, for example, "I baptize you..." or "I absolve you..."[11] Only in the Eucharist does he act *in persona Christi* and pronounce the words of Institution as if Christ himself were speaking.[12] Pieper points out that, while all believers are members of the priesthood of the faithful, the sacrament of orders consecrates priests and gives them "the authority to celebrate for the entire Church the Eucharist *in personal Christi*" and that "this authority can 'in no wise' be claimed by the laity."[13]

Using Thomas's distinction between "a human act" (e.g., a deliberated action of reason and will) and "an act of man" (e.g., a beating heart, a reflex), Pieper draws an analogous distinction between "priestly actions" and "actions that simply happen to be performed by priests," with the former being those actions performed by virtue of the authority received through sacred orders and the latter those that are not.[14] He further points out that both Aquinas and the Fathers of the Second Vatican Council identify the celebration of the Eucharist as the primary area of priestly action and that "he [Thomas] explicitly sees the 'Sacrament of Christ's Body' also as the sacrament of love and peace, and above all as the sacrament of Church unity, by whose

---

[9] Pieper, *In Search of the Sacred*, 70.
[10] Ibid.
[11] Ibid., 71.
[12] Ibid., 70.
[13] Ibid., 75.
[14] Ibid., 75.

power 'the many are united in Christ'"[15]

Pieper is not only concerned with sacred time, but also sacred space. He believes "a Christian church, in essence, is a sacred space."[16] It is consecrated in order to become an *aedes sacra*, a sacred space or sacred building.[17] What takes place there brings those gathered for the celebration of the sacred mysteries. Churches, in his mind, are built not to surround a book, but an altar.[18] For Catholics, this points to "the celebration of the Eucharistic mystery and... the actualization of the unique sacrifice of Christ himself."[19] Pieper here draws a sharp distinction between the "sacred mysteries" and the "proclamation of the word."[20] If this distinction is not maintained, the believing community runs "the risk of a demonstrative informality and familiarity in speech and comportment, devastating to the character of the 'sacred action;' or the risk of an aberrant idolizing of the 'word.'"[21] Sacred space, in his mind, should be set apart from the realm of ordinary use and explicitly dedicated to liturgical worship. To accomplish this task, he suggests that a boundary line be drawn in the form of a lobby or courtyard that would shut out the ordinary workaday world and that the entire church structure be reserved exclusively for divine worship.[22] The primary event of Catholic worship is the mystery of the Incarnation and the Christ's self-sacrifice on Calvary. The Eucharist makes Christ's saving mystery tangible. "The sacrament of the altar" is also "the sacrament of bread" and "the sacrament of Christ's presence." All three are cherished and

---

[15] Ibid., 76.
[16] Ibid., 85.
[17] Ibid., 99.
[18] Ibid., 103.
[19] Ibid., 105.
[20] Ibid., 109-10.
[21] Ibid., 110.
[22] Ibid., 114.

celebrated in sacred time and space.

Some Further Insights

Although much more can be said about Pieper's teaching on the Eucharist, these insights capture its main points and provide a good point of departure for further discussion. The observations that follow bring some of the implications of his teaching and look to their relevance for today.

To begin with, Pieper's insightful works on leisure and festivity provide us with an important context with which to view the Church's Eucharistic celebration. If philosophy begins in wonder, worship begins with awe and a deep desire to render thanks to God for his manifold gifts. The Mass, for Pieper, is a festival of thanksgiving that places our ordinary, workaday lives in proper perspective. It gives us the opportunity to pause for a time and to allow our hearts and minds to rise to the threshold of the sacred and honor the source of all that is. Rather than treating Sunday as just any other day, or simply a time to recharge our batteries so that we might do our work better and more efficiently, we need to set some time apart to relish creation, the gift of life, and all that God has given us through the Incarnation and Paschal Mystery of his Son. When seen in this light, the Eucharist is not simply another action that we add to our already very full and busy lives, but the center of our lives and the source from which everything flows. Care should be taken, therefore, to celebrate the Eucharist with reverence for God, respect for each other, gratitude for life, and a deep sense of the sacred.

Pieper reminds us that the Church celebrates the Eucharist both to receive Christ's saving mysteries and to affirm the whole of reality and existence through acts of glory, praise, and thanksgiving. In this respect, the sacrament embodies both God's gift to humanity and humanity's grateful and loving response to God. When celebrating this sacrament, God transforms not only time and space into sacred vessels of his loving presence, but also the empty and lonely corridors of the human heart. By participating in the Mass with reverence and devotion, we render thanks to God for his transforming presence in our lives. As the gift of God and the response of the body of the faithful, the Eucharist represents the very center of the Church's life and worship. As an action of Christ and his body, the Church, it represents, is at one and the same time, both a human and divine action. We respond to God's gift of Christ's saving mysteries with open hearts and hymns of praise and thanksgiving; God, in turn, blesses us and receives us in Christ as his adopted sons and daughters.

If, as Pieper maintains, the primary event of Catholic worship is the mystery of the Incarnation and Christ's self-sacrifice on Calvary, then the Eucharist as the "Sacrament of Sacraments" embodies these mysteries in a preeminent way. God becomes bread and wine so that he might divinize us and make us one with his flesh. Those celebrating the sacrament, moreover, are immersed in Christ's Paschal Mystery and incorporated more deeply into his passion, death, and resurrection. The Eucharist is the means by which God continues the mystery of his Incarnation and his sacrificial death on Calvary through time. It is a bridge between time and eternity, life and death, and God and humanity. It is central to the Church's life and worship, because it is an action of Christ's self-emptying made present in a concrete, visible way so that the members of the faithful might share in it themselves and thus be incorporated into his saving mysteries. The Eucharist represents the way Christ nourishes the members of his glorified body, the Church, and continues his salvific mission in time.

Although Pieper refers to Aquinas often and uses his categories to draw key distinctions in his own teaching on the

Eucharist, he does so in a way that remains faithful to this great scholastic master, yet is responsive to the needs of his time in creative and innovative ways. By embracing Thomas's sacramental realism, he points out the true depths of the Eucharistic mystery and highlights its central importance in the life of the Church and, indeed, in the life of every believer. Pieper has a unique way of seeing connections between the teachings of the masters and the current teaching of the Church. More than a mere popularizer, he cites important connections between the thought of the Thomas and the teaching of the Second Vatican Council that point to the continuity of the tradition and affirm the sacrament's central position as "the source and summit of the Christian life."[23] In this respect, Pieper incorporates elements both old and new into his teaching and ends up with a synthesis that is not only sound philosophically and theologically—but also thoroughly Catholic.

When discussing the relationship between the Eucharist and the priesthood, Pieper points out that the priest is ordained, first and foremost, to celebrate the Eucharist. The celebration of this sacrament is the *raison d'être* of this sacred order. The priesthood was established for the Eucharist, and the Eucharist cannot exist without the priesthood. When a priest celebrates this sacrament and says the words of consecration— "This is my Body...This is my Blood"—he acts not in his own name but "in the person of Christ" (*in persona Christi*), who is head of his mystical body, the Church. When at Eucharist, Christ acts in and through the person of the priest, whose priestly action becomes the action of Christ himself. When seen in this light, a priest's celebration of the Eucharist is a divine and human action and the means by which the faithful are both immersed in Christ's saving mysteries and divinized by receiv-

---

[23] Second Vatican Council, *Lumen gentium* ("The Dogmatic Constitution on the Church"), no. 11.

ing his Body and Blood. The dignity of the priesthood is thus intimately related to the dignity of the Eucharist. For Pieper, "[i]t is difficult to understand the thinking of those who consider the priesthood to be a 'part-time' occupation or even a 'hobby,' not a full-time job."[24]

For Pieper, churches are built around an altar, not the book of the word. The altar is the focal point of sacred space and should be prominent in any building erected for the purpose of Christian worship. Although the word is related to the altar, it is ancillary to it in that it prepares the heart for the proper reception of the sacrament. Although Christ is present in both the Liturgy of the Word and the Liturgy of the Eucharist, the fullness of his presence is found at the sacrifice celebrated at the altar by the priest and the community of the faithful. Pieper does not wish to place word and sacrament in opposition with each other, but merely highlight the centrality of Christ's sacrificial offering for Catholic worship and to underscore the importance that the Mass be a harmonious (and carefully coordinated) meeting of sacred time, space, and action. His insights into what make a church a church are closely related to those on what makes a priest a priest. Since, the Eucharist lies at the very heart of Catholic life and worship, every aspect of the Church's celebration should embody this underlying truth.

Finally, related to the above insight is Pieper's concern that a certain boundary line or border in the form of a narthex or lobby be created to separate the sacred from the secular, the place of worship from our ordinary, workaday world. Preserving a sacred space and setting it aside for nothing but worship says something about the relationship between the human and divine in Catholic worship. The purpose of the Eucharist is to immerse the faithful in the saving mysteries of Christ and, through them, to radiate outward into the world

---

[24] Pieper, *In Search of the Sacred*, 78.

around them—and not vice versa. While that is not to say that a place of Catholic worship should never be used for some other appropriate and tasteful form of cultural activity, care must be taken that the boundary between the sacred and the secular should be preserved at all times and that the place of worship not be cheapened in any way or, worse yet, secularized to the point where the harmonious balance of sacred time, space, and action is disrupted and possibly even disfigured. The Eucharist, for Pieper, is the most prominent of the sacraments just as bread is the most prominent of foods. It deserves a special dwelling place to mark its centrality to our lives and to recognize that our outer spaces of worship help to shape the inner spaces of the human heart.

Although these observations in no way exhaust the riches of Pieper's teaching on the Eucharist, they highlight its centrality for his thought and demonstrate his desire to explain the profound truths of the faith in a way that is, at one and the same time, creative, Catholic, and unabashedly orthodox. The impact of his thought on Catholic theology was calming, steady, inspiring, and profound. His works are widely read to this day, in learned as well as popular circles, and his legacy as one of the most profound Catholic writers of his day is clear and uncontested.

Conclusion

Josef Pieper could probe profound questions, uncover creative new insights about them, and express his findings in ways that were both easy to follow and in sync with his Catholic faith. He was a student of Aquinas in the best sense, someone who did not slavishly adhere to the conclusions of scholastic philosophy, but who was willing to explore new areas of inquiry, pose questions to the tradition, and integrate new learning into the body of Catholic knowledge.

Through his study of such areas as leisure, festivity, and the sacred, Pieper enriched the Catholic tradition and influenced a generation of Catholics on levels that affected both the highest levels of the academy and the popular practice and devotion of the faithful. He placed his philosophical learning at the service of the Church and, in doing so, unleashed a wealth of new insights into the perennial truths of the faith. To this day, many of his writings are not considered dated or "time-bound," but have a freshness and relevance about them that reveal the truth behind the perennial questions of the human situation.

Pieper's teaching on the Eucharist reflects his deep love for the Church and its worship. He considers this "sacrament of sacraments" central to the Church's life and its primary way of giving glory, praise, and thanksgiving to God. He sees the mysteries of the Incarnation and Christ's Paschal Mystery at the very heart of the celebration of the Mass and firmly believes that this action should be immersed in an atmosphere of the sacred. He emphasizes the intimate relationship between the Eucharist and the priest (who celebrates the sacrament *in persona Christi*) and believes that the altar should be the central focus of the Church's sacred space. For Pieper, everything about the sacrament says something about God's creative, redeeming, and sanctifying love. This "bread from heaven," he believed, was given to mortal men to heal them of their wounds, provide them with daily spiritual sustenance, transform their lives, and even divinize them, so that they might one day cross the threshold of the sacred, enter into the presence of the divine, and behold the very face of God himself.

Reflection Questions

- Pieper saw the Eucharist, as a festive celebration, a time for rejoicing in the love of Christ. Do you think of the Eucharist as a celebration? Do you look forward to participating in it? Do you find yourself rejoicing in Christ's love? How has Christ's love touched you? How has it touched others through you?
- According to Pieper, "The sacrament of the altar" is also "the sacrament of bread" and "the sacrament of Christ's presence." Do you see the Eucharist as sacrifice, banquet, and presence? Do you identify with one of these facets of the sacrament more than the others? Which of the three do you have the most difficulty understanding?
- Pieper emphasizes the close relationship between the Eucharist and the priesthood. How do you view the relationship between the two? Is it possible to have one without the other? What does the Eucharist reveal about the nature of the priesthood? What does it reveal about the priesthood of all believers?

Voice Seventeen

Karl Rahner:
Primordial Sacrament

Our next voice was a German Jesuit and arguably the most prominent Catholic theologian of the twentieth century. Karl Rahner, S. J. (1904-84) was born in Freiburg, entered the Jesuit novitiate in 1922, made his first vows in 1924, was ordained a priest in 1932, and professed his solemn vows in 1939. After his seminary training, he began graduate studies at the University of Freiburg in Breisgau, received his doctorate from there in 1936, and finished his postdoctoral work (*Habilitation*) in 1936. During his long academic career, he taught at various Jesuit seminaries and at such universities as Innsbruck, Munich, and Münster in Westfalen. In 1961, Pope John XXIII appointed him to advise Cardinal König to prepare the Second Vatican Council, and in 1962 he was named a theological expert (*peritus*) for the Council. He was a member of the International Theological Commission from 1969-71 and of the Synod of German Bishops from 1970-75. All in all, he received some fifteen honorary degrees as well as numerous honorary awards and professorships. He is most remembered for his multi-volume *Theological Investigations* (1954-84), a promoter of Transcendental Thomism, and such innovative theological concepts as the supernatural existential, transcendental freedom, and the anonymous Christian. His teaching on the Eucharist was known for its sensitivity to its transformative nature and its being the source of the other sacraments.[1]

Rahner's Spirituality

Although Rahner had many influences on his spiritual and theological outlook, he was very conscious of his formation in spirituality of St. Ignatius and once said that his Jesuit formation had a greater impact on him than all his philosophical and theological studies.[2] He found in the *Spiritual Exercises* an invitation to find God in all things and discovered in them one of the guiding principles of his theological vision: the intimate unity of the love of God and the love of man.[3]

With Ignatius, Rahner believed it was possible to enter into the mystery of God only through the humanity of Jesus. This process of immersion took place throughout a person's life and enabled him or her to become a disciple of Jesus by dying with him in God.[4] For this to occur, the Gospel narrative of Jesus' passion, death, and resurrection had to take root in one's life and become one's own. Rahner described his own vocation thus: "I have chosen the discipleship of the poor and humble Jesus, the poor and humble Jesus and no other. Such a choice has the underivability of specific love; it is a call which has its legitimization only in itself."[5]

Like Ignatius, Rahner believed that a person could exper-

---

[1] For a detailed chronology of Rahner's life, see Harvey D. Egan, *Karl Rahner: Mystic of Everyday Life* (New York: Crossroad, 1998), 14-18.

[2] See Ibid., 28.

[3] See Herbert Vorgrimler, *Understanding Karl Rahner: An Introduction to His Life and Thought* (New York: Crossroad, 1986), 36.

[4] Ibid.

[5] Ibid.

ience God's very self. He derived from this notion a belief that God could be experienced existentially. The supernatural, he asserted, formed the existential backdrop of all human experience. "One thing remains certain," he once wrote, "God can and will deal directly with his creature."[6] The Trinity, in other words, was directly involved with creation. Rahner was deeply influenced by Ignatius's Trinitarian mysticism, which stressed that a person could experience Father, Son, and Holy Spirit both in themselves and in relation to each other. From this insight, he developed his Trinitarian understanding of grace, a theory that led him to see an intimate connection between the inner relations and outward actions of the Godhead, that is, between the immanent and economic relations of the Trinity.

With Ignatius, Rahner also placed a great emphasis on discerning God's will and finding it in the circumstances of everyday life. He believed that discernment of spirits took place through the Ignatian concept of "consolation without previous cause," through which God entered a soul and drew it into the love of his Divine Majesty. This process, he believed, could even manifest itself in a group and form the basis of a communal logic of existential decision, the kind that gave birth to the Society of Jesus itself.[7] Ignatius's mystical spirituality permeates Rahner's thought and enabled him to see a close connection between action and contemplation, between what a person *does* and what a person *is*. This is true especially of the priesthood and the celebration of the Eucharist.[8]

---

[6] Egan, *Karl Rahner*, 33.

[7] Ibid., 44.

[8] For more on the influence of Ignatian spirituality on Rahner, see Philip Endean, *Karl Rahner and Ignatian Spirituality* (Oxford: Oxford University Press, 2001). For an overview of Rahner's spirituality and theological outlook, see *The Cambridge Companion to Karl Rahner*, eds. Declan Marmion and Mary E. Hines (Cambridge: Cambridge University Press, 2005).

Rahner's Teaching on the Eucharist

Rahner's views on the Eucharist must be viewed against his sacramental understanding of Christ and his Church. He calls Christ "the primordial sacrament of salvation" by which he means that Jesus represents "that historical event which, as an historical sign of God's will to save men, triumphantly succeeds in its purpose in spite of all the sins of men and from the beginning was implanted in the world as grace, brings about its own unmistakable historical manifestation, and establishes itself in the world and not just in the transcendent will of God."[9] Moreover, he calls the Church "the basic sacrament of salvation," by which he means "it is the sign that perpetuates Christ's presence in the world, the permanent and unsurpassable sign that the gracious entelechy of the whole of history, which brings this history into God Himself, will be victorious in the world despite all sin and darkness and will really prevail by bringing about the completion of the world in the form of salvation rather than judgment."[10] The Eucharist, in his mind, is the embodiment of Christ's sacrificial offering, for "in that hour Jesus accepted His death as the giving of Himself to God for the redemption of the world."[11] At the Last Supper, "He gave Himself to God as the eternal covenant of redemption, and He gave Himself to His disciples in the event and the symbol of a meal."[12]

Rahner believed that the Church was the "Church of the sacraments" and that the Eucharist was the "sacrament of the

---

[9] Karl Rahner, *Meditations on the Sacraments* (New York: The Seabury Press, 1977), xv.

[10] Ibid.

[11] Ibid., 29.

[12] Ibid.

new covenant."[13] By this he meant that the Church was the continuation through time of Christ's primordial sacrificial offering and that the Eucharist was "an absolutely central event in the Church."[14] "The Church," he believed, "is most manifest and in the most intensive form, she attains the highest actuality of her own nature, when she celebrates the eucharist."[15] In this sacrament, "everything that goes to form the Church is found fully and manifestly present: her separation from the world... her hierarchical structure...her dutiful receptivity to God, which forbids her to be an end in herself...her recitation of the efficacious words which render present what they proclaim... her unity...her expectation of the final kingdom...her penitential spirit...her profound readiness to serve others."[16] For this reason, he emphasizes the communal nature on the Eucharistic sacrifice and warns against an overly individualized devotion: "It is the Church that gives the individual the Body of Christ, which she has in her possession as the pledge of her redemption and the presence of grace in her, and she makes the individual share, for his sanctification, in the unity, love, and plenitude of the Spirit of this holy community of God's covenant, and so she fills him with all grace."[17]

Rahner also emphasizes the eternal dimensions of what took place at the Last Supper: "What happened there as an event once and for all is. It *is*."[18] He points out that "the Lord in this meal has wrought something that endures forever since His voluntary deeds come from the infinite primal grounds of the eternal *Word of God* itself and are a spiritual-human reality, like

---

[13] Karl Rahner, *The Church and the Sacraments* (new York: Herder and Herder, 1963), 11, 82.

[14] Ibid., 82.

[15] Ibid., 84.

[16] Ibid., 84-85.

[17] Ibid., 87.

[18] Karl Rahner, *Meditations on the Sacraments*, 33.

the creative words of Genesis."[19] In the Eucharist, Jesus "has wrought the 'new' and thus the final covenant."[20] For this reason, "He *is* the One whom He became in that time in His passion, ever and eternal: the crucified One and the resurrected One, the eternal ground for trusting oneself to the mystery of God, the lover who experienced the deepest helplessness of being human and endured all futility of utter devotion until it became victory itself. He *is* the one He became, and when we in holy Anamnesis proclaim His death until He comes again, we are not relating an incident from the scattered past, but proclaiming the once and for all presence with eternal validity."[21] The Eucharist, for Rahner, represents "the transfigured world in the transfigured flesh of the Resurrected, here is the beginning of the glorious validity of this earth!"[22] It is the "sacrament of the new creation," an eternal manifestation in time of the transformation of the world and all that we hope to become.

Some Further Insights

This brief exposition of Rahner's teaching on the Eucharist underscores its close connection to his understanding of Christ as the primordial sacrament, the Church as the visible extension of Christ's one redemptive sacrifice through time, and the Eucharist as the concrete manifestation that makes the Church what it is and heralds the coming of a new creation. The following observations highlight some of the spiritual and theological underpinnings of his view of the sacrament and their relevance for today's Catholics.

---

[19] Ibid.

[20] Ibid.

[21] Ibid.

[22] Ibid, 41.

To begin with, Rahner's Catholic faith, Jesuit formation, and background in Ignatian spirituality gave him a deep appreciation of the central role played by the Eucharist in humanity's redemptions the spiritual life of believers. Together, they gave him a deep sense of to the primary role the sacrament plays in the transformation of the human heart and the ultimate transfiguration of the world. He saw in the Eucharist the primary means through which believers were able to access the mystery of God through the humanity of Jesus, the Word-made-flesh. He recognized that eating Jesus' body and drinking his blood at the Eucharist gave believers the means to access in a unique way the self-communication of God that lies at the heart of their own experience. By becoming flesh and indeed by becoming humanity's food in the form of bread and wine, humanity is able to be divinized and thus realize its deepest hopes. Rahner's Eucharistic spirituality confirms God's presence in human experience and realizes humanity's latent hopes for living a transformed existence.

In keeping with one of the basic goals of Ignatian spirituality, Rahner views the Eucharist as a sacrament of contemplation and action, or rather, "contemplation in action." It embodies, at one and the same time, both Christ's prayer to the Father and his salvific self-offering manifested in his paschal mystery. As the prayer of the Church, it shapes the prayer of believers along these same lines. That is to say it unites being and action in the Church and its individual members, uniting the contemplative and active dimensions of their lives to make them "contemplatives in action." The Eucharist, in other words, conforms the Church and its members to the being and action of Christ. It not only heals their wounds, but elevates them in such a way that they are able to put on the mind of Christ and act accordingly. By eating Christ's body and drinking his blood, they have access to the life of the Spirit, who pray within them, acts within them, and empowers them to lives of authentic discipleship.

Rahner's belief in God's underlying self-communication in human awareness allows him to emphasize the Eucharist's role in bringing this awareness to heightened levels. His affirmation that "grace is everywhere" does not diminish the need for the sacraments, but places them in a new relation to human experience and its need for redemption. The Eucharist, in other words, builds upon and transforms the primordial self-communication of God present in all human beings. In his view, God's self-communication in human experience is not at odds with his self-communication through the Church and her sacraments, but confirms them and brings them to new heights. From this perspective, the Eucharist points to the complete transformation that God seeks to effect in all human hearts and in all creation and which his self-communication in human experience is but a faint reflection. It is the sacrament of humanity's and the world's transfiguration that has reached its concrete manifestation in Christ's passion, death, and resurrection.

Rahner believes that Christ is the "primordial sacrament" and that his abiding presence in the Church is "the official presence of the grace of Christ in the public history of the one human race."[23] As such, the Church is the fundamental and primal means by which Christ brings his redemptive love to humanity in the concrete circumstances of space and time. The Eucharist, in his mind, is the primary means by which the Church accomplishes this historical mission. It is the work of Christ's body on earth that makes the Church what it is and enables it to be "the abiding promulgation of his grace-giving presence in the world."[24] This means that Church cannot exist without the Eucharist; the Eucharist cannot exist without the

---

[23] Rahner, *The Church and the Sacraments*, 19.
[24] Ibid.

Church; and neither can exist without Christ. At the Last Supper, Jesus united his passion and death to a meal and told his disciples to celebrate it in memory of him. By uniting his body and blood to his death and the sharing of a simple meal, he united himself for all eternity to the members of his body and to the celebration of the Eucharist: the sacrament of his sacrificial offering, of his abiding presence in the Church, and of the heavenly banquet.

The Eucharist, for Rahner, is an action of Christ and his body, the Church. As such, it is communal in its orientation and private only in a secondary, derivative sense. Although he does not necessarily see a conflict between private devotion to the sacrament and its communal, liturgical celebration, he is wary of devotions that overly emphasize individual devotion to the detriment of the communal. He asserts that a person's access to the sacrament comes through the body of Christ's members and that his or her individual sanctification is mediated through the sacrament of the Church, which in turn mediates God's salvific mercy through the paschal mystery of Christ. For Rahner, authentic private devotion to the Blessed Sacrament gives a person a deeper appreciation of the Eucharistic liturgy as an action of Christ manifested through the community of believers for its collective good and the good of its members. In his mind, the Eucharist preserves an intimate balance between the individual and the community—and vice versa.

Rahner sees a close connection between the Eucharist and the priesthood. He says "the priest is he who, related to an at least potential community, preaches the Word of God by mandate of the Church as a whole and therefore officially, and in such a way that he is entrusted with the highest levels of sacramental intensity of this Word."[25] The Eucharist, he

---

[25] Karl Rahner, "What Is the Theological Starting Point for a Definition of the Priestly Ministry," in *The Identity of the Priest*, ed.

believes, is a sacramental intensification of the priests mission to preach the Gospel. As "an absolutely central event in the Church," it represents the fullest sacramental expression of Christ's salvific message and needs to be celebrated with dignity and great reverence. As a servant of the Gospel, the priest must be a servant of the Church and the Eucharist. In becoming a priest, he has taken on the great responsibility of being Christ for others and of feeding God's people with Christ's Word and with his Body and Blood. For a priest, to celebrate Mass and the sacraments is to preach the Gospel of Christ, a message of sacrificial love and divine mercy that resonates in both eternity and in time to heal the wounds of humanity and make it whole for the glory of God.

Finally, Rahner calls the Eucharist the "sacrament of the new covenant" and finds in it a transfigured world reflected in the transfigured flesh of the Risen Lord. This "sacrament of the new creation" embodies the hope not only of what humanity desires one day to become, but also the entelechy of the entire world. This eschatological orientation enables believers to have a glimpse of the eternal in the present moment and get in touch with their deepest, most intimate yearnings. In this respect, God's self-communication in human experience mingles with his sacramental self-communication in the consecrated bread and wine and gives way to a mystical vision of a fully transformed creation gathered around the table of the heavenly banquet. When seen in this light, the Eucharist affirms both God's presence in human experience and his desire to envelop it within the eternal through a process of historical divinization that makes it fully alive and able to cross the threshold of divine mystery.

Although these observations do not exhaust Rahner's

Karl Rahner, *Concilium* 43(New York/Paramus, NJ: Paulist Press, 1969), 85.

teaching on the Eucharist, they cover its main contours and point to the important role it plays in his understanding of how Christ mediates his redemptive love to humanity through the Church and the sacraments. They also reflect the various nuances of his spiritual outlook and how they impact his understanding and presentation of the Gospel message.

Conclusion

Karl Rahner was one of the great Roman Catholic theologians of the twentieth century. As a Jesuit, he was deeply influenced by the spirituality of St. Ignatius of Loyola and brought his deep desire to find God in everyday life to his philosophical and theological studies. He developed in his research a mystical understanding of existence based on the notion of God's self-communication in human experience. The experience of God, he believed, formed a natural part of human knowing and was not predicated on something coming from without human nature, but from within it. In making this assertion, he weakened the boundaries between the natural and supernatural, a stance for which he was criticized and, at times, even ridiculed by more traditional Catholic thinkers.

Rahner's stance on the Eucharist navigated the turbulent waters of twentieth-century Catholic thought. He was a theological innovator who sought to interpret the Gospel message through contemporary philosophical and theological categories. While doing so, he sought to remain faithful to the Catholic tradition, yet present it in a way that would be sensitive to both modern intellectual categories and human sensitivities. The Eucharist, for him, was the sacrament of Christ and his body, the Church. Through it, Christ continued to preach his message of divine mercy and actualized his redemptive action through time.

As an action of Christ and his Church, this sacrament was

communal in nature, but oriented toward the good of the individual. It was divinizing in its effects and played a major role in the transformation of humanity and all creation. It was rooted in history yet oriented toward the world to come. It provided daily bread, yet was eschatological in its outcome. It manifested the Gospel truth of a kingdom both in our midst and yet to come. The Eucharist, for Rahner, was the sacrament of the new covenant and the new creation. It constituted the Church and was constituted by it. It remembered the past, celebrated the present, and looked to the future. In this sacrament, eternity embraced time; infinity touched the finite; Christ's saving mystery crossed the threshold of the human heart; the Word-made-flesh became food for the soul and grace-filled light for the eyes of faith.

Reflection Questions

- Rahner thinks of the Eucharist as a central event in the life of the Church. Does the Eucharist have a central place in your life? Is your life oriented toward it? Does everything in your life flow from it?
- Rahner calls the Eucharist the "sacrament of the new creation." Do you see this sacrament as key to the world's transformation? Do you see it as the key to the trans-formation of the Church and your parish community? Do you see it as a means to your own personal trans-formation?
- Rahner maintains that everything that goes to form the Church is found fully and manifestly present in the Eucharist. Does this coincide with your view of the sacrament? Does it differ in any way? In what sense is the Eucharist a "sacrament of the Church?" In what sense is the Church most herself when she celebrates the sacra-ment?

Voice Eighteen

Jean Daniélou:
Mysterious Anticipation

Our next voice was a leading figure in the Nouvelle Théologie. Born at Neuilly not far from Paris, Jean Daniélou, S.J. (1905-74) was the son of a French politician and an educator and foundress of a well-known school for girls. He studied at the Sorbonne, passed his comprehensives in grammar in 1927, and entered the Jesuits in 1929. He taught for a time at a boys' school in Poitiers, did his theological training at Fourvière in Lyon, and was ordained to the priesthood in 1938.

During the Second World War, he served as a military chaplain in the French air force until the Nazi takeover of France in 1940, after which time he continued his studies in the Church fathers and ancient Christian literature. In 1943 he completed his doctoral thesis on the theology and mysticism of Gregory of Nyssa. That same year he was awarded a doctorate in literature from the Sorbonne and appointed to the prestigious Chair of Christian Origins at the Institute Catholique of Paris. From there, he embarked on a remarkable academic career that eventually made him one of the foremost Catholic theologians of his day. He served as a theological expert (*peritus*) at the Second Vatican Council, became a bishop and cardinal in 1969, and was elected to the Académie française in 1972.

A prolific author and founding member of both *Sources chrétiennes* and the international theological journal, *Communio*, his major works include, *The Bible and the Liturgy* (1956), *Primitive Christian Symbols* (1961), *Why the Church?* (1972), and his three-volume work on the history of Christian doctrine before the Council of Nicaea: *The Theology of Jewish Christianity* (1964), *Gospel Message and Hellenistic Culture* (1973), and *The Origins of Latin Christianity* (1976). He died in Paris in 1974 under what was thought at the time to be strange and unusual circumstances.[1]

Daniélou's Theological Outlook

Daniélou was one of the leading figures in the mid-twentieth century renewal known as the Nouvelle Théologie or the movement of Ressourcement, which was an attempt to address the pressing theological issues of the day by returning to the sources of the Church's past in the hope of getting in touch with the deeper (and often forgotten) truths of the faith and thus move the tradition forward. This attempt at theological renewal looked to the past not out of mere antiquarian interest, but to uncover its relevance for the present and make a genuine theological contribution for future generations. Along with such figures as Yves Congar, Henri de Lubac, and Henri Bouillard, he delved into the sources of the Church's antique past and found fertile soil from which to construct a theological vision that was

---

[1] For a brief biographical sketch, see Maurice F. De Lange, "Foreword" in Jean Daniélou, *Why the Church?*, trans. Maurice F. De Lange (Chicago: Franciscan Herald Press, 1974), xiii-xiv. For the unusual circumstances surrounding Daniélou's untimely death, see Brian Van Hove, "The Lasting Legacy of Cardinal Daniélou," *The Catholic World Report* (October 3, 2012), http://www.catholicworldreport.com/Item/1629/the-lasting-legacy-of-cardinal-danielou.aspx.

both continuous with the past and relevant for the believing community of his day.

Daniélou's study of the early sources of Jewish, Hellenistic, and Latin Christianity gave him a wealth of knowledge about the earliest Christian communities regarding their emerging beliefs, evolving structures, and developing modes of worship. They also led him to study the powerful symbols and typologies that permeated the mindset of early Christians and enabled them to weather the storms of external persecution and internal dissension. Such knowledge provided him with a firm basis from which to examine a wide range of issues within the Church of his day and led him to offer creative and innovative solutions, many of which received a warm welcome and others of which were severely criticized. His work and that of others in the Ressourcement movement laid much of the theological groundwork for the Second Vatican Council. Their attempt to renew the Church by returning to its sources enabled her to assess her present situation from a position of historical awareness and move into the future with a deep sense of confidence in God's abiding presence and providential care.

Daniélou's theological outlook was deeply tied to his service to the Church. After being made bishop and cardinal by Pope Paul VI, he focused his energies on a comprehensive program of apologetics, catechesis, and popular defense of the faith during the turbulent years immediately after the close of the Council. If his scholarly output suffered somewhat as a result of this decisive turn toward the general audience, his love for the Church deepened and grew all the more intense. His ability to combine deep scholarship with an ardent promotion of the Catholic faith reflects the deepest values of both the Nouvelle Théologie and his Jesuit order's educative mission within the Church. He worked tirelessly and suffered greatly to promote the purpose of renewal envisioned by the Council. His views on the Church, the sacraments, and the Eucharist reflect his deep love for the Church's theological tradition, its relevance for the present, and the hope it carries for the future.[2]

Daniélou on the Eucharist

In his teaching on the Eucharist, Daniélou emphasizes its common origin with all the other sacraments: "Christ formally institutes them during his ministry, he makes them efficacious by his death and resurrection, he causes them to be brought into use at Pentecost."[3] "The Eucharist," he maintains, "was instituted by Christ in the full reality of its signs and content by a mysterious anticipation of his redemptive action."[4] He is especially interested in examining the meaning of the various signs and symbols that make up the Eucharistic celebration. He points out that during the Easter Vigil the sacraments of Baptism, Confirmation, and the Eucharist formed a single whole and that they immediately succeeded one another to make up the rites of initiation and that, in this context, the Eucharist included three main parts: the preparation or Offertory, the Sacrifice or great prayer of thanksgiving over the bread and wine, and the Communion or distribution of the consecrated elements.[5] He further points out that two themes constantly occur in the Eucharistic catecheses leading up to the celebration; "the Mass is a sacramental representation of the sacrifice of the Cross; the Mass is a sacramental participation in

---

[2] See Brian Van Hove, "The Lasting Legacy of Cardinal Daniélou" (Internet access cited above). For an excellent synthesis of Daniélou's Biblical, theological, and spiritual vision, see his book *Christ Among Us*, trans. Walter Roberts (New York: Sheed and Ward, 1961).

[3] Daniélou, *Christ Among Us*, 135.

[4] Ibid.

[5] Jean Daniélou, *The Bible and Liturgy*, University of Notre Dame Liturgical Studies, vol. 111 (Notre Dame, IN: University of Notre Dame Press, 1956), 127.

the heavenly liturgy."[6]

According to Daniélou, the Easter Vigil represents the summit of the Church's liturgical commemoration of Christ's Paschal Mystery. He underscores the unity of the entire process of initiation: "from Baptism to Communion, this is all a participation in Christ dead and risen again."[7] In his mind, "[t]here is no other mystery than the Paschal mystery, this is the mystery which is the unique object of the whole sacramental life, and which renders present in all times and in all places to apply to souls its life-giving fruits."[8] The Eucharist, he points out, is full of Old Testament figures: "It is the anticipation of the eschatological banquet, the sacrament of union, the source of spiritual joy, the document of the covenant."[9] At the same time, he insists that it is important to remember the two themes that dominate the theology of the Eucharist from very early on: "that of the efficacious memorial of the Passion the Resurrection and the Ascension, and that of participation in the sacrifice and the banquet of heaven."[10] These themes form the basis of the Church's understanding of the Eucharistic celebration and must be included in any attempt at liturgical renewal.

In his study of the many symbolisms present in the Eucharistic celebration, Daniélou points to the Old Testament as the primary source for the Church's understanding of the ritual meal and sacrifice: "If we wish to understand why it was in the form of a meal in which bread and wine are shared that Christ instituted the sacrament of his sacrifice, we must refer to the allusions to the Old Testament contained in these rites, allusions which were present to the mind of Christ, rather than

---

[6] Ibid. 128.

[7] Ibid., 140.

[8] Ibid.

[9] Ibid. 141.

[10] Ibid.

to any symbolism that we might think up for ourselves."[11] For this reason, we see in the Eucharistic elements of bread and wine "an allusion to the sacrifice of Melchisedech, to the manna in the desert, to the meal in the Temple; by this we understand that the Eucharist is a spiritual and universal sacrifice; that it is the nourishment of the people of God in their journey toward the land of promise; that it is, finally, the participation of all nations in the communion of divine blessings."[12] For Daniélou, the Eucharist cannot be cut off or separated from its Old Testament roots, for to do so would undermine "the unity of the plan of God revealed by the correspondences between the two covenants."[13] The sacrament, for him, "represents "the central mystery around which the whole biblical significance of the Meal is developed."[14]

In his treatment of the Eucharist, Daniélou also makes a fundamental distinction between the universal priesthood and the ministerial priesthood. The latter, in his mind, is intimately related to the celebration of the Eucharist: "The *sacerdos* is the one who offers the sacrifice in the name of the community."[15] The Eucharist, in this respect, is intimately tied to the ministerial priesthood, for the latter possesses an ontological character specifically ordered to the offering sacrifice on behalf of the believing community.[16] The priesthood thus has a specific nature, a definitive character, and is closely linked to Christ's own celibacy and priestly mission.[17] It is through the Eucharist

---

[11] Ibid., 160-61.

[12] Ibid.

[13] Ibid., 176.

[14] Jean Daniélou, *The Lord of History: Reflections on the Inner Meaning of History*, trans. Nigel Abercrombie (London/Chicago: Longmans/Henry Regnery, 1958), 240.

[15] Daniélou, *Why the Church?*, 32.

[16] Ibid., 34, 37.

[17] Ibid., 38.

and the other sacraments that, assisted by the Holy Spirit, the Church "continues to be the source of that holiness which makes us living spiritual beings."[18]

Some Further Insights

This brief exposition of Daniélou's teaching on the Eucharist underscores its deep roots in the sources of the Catholic tradition and its importance for understanding God's presence and activity in the world today. The following observations highlight some of the spiritual and theological underpinnings of his view of the sacrament and their relevance for today's Catholics.

To begin with, Daniélou's views on the Eucharist were shaped by his interest in the Jewish, Hellenic, and Latin sources of the Christian tradition. His involvement in the Nouvelle Théologie led him to delve deeply into the foundational texts of the Church's spiritual, theological, and liturgical past with the hope of pointing the Church toward the path of renewal. In his examination of these sources, he gained an appreciation for the essential role the Eucharist played in nearly every aspect of the Church's life. The sacrament, he came to see, brought believers into close, intimate contact with Christ's paschal mystery and was considered both a participation in the heavenly banquet and an immersion in the Christ's sacrificial offering on the cross. From these key insights, he then saw how the Church in its early Eucharistic liturgies looked to the Old Testament for finding ways of explaining these aspects of the sacrament in the light of God's providential plan for the entire human family. When seen in this light, the Eucharist cannot be fully understood apart from its deep

---

[18] Jean Daniélou, *The Faith Eternal and the Man of Today*, trans. Paul Joseph Oligny (Chicago: Franciscan Herald Press, 1970), 100.

Biblical roots and the impact they had on the life of Jesus and his closest followers.

Daniélou's study of the doctrine and liturgy of the early Church had a direct impact on the reforms of the Second Vatican Council. Considered one of the leading voices of renewal in his day, his opinions on such themes as the nature of the Church, the centrality of the Eucharistic celebration, and the role of the ministerial priesthood carried great weight and were perceived as being very influential in shaping the direction of the Council's reforms. This influence represents that side of Ressourcement, which sought to bring the wisdom of the Church's past to bear on its present concerns and pressing issues of the day. He believed that only by remaining true to the deepest roots of its spiritual, theological, and liturgical traditions would the Church be in a position to be an effective evangelizing presence in the modern world. Daniélou thus looked to the past in order to shape the present and orient the Church toward the future. His insights into the Eucharist came from his deep appreciation of the sacrament's central role in the life of the early Church and a conviction that it should have a vital impact on today's believers.

In his study of the rites of initiation, Daniélou pointed out that in the early Church's Easter Vigil celebration the sacraments of baptism, confirmation, and the Eucharist succeeded one another immediately and were understood as forming a closely knit and integral unity. This insight highlighted the centrality of the Easter Vigil for the community of the faithful and demonstrated how it was seen as the most appropriate moment for catechumens to be immersed in Christ's paschal mystery and fully admitted into the Church's ranks. At the Easter Vigil, catechumens were consecutively (and in close order) immersed in the waters of baptism, strengthened by the gifts of the Holy Spirit, and nourished with the body and blood of the Risen Lord. Because this life-changing process of initiation took place within the context of the most important celebration in the liturgical year, it both highlighted the missionary character of the Church (by admitting new members) and reflected the threefold creative, redemptive, and sanctifying dimensions of Christ's paschal mystery. Through his paschal mystery, in other words, Christ made (and makes) all things new by healing humanity of its sinfulness and elevating it through the transforming grace of the Spirit. These insights gave shape to the development of the rite of adult initiation for the post-Vatican II Church.

Daniélou's insight that the Eucharist represents "a mysterious anticipation of his redemptive action" goes to the heart of the Church's evangelizing message. As a symbolic action of prophetic significance, the Eucharist both anticipates and embodies what it signifies. In this respect, it not only points to Jesus' salvific self-offering on Golgotha, but also makes it present. Moreover, since Jesus's death on the cross is itself intimately tied to the empty tomb, it follows that the Eucharist embodies the entire redemptive action of Jesus' passion, death, resurrection, and ascension. The Eucharist, in this respect, puts us in direct contact with Jesus' paschal mystery and enables us to participate in the life of the Risen Christ. It looks to the redemptive mysteries of the past, makes them present for today's believers, and instills in them a hope of their ultimate transformation in the life of the glorified Lord. It embraces every dimension of time—past, present, future—and spreads Christ's redemptive action throughout the concrete dimensions of space and time.

Daniélou's study of the Old Testament figures (e.g., eschatological banquet, the sacrament of union, the source of spiritual joy, the document of the covenant) shows us what gave the fathers of the early Church the conceptual tools with which to understand the meaning of the Last Supper, and are especially significant because they are the very images and symbols that inhabited Jesus' prophetic imagination and inspired him to leave this sacred ritual in the hands of his disciples. These figures stand in strong continuity with the Old Testament prophets, Jesus' own prophetic vision, and the tradition of the early Church. As the sacrament of the New Covenant, the Eucharist thus represents the continuation of God's loving and providential care for his people, who are now understood as extending beyond the Jewish race to include anyone who looks to Jesus as their paschal lamb, priestly mediator, and redeeming Lord. By making present Christ's eternal sacrifice and giving believers a foreshadowing of the messianic banquet, it offers a concrete way for them to gain access to the mysteries of their faith in their everyday lives.

Daniélou finds an intimate link between the Eucharist and the ministerial priesthood and identifies the priest as one who offers sacrifice on behalf of the community. This close connection between priest and Eucharist does not undermine the universal priesthood of all believers, but simply affirms their different degrees of participation in the one priesthood of Christ. Just as baptism gives an ontological sharing in the universal priesthood of Christ, so does ordination give a deeper ontological sharing in the Christ's salvific self-offering. Daniélou maintains that there is "a difference of nature between the two" and that "[t]hey correspond to two dimensions of the Christian mystery which are opposite and complementary."[19] In his mind, there is no universal priesthood without the ministerial priesthood: "Just as the Incarnation is the condition of the Ascension, so too the ministerial sacrifice is the condition of the universal priesthood."[20] The first belongs to the order of efficient causality; the second, to the order of finality.[21] He

---

[19] Daniélou, *Why the Church?*, 31.
[20] Ibid., 33.
[21] Ibid., 33-34.

believed that the crisis in the priesthood after Second Vatican Council stemmed from a failure to make a clear distinction between the two.

Finally, when Daniélou was consecrated bishop and made a cardinal in obedience to the request Paul VI, life for him became markedly different. While so much of his work prior to the Council was dedicated to a meticulous scholarly examination of the sources of the Christian tradition with a view toward Church renewal, after the Council much of his energy was devoted to implementing the reforms of the Council and defending them from possible misinterpretations. This change in focus represented not a departure from the movement of Ressourcement, but a deeper understanding of its purpose and scope. For the reforms of the Council to be fully implemented, it was necessary to have authorities in place who understood their origin, scope, and purpose. Paul VI identified Daniélou as someone who would help him implement the changes initiated by the Council and suffer with him for the sake of the Church. Until his untimely death in 1974, he worked tirelessly to promote the theological, liturgical, and spiritual reforms of the Council. The centrality of the Eucharist for the life of the Church and its roots in and mediation of Christ's paschal mystery were foremost in his mind.

Although these observations do not do justice to the breadth and scope of Daniélou's teaching on the Eucharist, they underscore some of its major features and highlight the impact it had on the Church's program of renewal. If nothing else, they show how his deep interest in Ressourcement helped to shape the Church's thinking on a wide range of issues and how it placed the mystery of Christ passion, death, and resurrection at the very heart of Christian theology and worship.

Conclusion

Jean Daniélou was one of the leading Catholic theologians of the twentieth century and an outspoken agent of renewal before, during, and after the Second Vatican Council. His involvement in the Nouvelle Théologie and its work of ressourcement brought to the fore insights that had previously been over-looked, marginalized, or simply forgotten. His study of the sources of the Church's Jewish, Hellenistic, and Latin sources of the Church's past brought a badly needed historical con-sciousness to a tradition that until then had relied too heavily on scholastic manuals that were overly abstract and removed from their sources.

His teaching on the Eucharist reflects both a return to the sources of the Church's spiritual, theological, and liturgical past and a capacity to discern the central elements of the tradition. In his sifting through these ancient Christian texts, he was able to identify the Eucharist's roots in Christ's paschal mystery, its intimate connection with the other sacraments of initiation, its reliance on Old Testament figures for the conceptual and imaginative exposition of its meaning, and its constituent relationship to the ministerial priesthood.

These and many other insights of Daniélou's related to the nature of the Church and her sacraments contributed greatly to the theological groundwork prior to the Council, influenced the deliberations, and affected the implementation of its reforms. In this respect, his influence on the Council was insightful, profound, and lasting. He was one of the great twentieth-century voices for Church renewal and his legacy continues to inspire those both within and without the Church who yearn for authentic development and a program of seasoned change.

Reflection Questions

- For Daniélou, the Mass is "a sacramental representation of the sacrifice of the Cross." To what extent does the Church share in the sufferings of Christ? To what extent do you yourself share in his sufferings? Does your participation in the Eucharist constitute a participation in this sacrifice?
- For Daniélou, the Mass is "a sacramental participation in the heavenly liturgy." In what sense is the Eucharistic celebration both in and out of time? To what extent does it transcend time? What elements in the Eucharistic liturgy point to the heavenly one?
- For Daniélou, the Eucharist and the Church's other sacraments make us and keep us alive as living spiritual beings. Is the Eucharist the focal point of your spiritual life or does it lie somewhere on the periphery of it? Do you look upon it as something essential for your spiritual well-being? Could you live without it? How does the Eucharist satisfy the hungers of your heart?

Voice Nineteen

Hans Urs von Balthasar:
Work of the Spirit

Our next voice has much to add to our understanding of the Eucharist. Hans Urs von Balthasar (1905-1988) was born in Lucerne, Switzerland and steeped in literature and the arts from an early age. He entered the Jesuits in 1929, was ordained a priest in 1936, and became the student chaplain at the University of Basel shortly thereafter. During his time in Basel, he met the physician Adrienne von Speyr, was instrumental in her conversion, and played a role in helping her interpret her mystical experiences. In 1950, he left the Jesuits to found with her the Community of St. John (*Johannes Gemeinschaft*), a secular institute dedicated to living the evangelical counsels within their secular professions. He eventually became incardinated into the diocese of Chur and spent the rest of his life as a diocesan priest and leader of the institute he founded. Although he never held an academic position, Balthasar was a prolific author with varied interests and profound insights into the mysteries of the Catholic faith. He was a member of the International Theological Commission in the years immediately following the Second Vatican Council and, along with Josef Ratzinger, one of founders of the theological journal *Communio*. He died on June 28, 1988, just two days before he was to be received into the College of Cardinals by Pope John

Paul II.[1]

Balthasar's Theological Outlook

Balthasar's wide and varied interests gave an eclectic shape to his writings. His enormous literary output spanned much of the twentieth century and covered such areas as the Church Fathers and the lives of the saints, as well as topics related to language, literary analysis, and philosophy. In addition to systematics, he wrote on Christian ethics and spirituality, but in a way that united rather than separated them from each other. To this end, he refused to sever ethics and concrete social concerns from spirituality and often spoke of the marriage, divorce, and remarriage of Christian theology and spirituality. An expert on the thought of Karl Barth, his 1951 work remains a classic introduction to the thought of this seminal Protestant thinker. He also wrote important works on Henri de Lubac, George Bernanos, and Romano Guardini. He was especially influenced by de Lubac and the thought of the *Nouvelle Théologie,* the concerted attempt among some noted twentieth-century Catholic theologians to go back to the sources and of theology and break out of the neo-scholastic mindset prevalent in their time. The comprehensive yet exploratory nature of Balthasar's work led him to treat many difficult questions of Catholic theology and moral thought. Nor was he afraid to take

---

[1] For general biographical and detailed bibliographical information, see "Hans Urs von Balthasar: An Internet Archive," http://hansursvonbalthasar.blogspot.com. See also Peter Henrici, "Hans Urs von Balthasar: A Sketch of his Life," *Communio* 16(no. 3, 1989): 306-350, http://www.communio-icr.com/articles/PDF/henrici16-3.pdf; Stratford Caldecott, "An Introduction to Hans Urs von Balthasar," *Catholic Education Resource,* http://www.catholiceducation.org/en/culture/catholic-contributions/an-introduction-to-hans-urs-von-balthasar.html.

up such varied (and, at times, controversial) subjects as the nature of Christ's divine knowledge, the authenticity of recent apparitions of the Blessed Mother, and the possibility of humanity's universal salvation (*apokatastasis*).[2]

Balthasar believed that theology should be a study of the fire and light burning at the heart of the world rather than a static collection of dusty ideas. He is probably best remembered for his multivolume systematic theology: *The Glory of the Lord* (7 volumes), *Theo-Drama: Theological Dramatic Theory* (5 volumes), and *Theo-Logic* (3 volumes), along with a closing Epilogue (1 volume). Taken together, these learned tomes offer a comprehensive theological outlook that comprises a sophisticated Christian aesthetics based on the transcendental values of the One, the True, the Good, and the Beautiful. What is more, they go to the heart of the Christian message by showing how God manifests these values in Christ's paschal mystery, the dramatic foundational events that took place on Good Friday, Holy Saturday, and Easter Sunday. In these volumes, he also emphasizes how God revealed his love for humanity through Christ's embrace of the Cross and how in this single act of selfless love, God revealed the Beauty of Divine Love in the crucified person of his Only Begotten Son.[3]

Balthasar placed the reality of God's love at the very heart of his theology. When understood in its deepest sense, Love is the Glory of God, the very essence of Truth, Beauty, and Goodness. For him, the whole history of the world can be seen as the story of our response (or lack thereof) to God's call of love within our

---

[2] See "Hans Urs von Balthasar: An Internet Archive," http://hansursvonbalthasar.blogspot.com; S. Joel Garver, "An Overview of Balthasar's Project," http://www.joelgarver.com/writ/theo/balt/overview.htm; Idem, "Balthasar's Formative Influences,' http://www.joelgarver.com/writ/theo/balt/influences.htm.

[3] Ibid.

hearts and the heart of the world. In his *Theology of History*, he shows how Christ "stands in time and in history as the heart and norm of all that is historical" and how "the disclosure of God through time is identical with grace: access to him granted by himself."[4] By recapitulating all of history in himself, Christ becomes its norm and guarantor through the work of the Holy Spirit, who manifests himself in the incarnate Son himself, in the forty days after his Resurrection, in the historical Church as expressed through the sacraments, and in the subsequent missions of the whole Church in the lives of believers.[5]

Balthasar on the Eucharist

Although Balthasar treats the Eucharist at a number of places in his writings, its central role in humanity's redemption comes across most clearly in his *Theology of History*, where he places the sacrament in the larger context of the Spirit's work in the Resurrection and the missions of the Church. He believes that through his paschal mystery Christ recapitulated all of history into himself and that his individual existence was universalized by the work of the Spirit to become the immediate norm for each person's life.[6]

According to Balthasar, the Spirit acted powerfully in the forty days after Jesus' resurrection, a period marking its first universalizing action in historical time. Belonging to both Jesus' earthly and heavenly modes of existence, the days before and after his resurrection were not discontinuous, but closely tied. This intimate unity is evidenced by the Gospel accounts of the

---

[4] Hans Urs von Balthasar, *A Theology of History* (New York: Sheed and Ward, 1963), 20, 34. The original German publication, *Theologie der Geschichte*, appeared in 1959.

[5] Ibid., 80

[6] Ibid.

Risen Christ appearing to his disciples several times before his ascension, eating and drinking with them, as well as allowing them to examine the bloody wounds of his passion. Such reports imply that, after his resurrection, Christ manifested himself to his disciples in actual historical time. Unlike the period between his birth and passion, however, Jesus was no longer subject to death. In this respect, the forty days after his resurrection represent both a continuation and a break with the past. They comprise a new mode of time brought about by the power of the Spirit and which continued after Our Lord's Ascension.[7]

Balthasar further maintains that this universalizing movement in the Risen Christ has special relevance for the Church, since the same Spirit who brought about the incarnation of the Son in the womb of the virgin now enters the womb of his spiritual and universal bride, the Church.[8] For him, the Church and her sacraments represent the second great universalizing work of the Spirit in history. This action takes place in the sacramental order through the Church and her celebration of the mysteries of salvation. Christ's glorified mode of existence flows from his mode of existence during the forty days after his resurrection and endures in the Eucharist and the sacraments: "Here, again, he is the risen Lord, living in the eternity of the Father, his earthly time transfigured into his eternal duration, the eternal Christ accompanying 'his own' throughout time."[9] Our author affirms the close connection between the time of the forty days and the time of the Church. For him, the only difference between them is that in the former Jesus openly reveals his intimate companionship with us, while in the latter it is concealed in sacramental forms.[10]

---

[7] Ibid., 81-90.

[8] Ibid., 90.

[9] Ibid., 91.

[10] Ibid.

Balthasar further maintains that a sacramental, even Eucharistic, mode of time comes into existence in the deeply personal communion between the Lord and his Church.[11] At Mass, the eternal Lord comes to his people anew, but without being subject to the limitations of time. In making himself present to believers in the sacramental form of bread and wine, he gives himself to them in a manner unmarked by corruption. This encounter continues the transforming and universalizing process begun at Baptism and is limited only by death and the last judgment. At these moments, such forms of encounter will be unnecessary, since the Lord will no longer conceal himself under sacramental veils limited by space and time.[12]

For Balthasar, the Lord's presence in the Church, sacraments, and especially the Eucharist, is the work of the Spirit: "Just as it is he who awakens the flesh to life, so it is he who brings about sacramental presence. The miracle that achieves the sacrifice, transubstantiation, must be ascribed neither to the Father, who receives the sacrifice, nor to the Son, who is the offering, nor to the Church, who, as a corporate community, prays and brings forth the offering, but to the *Creator Spiritus*, the creating Spirit."[13] The Spirit is "the Lord of the sacraments," in both a hierarchical and personal sense. He is hierarchical because, as the Spirit of the Church, "he prepares the vessels, sets up the universal, valid framework, forming out of the life of Christ these seemingly rigid and lifeless images." He is personal because, as the Spirit of Love, "he breathes the life of Christ into them, and fills them with all the uniqueness and historical reality of the divine encounter."[14] For this very reason, the Spirit is also the "Lord of the Eucharist."

---

[11] Ibid., 95.

[12] Ibid.

[13] Ibid., 96.

[14] Ibid., 96-97.

The third universalizing work of the Spirit in history, for Balthasar, comes in the missions of the Church and individual Christians. These missions perfect the Spirit's work of the forty days and the sacraments. They do so by setting the Church as a whole and each believer in particular under the enduring spiritual norm of Christ's glorified life.[15] At this level, the Christian does not merely encounter Christ in the sacraments, but now lives according to his law of love. He does so by following the supreme example of Jesus, the God-man, through a life of discipleship. The Christian is empowered to love by the work of the Spirit, who does not impose himself, but works from within a person's spirit so that he often is indistinguishable from it.[16] At this point, thinking with the Church is inseparable from thinking with the Spirit. One's mind and thought processes are deeply in tune with the promptings of Christ's Spirit, who inspires new missions by calling forth saints to present the truth of Christ ever anew to each succeeding age.[17]

The Eucharist, for Balthasar, is a part of a larger movement of the Spirit through history which, after Christ's earthly life, manifests itself first in the forty days after the Resurrection, then invisibly in the sacramental life of the Church, and finally spiritually in the life of discipleship as manifested in the missions of the whole Church and of each individual Christian. His teaching on the Eucharist is intimately tied to the work of the Spirit, whose purpose is to reveal the glorified presence of the living Lord in the present and throughout all of human history.

---

[15] Ibid., 97.
[16] Ibid., 99.
[17] Ibid., 104.

Some Further Insights

This brief exposition of Balthasar's teaching on the Eucharist highlights the important role the Holy Spirit plays in making Jesus Christ central to the mission and life of each believer. The following remarks seek to develop some of the key insights of his understanding of Christ as the norm of history and to find its specific relevance for having a vital Eucharistic spirituality in the life of the Church.

Balthasar's teaching on the Eucharist must be seen in the context of the entire sweep of salvation history. The sacrament, for him, is a work of the Spirit that continues the presence of the risen and glorified Christ among his people and sends them out on the mission of authentic discipleship. It is the concrete, visible means by which the people of God not only come into direct contact with the person of their Lord but also are empowered by his Spirit to follow in his footsteps. Balthasar gives the Eucharist an important place in his theology of history. God revealed his Word through the mouths of the prophets, gave it flesh in the person of Jesus Christ, affirmed its power over death through his resurrection, and universalized it through his post-resurrectional appearances. The Church continues the historical presence of the risen Lord in the world through her celebration of the sacred mysteries. Although it presently does so in a hidden and concealed form, it recognizes that the time will come when these sacramental veils will no longer be necessary and the historical mode of time will itself be elevated to new heights.

According to Balthasar, Christ recapitulates all of history in himself and carries it into an elevated mode of time. Through his incarnation, death, and resurrection, he has become the norm of history, the standard by which it is measured and by which humanity will be judged. Christ's paschal mystery immerses not only humanity, but also history itself into the mystery of God's transforming love to establish a new creation. Christ, the New Man, places us in a new relationship to the Father as his adopted sons and daughters. As a father loves, protects, guides, and nourishes his children, so now God relates to us; the Eucharist is the concrete means by which he does so. Through it, we join Christ, in the Spirit, as members of his body, the Church, in rendering glory and praise to the Father. In this respect, the Eucharist concretizes God's universal redemptive love for each individual believer. It is the visible sign of the new creation and ushers in the new, elevated mode of time established by Christ into our midst.

For Balthasar, ever since the time of Christ all of history is fundamentally "sacred:" everything before leads up to him; everything after flows from him. Old Testament history culminates in Christ and is transformed by him into a New Covenant forged between God and humanity through the shedding of his blood. As a result, his passion, death, and resurrection have been woven into the fabric of history itself and, in a special way, into the warp and woof of every believer's life. As the sacrament of the New Covenant, the Eucharist sanctifies time and space and, in doing so, transforms the narrative of human history. It represents both the goal toward which history is moving and the means by which it arrives. It does so, however, in a hidden and concealed manner, and points to the eschatological consummation of time when the risen and glorified Christ will establish the fullness of his kingdom for the glory of God in the new creation.

Since the Spirit represents the bond of love between the Father and the Son, God's presence in the world manifests itself in ever deepening relations of communio. According to Balthasar, the movement of history is oriented toward the Trinitarian community of love. This final goal manifests itself in the present in a variety of ways. For the disciples, it had very much to do with the time Jesus spent with them in the forty days after his resurrection and in their experience of the Spirit on the day of Pentecost. For the Church, it has to do with the hidden presence of the risen and glorified Christ in her celebration of the sacraments and the mission given to all believers to spread his message of love in all they do. For Balthasar, Christians are called to build up the kingdom of God in the present and throughout all of history. They do so by staying in close institutional and personal contact with the Lord so that they may experience something of the close bond he shares with the Father and then share it with others. As a work of the Spirit, the Eucharist represents the deepest dimension of this "holy communion" with God, with the members of Christ's body, the Church, and with all humanity.

Finally, the Eucharist, for Balthasar, plays an important role in connecting the early Christian experience of the risen Lord with the mission of the Church in the world today. It does so by continuing the universalizing process begun by the Spirit at the moment of the Resurrection, concretizing it in a commemorative meal it, and then spiritualizing it in the missionary faith of the Church and all believers. The presence of the risen and glorified Lord, in other words, continues throughout history in the Church's celebration of the Mass. This meal recalls the Lord's Last Supper with his apostles and points to all the meals he shared with them in his post-resurrectional appearances. When Christians receive the Body and Blood of their Lord, they come in direct contact with their risen and glorified Lord and his redemptive mission to humanity. The Eucharist deepens their communion with the Lord and strengthens them for their missionary journey through time.

Although these remarks do not exhaust Balthasar's teaching on the Eucharist, they go a long way in establishing its major themes and demonstrate the central role it plays in his theology of history. They also reflect the comprehensive nature of his thought in general and the main contours of his overall theological outlook.

Conclusion

Hans Urs von Balthasar's writings have made an indelible mark on twentieth-century Catholicism and beyond. He was a seminal thinker who came up with profound insights into the fundamentals of Christian belief and their relevance for the world today. He believed in the close connection between drama within God and the way it played itself out in salvation history, culminating as it did in Christ's paschal mystery and in the historical journey of the community of believers.

Balthasar's teaching on the Eucharist focuses on the mystery of divine love revealed in Christ's sacrificial gift of self and the imprint it has made on the course of history by releasing the eternal dimension of time and transforming humanity's sojourn through it. The Eucharist, he believed, continues the presence of the risen and glorified Christ throughout history in a hidden, sacramental form. It is a work of the Spirit that nourishes and supports the mystical communion of the Church as it sends it and all of her members out to proclaim the good news of God's redeeming love. This mission will continue throughout the course of history until it reaches its goal in the recapitulation of all things in the risen and glorified Christ, when the transformation of history will be complete.

As the visible sign of Christ's continuing presence in time, the Eucharist holds a central place in Balthasar's theology of history. It is the "sacrament of the Spirit" that continues the work begun by Christ's paschal mystery and unleashed in the community of disciples at Pentecost. Through it and by means of it, the risen and glorified Lord accompanies the body of believers throughout history and empowers it to carry on his redemptive mission to the world. It represents the beginning of the new creation, the point towards which all created things tend and find their final shape and mode of transformed existence.

Reflection Questions

- For Balthasar, the Eucharist plays a central role in the history of redemption, because it extends the action of Christ's salvific action through time. What role has the Eucharist played in your own salvation history? Do you see this role as an ongoing one? Have you taken full advantage of it?
- For Balthasar, Christ's glorified resurrected life continues in the Eucharist. Do you believe that the same risen and glorified Christ is present in the Eucharist? How is his presence manifest to you? How is it hidden? What does it mean to perceive this presence through the eyes of faith?
- For Balthasar, the transforming action of the Eucharist is a work of the Spirit. It is for this reason that the Spirit is the "Lord of the Eucharist." How do you relate to the Holy Spirit? What does it mean to pray "in the Spirit?" How does the Eucharist lead one to a deeper intimacy with the Spirit of God?

Voice Twenty

Bernard Häring:
Vital Center

Our next voice was a Redemptorist priest and a leading voice of Catholic moral theology in the twentieth century. Bernard Häring, C.Ss.R. (1912-1998) was born in Böttingen, Germany, entered the Redemptorist seminary at an early age, professed his religious vows in 1934, and was ordained to the priesthood in 1939. Soon afterwards, his religious superiors sent him to the University of Tübingen to specialize in moral theology. His studies were interrupted, however, by the outbreak of the Second World War, during which time her served as a priest-medic in the German army in France, Poland, and the Russian front. After the war, he resumed his doctoral studies, went on to teach in the Redemptorist seminary at Gars in the Münich Province of the Redemptorists, and later was an ordinary professor at the Alphonsian Academy of the Pontifical Lateran University in Rome, where he taught moral theology from 1949-1987. A prolific author, he is most remembered for the pastoral approach to moral theology that he developed in his multi-volume works on moral theology, *The Law of Christ* (1954) and *Free and Faithful in Christ* (1978-81). His teaching on the Eucharist reflects this deep pastoral concern and concern for authentic Christian living.[1]

Häring's Spiritual Outlook

Häring's spirituality is closely tied to the Redemptorist order, a congregation of priests and brothers founded by St. Alphonsus de Liguori (1696-1787) and dedicated to preaching the Gospel message of plentiful redemption to the poor and most neglected. The Redemptorists preach fundamental conversion (*metanoia*) through home and foreign missions and are known for their pastoral zeal, their competence as confessors and spiritual directors, and their closeness to the people.[2]

The Alphonsian Academy in Rome where Häring taught for almost forty years brings this deep pastoral concern to the study of Catholic moral theology. Häring's work in the Academy brought it to international prominence in the early 1950s, especially through the appearance of what is now considered a classic in modern moral theology, *The Law of Christ*. This three-volume work contributed much to the movement away from the manualist tradition of moral theology that had been in place for almost four hundred years and laid the groundwork for a new approach to the discipline, one based on Scripture and dialogue with modern thought. A *peritus* (or theological expert) at the Second Vatican Council, Häring played a major role in the shaping of *Gaudium et Spes*, "The Pastoral Constitution on the Church in the Modern World" (1965) and is recognized by many as the father of modern Catholic moral theology.[3]

---

[1] For a brief chronology of Häring's life, see Bernard Häring, *Free and Faithful: My Life in the Catholic Church—An Autobiography* (Liguori Publications: Liguori, MO, 1998), 185.

[2] Ibid., 15-22.

[3] Ibid., 69-103.

Häring's spirituality reflects his deep roots in the mind and message of St. Alphonsus, the patron saint of confessors and moral theologians. Just as Alphonsus was someone who used his theological acumen in his day to steer a *via media* between the extremes of rigorism and laxism, Häring promoted the responsibility of believers who, through Christ and in the Spirit, live under the law of freedom as adopted sons and daughters of the Father. His spirituality focuses on turning one's heart to God through dedicated prayer and responsible action. His teaching on the Eucharist reflects a pastoral concern rooted in the spirit of the Gospel and a deep love for Christ.[4]

Häring's Teaching on the Eucharist

For Häring, the sacraments are the means through which believers are able to worship God in Spirit and in Truth. They consecrate us sacramentally to God's Glory and enable us to celebrate them as Jesus' disciples in order to render worship to God and be sanctified by his grace. In this respect, the sacraments are actions of Christ that lay out the plan of salvation for us. When received with the proper dispositions, they mediate for us a personal encounter with Christ, are concrete signs of our membership in the Church community, and are the ordinary means for receiving grace and for working out our salvation. As actions of Christ, they are also actions of his body, the Church. The entire Church celebrates the sacraments, not simply those who have gathered for them at any particular place or time. This deep communal dimension of the sacraments emphasizes the catholic (i.e., universal) dimension of the Church and brings with it the responsibilities of living in

_____

[4] Ibid., 147-76.

union with the Church and her teachings.[5]

Häring's teaching on the Eucharist reflects this profound sacramental spirituality. He calls it "the foregathering of the sacred assembly around the risen Christ, who sits on the throne at the right of the Father, and the most intimate communion with Him in commemoration of His Death until He comes again."[6] The Eucharist, for him, is the center of Catholic life and worship: "'Mass as center' means above all a life with the Church, for the vital center of the Church is the Eucharistic Sacrifice: this is the whole Sacrifice of Christ and of His Holy Bride, the Church. *Sentire cum ecclesia* (a bond of feeling with the Church, and work in union with her and for her) presumes a partnership in her life."[7] He also points out Sunday should be "a day of fellowship in the breaking of bread."[8] The Liturgy of the Word and the Liturgy of Sacrifice, moreover, complement each other so that the Eucharistic bread and the bread of the divine word are both broken and distributed to the faithful.[9] In his mind, "the Logos, the Second Person who is the Word of the Father, gives both to us through the Church."[10]

One of Häring's key insights is the centrality of the Eucharist for the moral and spiritual life: "If the most holy Eucharist is the center of our faith and our worship, then the whole of Christian life—both moral and religious—must be based on this central mystery."[11] He sees an intrinsic unity between liturgy and ethics and deplores "that unfortunate catechetical and theological

---

[5] Bernard Häring, *The Law of Christ*, trans. Edwin G. Kaiser, vol. 29Westminster, MD: The Newman Press, 1963), 139-88.

[6] Ibid., 150.

[7] Ibid., 309.

[8] Ibid., 309.

[9] Ibid., 312.

[10] Ibid.,

[11] Bernard Häring, *A Sacramental Spirituality* (New York: Sheed and Ward, 1965), 125.

systematization which treated the sacraments *after* the commandments, or only as an *adjunct* to the commandments of the covenant of *Sinai*, and which regarded them principally as a new 'set of duties' and at most as a special 'means of grace' given to help us to keep those commandments, which are expounded without any reference to the 'sacraments of the new law.'"[12] From this insight, he concludes that the Eucharistic celebration must be a pastoral liturgy that "speaks with a living voice to Christian people, restores full meaning to the symbolic language of the sacraments, together with the words through which we understand them."[13] In this way, it will have a powerful effect on our lives and its fundamental themes will "direct us towards a way of life based on the mystery of salvation."[14] These themes include: the mystery of God's holiness (*mysterium tremendum*), the mystery of blessedness (*mysterium fascinosum*), the mystery of faith (*mysterium fidei*), and the mystery of unity and love (*mysterium unitatis*).[15] The holiness of God, in other words, reaches out to us through the liturgy to divinize us so we might be able to commune with him and one another in oneness of faith and in the unity of his love.

Some Further Insights

This brief exposition of Häring's teaching on the Eucharist highlights the centrality of the sacrament for the life of the Church and its members. The following remarks focus on the implications of his teaching for moral theology and the believer's life of faith.

To begin with, Häring's formation in the pastoral life of the

---

[12] Ibid., 123-24.

[13] Ibid., 125.

[14] Ibid., 126.

[15] Ibid.

Redemptorists and the spiritual outlook of their founder, St. Alphonsus, had a profound influence on his understanding of the Eucharist and its relationship to the Christian moral and spiritual life. The Redemptorists' emphasis on closeness to the people, meeting their needs, and even being evangelized by them, helped him realize that moral and spiritual theology were meant to serve the faithful, not be a burden to them. The moral law of the Gospel, in his mind, was a law of freedom in the Spirit, not a duty-oriented law of obligation. For Häring, the Christian moral life was rooted in the love of God for humanity as embodied in the person of Jesus Christ. The Eucharist, for him (as for St. Alphonsus) was the "sacrament of love" and the primary means for personally encountering Jesus in their lives.

Häring's life as a Redemptorist preacher and missionary also shaped his approach to the Eucharist and its impact on the moral and spiritual life. Preaching, for St. Alphonsus, could take place in one of three ways: the spoken word, the written word, and through deeds. Of the three, personal witness was the most important, for it brought credibility to all that the preacher said and wrote. As a Redemptorist, Häring was deeply aware that St. Alphonsus wanted the Redemptorist Congregation to be a community of saints and that prayer and participation in the sacramental life of the Church were the primary means through which their sanctification would take place. Devotion to the Blessed Sacrament through regular visits has a special place in Redemptorist spirituality, for it was seen by St. Alphonsus as a way of shaping the soul and extending the grace of the Liturgy into daily life. The Eucharist, in other words, makes saints of the faithful and enables them to preach the Good News of plentiful redemption through their actions. This witness, rooted in a personal encounter with Christ in the Eucharist, was essential to Häring's approach to the Christian moral and spiritual life.

Häring sees the Eucharist as an important unifying bridge between the spiritual and moral lives of believers. The sacrament, for him, unites rather than divides these two important dimensions of Christian discipleship. It tells us that faith and action are intimately related and gives us a concrete way of rooting moral action in the Church's sacramental practice and experience. As "the source and summit of the Christian life,"[16] the Eucharist is the "sacrament of the new covenant" which not only inspires us to follow the way of the Lord Jesus, but also empowers us to walk it. It is central to the Church's life and worship and lies at the very heart of all authentic Catholic spirituality. Häring believes the Church needs to highlight this intimate relationship between the Church's sacramental worship and the daily lives of the faithful through sound teaching, preaching, and catechesis. To neglect this important link is to place the very life of the Church and the lives of the faithful at risk.

The Eucharist, for Häring, offers believers a chance for a personal encounter with Christ. Because this encounter is mediated through the Church, it is at one and the same time both personal and communal. These two dimensions complement each other for the well-being of the Church and that of each individual. Häring would be against any approaches to the sacrament that would, on the one hand, emphasize personal piety to the detriment of the communal participation in worship or, on the other hand, focus on communal conformity to the detriment of the dignity of the human person. This dynamic tension between the individual and the community lies at the very heart of the Church's Eucharistic worship and flows into the way her members are called to interact with the world. The Church's concern for the common good and the dignity of the human person, in other words, flows from its central act of worship. By promoting these values through its actions in the world, the faithful give glory to God in

---

[16] Second Vatican Council, *Lumen gentium*, no. 11.

the concrete circumstances of daily life.

Häring points out that a person must have the proper dispositions for this personal encounter with Christ in the Eucharist to take place. These dispositions include such things as a proper intention, freedom from serious sin, humility before God, faith in Christ's paschal mystery, hope in its redemptive powers and ability to transform the human heart, docility to the will of God, openness to the Spirit and its fruits, and a spirit of gratitude—to name but a few. Although Christ is personally present in the Eucharist, he emphasizes our responsibility to prepare ourselves appropriately with the proper internal dispositions. Not to do so denigrates the sacrament and obstructs the flow of God's transforming grace into our hearts. The personal encounter with Christ, in other words, requires reciprocity between Christ and the believer. We will meet Christ in the sacrament only if we have prepared a proper place for him to dwell. The Eucharist cannot transform the human heart, if we have darkened it by sin and cluttered it with inordinate attachments. To unleash the transformative power of Christ in our hearts, we must open them and allow the grace of his Spirit to do his work.

Häring's sacramental spirituality roots the Eucharist in the glory of the risen Christ and sees it as a celebration of the saints who have been, are being, and will be redeemed by him. As such, the sacrament offers the faithful hope in the power of God's redemptive love and inspires them to open their hearts to Christ and allow his Spirit to penetrate their lives. This sacramental spirituality is rooted in the notion that the grace of the Spirit is mediated through Christ and through the Church and her sacraments. As Christ is the sacrament of God, and the Church is the sacrament of Christ, so is the Eucharist the "sacrament of the Church" and the "sacrament of sacraments." Through the Eucharist, his power of mediation extends itself to the very lives of the faithful so that the power of Christ's love manifests itself in a concrete, visible way. From this perspective, the Eucharist brings the glory of the risen Christ not only to the faithful, but also to the world. It enables the faithful to enter into the friendship of Christ and empowers them to live the Gospel message in Spirit and in Truth.

Finally, the Eucharist, for Häring, is a multi-faceted mystery, one that embodies in a simple act of consecration, the mystery of God's holiness, the mystery of humanity's sanctification, the mystery of faith, and the mystery of unity and love. Aware that no theory or systematic presentation could ever fully exhaust the meaning of the sacrament, he focuses on a very limited area of inquiry: the importance of the Eucharist for the Christian life. Once again, this concern reflects his deep pastoral sensitivities and his awareness that Christ came to set us free from the slavery of sin and death. Christ does so by immersing the faithful in his paschal mystery and effecting a gradual healing, restoration, and transformation of our wounded natures. Even here, Häring does not purport to exhaust the full impact of the sacrament for the moral and spiritual life. He seeks merely to emphasize its importance as the "sacrament of the new covenant" for the freedom it brings under the New Law of the Spirit and its central importance for the life of discipleship.

Although these observations do not exhaust Häring's teaching on the Eucharist, they cover its major themes and demonstrate the important role it plays in the life of Christian discipleship. They also point to the integrated nature of his theological outlook and highlight the centrality of Eucharistic worship for the Catholic moral and spiritual life today.

Conclusion

Bernard Häring was one of the great Catholic authors of the twentieth century and arguably the greatest moral theologian of his day. Seen by many as the "father of modern Catholic moral theology," he played an instrumental role in steering the Church away from a manualist tradition that over the years had become an overly rigid and systematized set of rules and regulations. His ground-breaking multi-volume moral theology, *The Law of Christ*, set the stage for the renewal of moral theology by rooting it in the Gospels and by initiating a dialogue with current modes of contemporary thought. He continued these efforts as a theological expert at the Second Vatican Council and made a major contribution to its message in the important role he played in the drafting of *Gaudium et Spes*, "The Pastoral Constitution on the Church in the Modern World." As a professor at the Alphonsian Academy in Rome for almost forty years, he educated many generations of priests, religious, and laity in his vision of a renewed Catholic moral theology. This message of renewal was further extended through his many writings, not the least of which was his second multi-volume work of moral theology, *Free and Faithful in Christ*. As a Redemptorist missionary and in the spirit of St. Alphonsus, he also used the spoken word to spread his message of renewal: as a visiting professor at numerous universities, on the lecture circuit, and through countless workshops, retreats, missions, and preaching engagements.[17]

Influenced by his Redemptorist roots and his formation in Alphonsian spirituality, Häring emphasized the centrality of the Eucharist for the moral and spiritual life of the faithful, focusing especially on its closeness and accessibility to the people and its ability to lead them to a personal encounter with Christ and empower them to the Gospel message freely and responsibly in the Spirit. This deep pastoral concern represents the hallmark of his moral and spiritual vision, and it should come as no surprise that the Eucharist, as the "sacrament of the new

---

[17] See Häring, *Free and Faithful*, 131-76.

covenant," lies at its very heart. This sacrament, in his mind, captures the essence of the Christian life. By immersing us in the mystery of Christ's passion, death, and resurrection, it puts us in touch with the mystery of God's holiness, sets us on the path of holiness, and empowers to live authentic lives of Christian discipleship. It does this by shaping our souls and forming our characters in conformity with that of Christ and his Spirit.

As a moral theologian, Häring was involved in many of the controversial ethical issues of his day: abortion, contraception, euthanasia, the just war, nuclear disarmament—to name but a few. He always tried to examine these issues in the light of Gospel values and authentic Church teaching as interpreted by the magisterium. Although he disagreed, at times, with official Church teaching, he did so from a conviction of conscience and a deep love for the Church and its well-being. Although he was often misunderstood and sometimes even suffered for his controversial opinions, he was never discouraged and firmly believed that he was a prophetic voice for the Church for both present and future generations. Through it all, he was sustained by a deep love and devotion to the Holy Eucharist, a sacrament which brought him close to God and to God's people, and which led him along the way of holiness into the mystery of divine love.

Reflection Questions

- Häring highlights the centrality of the Eucharist for the moral and spiritual life. What does the Eucharist have to do with the moral life? What does it have to do with the spiritual life? How are these two spheres related? Why is it important to view them in a complementary and integrated way? Do you?
- Häring believes that the Eucharistic celebration should speak with a living voice to Christian people. What are

the pastoral implications of the Eucharistic liturgy? What relevance should it have for the way you live your daily life? What significance do the words of the priest have for you when he says, "Go forth. The Mass is ended?"

- For Häring, the holiness of God reaches out to us through the Eucharistic liturgy to divinize us so that we might commune with him and one another. Do you believe that God reaches out to you when you share in the Eucharist? Does the Eucharist fortify your relationship with God? Does it draw you closer to those you love? Does it help you to reach out to those who are distant from you?

Voice Twenty-One

Louis Bouyer:
Body of Christ

Our next voice was a master of the Christian spiritual life. Louis Bouyer (1913-2004) was born in Paris and studied at the Sorbonne and the Protestant faculties at Strasbourg and Paris. Raised a Protestant, he began his service in the Church as a Lutheran minister in 1936 and converted to Catholicism in 1939 by way of his study of Eastern Orthodoxy. He was ordained a Catholic priest of the French Oratory in 1944, earned his doctorate at the Catholic Institute of Paris in 1946, and was a professor there until 1963. He eventually became one of the leading figures in the French movement of *Ressourcement* (or *Nouvelle Théologie*), which emphasized a return to the sources as a way of deepening our insights into the Catholic faith. He looked to the Scriptures as the primary resource for Catholic renewal by interpreting them in the light of the living tradition of the Church, especially through the eyes of the early Church fathers.

Bouyer's interests spanned a wide range of topics: Scripture, the history of spirituality, systematics, Mariology, ecumenism, literature, biography—to name but a few. He was a peritus at the Second Vatican Council, a co-founder of the theological journal *Communio*, one of the original members of the International Theological Commission, and would have been made a cardinal by Pope Paul VI, but for his own humble and self-effacing refusal of the honor. His ideas on the liturgy inspired many of the reforms of Vatican II, although he cautioned that they be implemented gradually over time and with great restraint. A prolific author, his most noted works include: *The Paschal Mystery. Meditations on the Last Three Days of Holy Week* (1951), *Life and Liturgy* (1955), *The Spirit and Forms of Protestantism* (1956), *Newman: His Life and Spirituality* (1958), *Introduction to Spirituality* (1961), *The Word, Church and Sacraments in Protestantism and Catholicism* (1961), *The Spirituality of the New Testament and the Fathers* (1982), *The Spirituality of the Middle Ages* (1982), *The Church of God* (1982), and *Eucharist: Theology and Spirituality of the Eucharistic Prayer* (1989). He teaching on the Eucharist touches the very heart of his spiritual outlook.[1]

Bouyer's Spiritual Outlook

An examination of Bouyer's thought shows that he sees an intimate connection between theology, spirituality, and liturgy.[2] In his mind, there is one Christian spirituality, the Gospel of Jesus Christ, which down through the centuries has had numerous manifestations in the life of the Church. "All Christian worship," moreover, "is but a continuous celebration of Easter: the sun, rising and setting daily, leaves in its wake an

---

[1] Michael Heintz, "Introduction," in Louis Bouyer, *Introduction to the Spiritual Life*, trans. Mary Perkins Ryan (New York: Desclee, 1961; reprint, Notre Dame, IN: Christian Classics, 2013), 2-3. See also http://ldysinger.stjohnsem.edu/@books/Bouyer_In-Sp/00a_start.htm. The dates after Bouyer's works refer to the appearance of the first English edition.

[2] Louis Bouyer, *Life and Liturgy* (London: Sheed and Ward, 1956; fourth impression, 1978), 257-71.

uninterrupted series of Eucharists."[3] He recognizes the uniqueness of Gospel spirituality and recoils from those attempts to proliferate Christian spirituality into a variety of competing subsets. "Catholic spirituality," for him, is "simply Christian spirituality in its fullness."[4] It represents "a spiritual life in which our own most interior, most personal life opens out and develops, only in development of that personal relationship which God wishes to establish with us in speaking to us in Christ."[5]

Bouyer draws a radical distinction between God and his creation. Man is not a divine spark sharing the very essence of the divinity, but a creature made in God's image and likeness. God, moreover, is not some *thing*, but an actual someone, a *person* whose Triune being radiates the very mystery of love itself.[6] "God is love," the First Letter of John reminds us (1Jn 4:8).[7] He takes this basic Scriptural insight and places it at the very heart of Christianity spirituality. God's immanent self-relations as well as his external relations with his creation flow from this love and return to it. God's love, moreover, is self-diffusive and pours itself out freely in the creative, redemptive, and sanctifying actions of the Trinity, associated respectively with the work of the Father, Son, and Holy Spirit.[8]

Christ reveals to us the Trinitarian communion of love and

---

[3] Louis Bouyer, *The Paschal Mystery: Meditations on the Last Three Days of Holy Week*, trans. Sister Mary Benoit (Chicago: Henry Regnery Company, 1950), xiii.

[4] Bouyer, *Introduction to the Spiritual Life*, 29.

[5] Ibid.

[6] Ibid., 20, 187.

[7] All Scripture quotations come from the *New American Bible*, revised ed. (New York: Oxford University Press, 2011).

[8] See Louis Bouyer, *The Church of God: Body of Christ and Temple of the Spirit*, trans. Charles Underhill Quinn (Chicago: Franciscan Herald Press, 1982), 235-73.

through the Church extends this love to all humanity.[9] The life of the Trinity, for Bouyer, is mediated to us today through the life of the Church, especially through its celebration of the sacraments, the visible signs of Christ's redemptive and sanctifying grace. These Trinitarian, ecclesial, and sacramental dimensions permeate his entire theological outlook and touch the very core of the Christian faith. Christ, in other words, mediates to us the life and love of the Trinity by continuing to live out his Incarnation and Paschal Mystery through the Church and its celebration of the sacramental mysteries. As our sole mediator and high priest before God the Father, Christ intercedes with him on our behalf and channels God's love to us through the Church in its proclamation of the Word and its celebration of the sacramental mysteries. In this respect, the Church lies at the very heart of salvation history and is the primary means through which Christ accomplishes his redemptive will for humanity.[10]

Salvation history, for Bouyer, is a gradual unfolding of this mystery of love to God's chosen people which reaches its fullness in the person of Jesus Christ, who bids his followers to pick up their cross daily and follow him. The cross, in his mind, lies at the heart of Christian spirituality. A Christian embraces the cross not as an end in itself, but because it can be united to Christ's own suffering and contribute in some small way to the world's redemption. Christ, in other words, lives out his paschal mystery in the lives of his followers.[11] This active participation is made possible by the gift of his Spirit who unites the community of the faithful to the narrative of Christ's Incarnate and Paschal mysteries. Christ, we might say, is the Word made flesh who continues to be born, live, suffer, die, and rise, in the

---

[9] Bouyer, *Introduction to the Spiritual Life*, 29.

[10] Bouyer, *The Church of God*, 235.

[11] Bouyer, *Introduction to the Spiritual Life*, 54-57.

members of his body, the Church. Just as there is only one Christian spirituality, there is for Bouyer only one Body of Christ. Christ's presence in the Church is real and substantive, and the Eucharist is its clearest and most manifest expression.[12]

Bouyer on the Eucharist

Bouyer's teaching on the Eucharist flows from his understanding of the relationship between Word and Sacrament. God has revealed himself gradually through time through his Word and manifests himself fully in the Person of Jesus Christ, the Sacrament of God. Through the outpouring of the Holy Spirit at Pentecost, Christ continues his revelatory activity through the Church and her sacraments. Word and Sacrament, for Bouyer, are thus intimately related. He criticizes the attitude, prominent among some Protestant denominations, that reduces the sacraments to nothing but a visible manifestation of the Word. To do so, he maintains, empties the Word of its very content.[13]

The Word, for Bouyer, is intrinsically oriented toward the manifestation of God's Presence, which is precisely what the sacramental mysteries reveal. Word leads to Sacrament, just as revelation leads to presence: "And the Word was made flesh and lived among us" (Jn 1:14). These words from the Gospel of John display the intrinsic link between the revelatory nature of the Word and its orientation toward Presence. This Incarnational relationship sheds light on the connection between the Liturgy of the Word and the Liturgy of the Eucharist. At Mass, Word and Sacrament come together in a unique way; the Living Word reveals the Real Presence, the very presence of the Risen Lord himself. The Eucharist is the continuing manifestation of

---

[12] Ibid., 148-49.
[13] Ibid.

Christ's personal presence to the community of believers.[14]

The Eucharist, for Bouyer, is the focus of the Church's sacramental life: "we go quite naturally from the mystery *proclaimed* by the word of the Gospel to the mystery *made present* by the words of consecration."[15] What is more, "we perceive the whole meaning of the proclaimed Word only in the sacramental celebration."[16] In the words of St. Paul: "Whenever you eat this bread and drink this cup you *proclaim* the death of the Lord, until he comes" (1Cor 11:26).[17] The meaning of the Word, we might say, reaches its fullness when we gather for the Eucharist to break bread together and to share the cup. That fullness is the presence of Christ himself who is present in the person of the priest, in the sacramental presence, and in the believing community.[18]

For Bouyer, the Body of Christ present in the Blessed Sacrament and in the community of the faithful are intimately related: "The Body of Christ which is the Church is called so because in it we are all united in one single body by the fact of being all nourished by the Body of Christ which once died on the Cross and today nourishes the life of the mystery in us."[19] The Eucharist plunges us into the paschal mystery of Christ who, as high priest and sacrificial victim, makes an offering of himself on our behalf and empowers us through the gift of his Spirit to offer our prayers to the Father, give him our sacrifice of praise

---

[14] Louis Bouyer, *The Word, Church, and Sacraments in Protestantism and Catholicism*, trans. A.V. Littledale (New York: Desclee Company, 1961; reprint, San Francisco: Ignatius Press, 2004), 84-88.

[15] Bouyer, *Introduction to the Spiritual Life*, 141. See also Bouyer, *Life and Liturgy*, 70-85.

[16] Bouyer, *Introduction to the Spiritual Life*, 141.

[17] Ibid.

[18] Ibid. 142-43.

[19] Ibid., 143. See also Bouyer, *The Church of God*, 294-305.

and thanksgiving, and enter into intimate communion with him.[20] In a particular way, the "consecrating word" is "the soul of the Eucharistic Prayer of the Word made flesh" and "re-creates in us the new self, just as the original word of creation drew us out of nothingness."[21] As a result, we become one body with Christ: "it is impossible to take the 'Body' of Christ in two senses rigorously distinct from one line to the other."[22] In this respect, "this 'Body' of Christ which is the Church and which we all form together exists only in and by effective participation of all in the one 'Body' of Christ dead on the Cross and risen to divine life."[23]

Some Further Insights

This brief exposition of Bouyer's teaching on the Eucharist shows the central place it holds in his theology and overall spiritual outlook. It also clearly indicates why the Mass is the focal point of the Church life, ministry, and worship—and must remain so. The following observations develop some of the implications of his view of the sacrament and their relevance for today's Catholics.

To begin with, Bouyer points out that Christianity centers around two central claims: "God has spoken to us," and "He has given himself to us in his Word."[24] The Eucharist, he maintains, is God's way of speaking to the community of the faithful during its historical pilgrimage. It proclaims that God did not merely visit his people some 2,000 years ago, but that Jesus himself continues to be present to his people in the life of

---

[20] Ibid., 146. See also Bouyer, *The Paschal Mystery*, 218-228.

[21] Bouyer, *Introduction to the Spiritual Life*, 147.

[22] Ibid. 148.

[23] Ibid.

[24] Ibid., 23. See also Bouyer, *The Church of God*, 175.

the Church, especially in its sacramental worship. The Eucharist, in other words, is the concrete sign that Jesus' words to his disciples remain true: "I am with you always, to the end of the age" (Mt 28:20). Through it, God continues to speak and be present to his people. It is a visible sign of his abiding presence in the life of the Church and a reminder that through the power of his Spirit "...nothing will impossible with God" (Lk 1:37).

Bouyer's emphasis on the close connection between Word and Sacrament has important implications for the Eucharist. The revelatory nature of God's Word leads to the visible presence of that Word in time and space. That is to say that it tends by its very nature towards God's presence in the midst of his people and finds its deepest meaning by resting in that presence. This was true for the Jews as seen in the centrality of the Ark of the Covenant in their life and worship, and it is what Christians see in Jesus, who is "Emmanuel, which means, God is with us" (Mt 1:23). For Catholics, it has special significance for Christ's presence in his body, the Church, and in the Eucharist. Christianity, we might say, is a religion of Word and Sacrament. Catholicism, for Bouyer, represents the fullness of the Christian message, since it reveres each of these aspects of God's revealing presence by keeping them distinct yet insisting upon their intrinsic relation.[25]

Bouyer is also quick to point out that the union between the Eucharist, the Church, and the crucified and risen Lord is not a matter of fusion, but of close, intimate union. Although it is more than a union of wills, it falls short of an actual physical unity, for the relationship between the human and divine always remains intact. He identifies the Pauline imagery describing the Church as the "Bride of Christ" (Eph 5:22-23; 2Cor 11:2) as an apt metaphor for describing this relationship: "Certainly the Bridegroom and Bride are no longer more than one flesh. Yet

---

[25] Bouyer, *Introduction to the Spiritual Life*, 139-41.

the Bride, far from being annihilated in the Bridegroom can find, can realize her full personality as Bride only in her union with the Bridegroom."[26] In this relationship, the Eucharist plays a fundamental, constitutive role, for it mediates the life of the crucified and risen Lord to the believing community and is the covenantal bond that both constitutes their spousal relationship and makes it a vibrant, living reality.[27]

Bouyer also points out that, because the Eucharist lies at the heart of the Church's life and mission, all the other sacraments are all in some way oriented to it. That is to say, they "...introduce us and adapt us, or else they extend it to our whole existence."[28] This insight echoes the same sentiment expressed by the fathers of the Second Vatican Council that the Eucharist is "the source and summit of the Christian life,"[29] an insight that, if not unique to Bouyer, was certainly close to his heart and is a consistent theme throughout much of his writing. As a major theological voice in his day, Bouyer played an important role in shaping the program of renewal initiated by Vatican II, especially with respect to the reform of the Liturgy. His painstaking work on the sources of the Eucharistic celebration helped the Council fathers to recover lost emphases and focus their work on a reform of the liturgy that was, at one and the same time, both faithful to the tradition and relevant to the lives of the faithful.

Bouyer's teaching on the Eucharist has clear implications for the ministry of the priesthood. While all Christians are called to embody the one and the same priestly spirituality, they are called to do so in different ways. The ministerial priesthood

---

[26] Ibid., 148. See also Louis Bouyer, *The Church of God*, 163-64.

[27] See Bouyer, *The Church of God*, 294-305.

[28] Bouyer, *Introduction to the Spiritual Life*, 149.

[29] Second Vatican Council, *Lumen gentium,*("The Dogmatic Constitution on the Church), no. 11.

stands out in its dedicated service to the work of the Church. "Every Christian priest," he maintains, "should consecrate his entire life to the union of Christ and the Church in all his members."[30] The priest, in other words, is married to the Church and gives his life to her as an *alter Christus* (another Christ). This shines through most clearly in the Church's liturgical celebrations when he leads the people in prayer and mediates God's redemptive action to them on Christ's behalf. Bouyer is skeptical of the tendencies such as the worker-priest movement that seek to bridge the gap between priests and laity by encouraging priests to enter full-time into the secular working force. In his mind, one thing alone distinguishes priestly spirituality from its lay counterpart: "the performing of priestly work *instead of* all other kinds of human work."[31]

Bouyer maintains that "the bread and wine ... 'sanctified' in the Eucharist are the nourishment of eternal life."[32] By eating the body and blood of the crucified Lord we become sharers in his humanity, which divinizes our own and enables us both to worship the Father with him and to share in the very reality of his being the Son. The Eucharist, in other words, nourishes our filial relationship with the Father. As the "Sacrament of the New Creation" it nourishes the "new self" given to us at Baptism and empowers us to live in holiness and experience a foretaste of the life to come. This "new self" is distinct but not isolated from the other members of the community of the faithful. It is a living member of Christ's Body, the Church, who derives her very life and being from the crucified and risen Lord himself. In this respect, St. Paul's words to the Galatians holds true for every Christian: "it is no longer I who live, but Christ who lives in me" (Gal 2:20).

---

[30] Bouyer, *Introduction to the Spiritual Life*, 161.

[31] Ibid., 162.

[32] Ibid., 147.

Finally, Bouyer's Protestant background and interest in the theology of Eastern Orthodoxy gives a marked ecumenical flavor in much of his writing, one that enables him to sense both the strengths and weaknesses the various Christian traditions and enables him to retrieve those elements of the Catholic faith that, for various reasons, have either been downplayed or overlooked. He notes, for example, that while the Jewish people highlight the power of God's revelatory Word, and while the Protestants find the fullness of this revelation in the person of Jesus Christ, Catholics emphasize Christ's continuing presence and revelatory activity in the Church. As the Bride of Christ, the Church is so closely united to Christ that it acts in conformity with him, especially in its celebration of the sacraments, and most especially at Mass, when the messianic banquet, the sacrifice of Calvary, and the presence of the Risen Lord become present in a single liturgical action that continues his redemptive mission through time.

Although these observations do not do justice to the depth of Bouyer's teaching on the Eucharist, they underscore its main contours and highlight the impact it had on the forces of renewal within the Church before, during, and after the Second Vatican Council. They also reflect his desire to steer a *via media* between a "false traditionalism" and a "rash modernism" in the Church's search for reform, particularly with regard to the liturgy.[33] If today his insights seem ordinary and commonplace, it is because they have gradually moved into the mainstream of Catholic belief and practice.

Conclusion

Louis Bouyer was one of the leading Catholic voices of renewal of the twentieth century. Once described as "the least

---

[33] Bouyer, *Life and Liturgy Liturgical Piety*, 70.

conformist of theologians and among the most traditional,"[34] he was noted for his orthodox yet unconventional approach to many of the issues facing the Church of his day. His Protestant background gave him a special sensitivity to the way the Church was perceived by other faith traditions and deep insights into the various neglected aspects of its own rich tradition. His involvement in the *Nouvelle théologie* led him to tap into new areas of research that brought fresh insights into the theological thinking of his day and provided an impetus for many of the reforms of the Second Vatican Council.

A *peritus* at the Council, he worked to insure that the Church's theological *ressourcement* would be inspired by Scripture, rooted in the Church's liturgical worship, and steeped in a vibrant and living Gospel spirituality. His insistence on the unity of Christian spirituality led him to affirm the oneness of Christ's Body in its Risen, Eucharistic, and Mystical states. The Church, in his mind, was one with the body of the glorified Lord, and the Eucharist was the covenantal bond uniting them. The centrality of the Eucharist in the spirituality, theology, and worship of the Church was a central theme in his writing. His deep love for the Eucharist stemmed from his own personal journey to the Catholic faith and a deepened understanding that the divine Word tends by its very nature to the dynamic, living reality of God's presence in our midst.

The Eucharist, for Bouyer, is the mainstay of Catholic worship, belief, life, and practice. It is the sacrament of Church unity, the source of its faith, and the strength behind its convictions and actions in the world. It is a constant reminder that Christ is always present in his Church and that he continues to live out his paschal mystery in the lives of the community of

---

[34] Attributed to Cardinal Jean-Marie Lustiger. See http://www.theanglocatholic.com/2010/03/introducing-father-louis-bouyer/.

the faithful. The Eucharist, for Bouyer, constitutes the Church and is constituted by it. It is an act of Christ rendering worship to the Father in the Spirit and through the living members of his body, the Church. It is an act of worship with one foot in time and another in eternity and gives to each person who partakes of it a foretaste of the heavenly banquet.

Reflection Questions

- Bouyer's teaching on the Eucharist flows from his understanding of the relationship between Word and Sacrament. In what sense does Christ's presence in the Eucharist flow from the proclamation of the Word? In what sense is the proclamation of the Word enriched by Christ's Eucharistic presence? How have each of these dimensions of the Eucharistic celebration nourished your life of faith?

- Bouyer presents the Eucharist as the continuing manifestation of Christ's personal presence to the community of believers. Does Christ manifest himself to the community of believers first and then to each individual believer—or vice versa? Which of these possibilities best fits your own personal experience? Can Christ reveal himself to the community and to its individual members at the same time?

- Bouyer asserts that through the Eucharist we become one body with Christ. What does this mean for our membership in the Church? What does it say about the way we should relate to God and one another? What significance does it have for the way we relate to our very selves?

Voice Twenty-Two

F. X. Durrwell:
Paschal Sacrament

Our next voice was a French Redemptorist of the Strasbourg Province, a noted biblical scholar and theologian, and one of the first of his day to emphasize the centrality of the Resurrection for Christian spirituality. François-Xavier Durrwell (1912-2005), was born in Soultz, France and studied at the Redemptorist seminary in Alsace and later in Switzerland. He professed his religious vows in 1931 and was ordained a priest in 1936. He studied in Rome at the Pontifical Gregorian University and the Biblical Institute from 1937-1940 and began teaching New Testament exegesis at the Redemptorist scholasticate in Echternach in Luxembourg in 1940. In 1950, he published his groundbreaking work, *The Resurrection: A Biblical Study* (*La Résurrection de Jésus, mystère de salut*; English translation, 1960). He served as Provincial of the Strasbourg Province from 1952-1961 and taught at the *Lumen Vitae* Institute in Brussels from 1961-1971. A prolific author, he is probably best known in the English-speaking world for his theology of spirituality, *In the Redeeming Christ* (*Dan le Christ rédempteur*, 1960; English translation, 1963). His writings on the Eucharist include such works as *The Eucharist, Presence of Christ* (*L'Eucharistie présence du Christ* ,1970), *The Eucharist,*

Paschal Sacrament (*L'Eucharistie, sacrement pascal*, 1980), and his final work, *To the Sources of the Apostolate: The Apostle and The Eucharist* (*Aux sources de l'apostolat. L'apôtre et l'eucharistie*, 1999). In 1996, he was awarded a doctorate *honoris causa* from the Alphonsian Academy of Rome's Pontifical Lateran University.[1]

Durrwell's Theological Outlook

The Resurrection lies at the heart of Durrwell's theological outlook, which is best presented in his seminal work, *The Resurrection*.[2] There and elsewhere, he points out that there was a time when theologians would not even mention Christ's resurrection from the dead when discussing the doctrine of the Redemption: "Christ's work of redemption was seen as consisting in his incarnation, his life and his death on the cross."[3] As a result, the mystery of Christ's resurrection was marginalized in Catholic theological reflection and had little, if any, direct relevance for understanding the nature of salvation. In his mind, "Christ's resurrection was shorn of the tremendous significance seen in it by the first Christian teachers, and relegated to the background of the redemptive scheme."[4]

To rectify this impression, Durrwell brings the Resurrection front and center in his theological reflection. He develops a biblical theology that presupposes faith and seeks to grasp the Christian reality itself on the meaning and purpose of the Christ event. He values this approach as an alternative to strict

---

[1] For the important dates and other biographical information on Durrwell's life, see: http://www.durrwell.fr/content.php?article.10.

[2] F. X. Durrwell, *The Resurrection: A Biblical Study*, trans. Rosemary Sheed (New York: Sheed and Ward, 1960).

[3] Ibid., xxiii.

[4] Ibid.

historical exegesis and highlights its ability to create a synthesis of the Christian mystery, one that touches the heart of the early apostolic message. For this reason, his writings focus on the experience of early Christian writers such as St. Paul, who insisted that if Christ did not rise, our faith was in vain (1 Cor 15:17), that he died for our sins (2Cor 5:15), and rose for our justification (Rom 4:25).[5]

From this point of departure, he establishes a connection between Jesus' resurrection with his incarnation, passion, and death and then identifies the unique role it plays in our salvation by unleashing the power of the Holy Spirit upon the world. This unprecedented release of the Spirit's power has dramatic repercussions on Christ himself and the Church, both in its paschal life and its voyage through time. Durrwell sees the Easter mystery spreading outward from the empty tomb to the upper room and from there to all the corners of the earth. This mystery lies behind the force of the Gospel message and will culminate in Jesus' second coming. The Eucharist plays a special role in this regard, for it accompanies the Christian community in its historical sojourn and looks forward to the final consummation of all things in Christ.[6]

Durrwell's Teaching on the Eucharist

The main contours of Durrwell's teaching on the Eucharist are also present in his seminal work on Christ's Resurrection. For him, this sacrament is a ritual meal that joins Jesus' Last Supper with his apostles with the meals they shared with him as the Risen Lord. In this sense, it unites the sacrificial meal of the Cross and mediates the presence of the Glorified Christ to those

---

[5] Ibid., xxiii-xxv.
[6] Ibid., 319-332.

who partake in it. For this reason, it is the "paschal sacrament"[7] for it immerses us in Jesus' Death and Resurrection and brings the fullness of Christ's paschal mystery into his earthly body, the Church.

Durrwell also emphasizes the close connection between the Eucharist and the sacrament of Baptism: "Both rites cause the paschal life of Christ to extend to the faithful, opening for them in his body an entry into the act of redemption".[8] What is more, "[i]n both the believer is united to the body of Christ, immolated in the flesh and consecrated in the Spirit of God; by both he takes part in Christ's own communion in his sacrifice—the Resurrection. In this communion he is himself sacrificed, for he becomes joined to a body in which the sacrifice is forever actual."[9] Both sacraments are a celebration of Jesus' paschal mystery because they immerse us in his passion, death, and resurrection. Baptism makes us adopted sons and daughters of the Father and members of Christ's body, the Church. The Eucharist enables us to share in Christ's redeeming act. Whenever we celebrate it, we celebrate the great mystery of our redemption, for we participate anew in Christ's dying and rising.

For Durrwell, the Eucharist is also the "Sacrament of the Parousia."[10] At one and the same time, it both realizes God's kingdom in our midst and points to it future consummation with Christ's coming at the end of time. This "already-but-not-yet" quality of the sacrament enables to celebrate the gift of our Redemption, made possible through Jesus' passion, death, and resurrection, and also to live in the hope of one day seeing God face-to-face. Durrwell maintains that the Eucharist "is a complex mystery, uniting the believer to both ends of history, to

---

[7] Ibid., 319.

[8] Ibid.

[9] Ibid., 332.

[10] Ibid., 328.

the Lord's resurrection and his *parousia*."[11]

Some Further Insights

This brief exposition of Durrwell's teaching on the Eucharist highlights the centrality of the Resurrection for his overall theological outlook and its impact for Catholic spirituality. What follows are some observations on how these insights shape the daily lives of believers.

By bringing Jesus' Resurrection to the very center of his theological reflection on the meaning of the Christ-event, Durrwell breathes new life into Catholic theology and encourages believers of all ages to think of their faith in an entirely new light. The reality of Jesus, the Resurrected Lord, should permeate everything the Church does and says. To the extent that it does not, then the Church and her members are not remaining faithful to the foundational and formative witness of the early Church. The belief in Jesus' Resurrection propelled his earliest followers onto the world stage and made them willing to give up their lives for the sake of the Gospel. When Christians lose touch with this central proclamation of the nascent faith, their message is emptied of its deeply spiritual and life-changing power. For Catholics today, the Eucharist should lie at the very heart of their message of the Resurrected and Glorified Lord's presence in their midst.

Durrwell calls the Eucharist "a complex mystery," because it unites Jesus' Last Supper with other meals he shared with them after his resurrection. As such, it links Jesus' cross with the empty tomb and mediates his paschal mystery to the members of his body as they continue their sojourn through time. When seen in this light, the Eucharist is both a sacrificial meal, pointing to Jesus' passion and death, and a heavenly

---

[11] Ibid., 329.

banquet, revealing our hope in future glory. This juxtaposition of the sacrificial and the glorious, the earthly and the heavenly, highlights the sacrament's eschatological nature and bids believers to shape their lives accordingly. When receiving the sacrament, they are encouraged to live with their feet firmly planted on the ground, but with eyes that are constantly looking and waiting for things still to come. They are to celebrate the kingdom in their midst and patiently await its coming.

Durrwell's teaching on the Eucharist arises out of his reading of the Scriptures and his deep awareness that God's Word and the sacrament of the breaking of the bread are intimately related. His methodology departs from the historical critical exegesis popular in his day and adopts a more synthetic approach that seeks to honor the Christian mystery as it was lived by the earliest Christians. While he deeply respects the historical critical method, he understands its limitations and is willing to go beyond it in the name of faith. Durrwell does not leave his faith behind when reflecting on the Scriptures, but carries it with him and gives it primary place in his reflections. This faith leads him to see the centrality of the Christian Scriptures for a proper understanding of the Eucharist—and vice versa. It also helps him see that a careful, reflective reading of God's Word and a reverent celebration of the Lord's Supper can do nothing but strengthen the faith of today's Christians.

As "the paschal sacrament," the Eucharist is related to all the sacraments, but in a special way to Baptism. If we are immersed in Christ's paschal mystery at Baptism, that same redemptive mystery of Jesus' passion, death, and resurrection becomes present every time we gather to celebrate the Eucharist. As the fathers of the Second Vatican Council remind us, the Eucharist is "the source and summit of the Christian life."[12] Durrwell recognized this fundamental truth of the

---

[12] Second Vatican Council, *Lumen* gentium, no. 11.

Christian faith years before the convening of the Council and, in many respects, laid much of the theological groundwork for this important conciliar teaching. The Church's strong preference that the other sacraments take place during the celebration of the Mass point to the privileged place the Eucharist has in its spiritual and theological outlook. Because it brings the reality of Christ's paschal mystery into our midst the Eucharist represents the visible fullness of Christ's redemptive action on earth and the concrete sign of God's salvific presence in our midst.

The Eucharist, for Durrwell, is also intimately related to the apostolate. The Lord established the priesthood when he celebrated his Last Supper with his disciples, making the two inseparable and placing them at the very heart of the Church. This ministry is the work of the body of Christ, the Church. It flows from the Eucharist, because the ecclesial body of Christ and the sacramental body of Christ cannot be separated from one another. In this respect, the Eucharist is the "sacrament of the Church," the "sacrament of the apostolate," and the "sacrament of unity." What is more, both the Eucharist and the apostolate are actions of Christ and powerful channels of his Spirit. The apostolate finds its origin in the Eucharist, goes out from it (*Ita missa est*), and returns to it for strength and sustenance. The Eucharist exists to give glory and praise to the Father and to draw as many as possible into the mystery of Christ's redeeming love.

As the "sacrament of the parousia," the Eucharist unites believers both to the Lord's resurrection and to his second coming at the end of time. In looks back to the glorious end of Jesus' first coming and looks forward to his glorious return in his second. By uniting these two important ends of history, the Eucharist highlights the glorious destiny all believers have in Christ by virtue of their being members of his mystical body, the Church. By uniting Jesus' first and second comings, it offers the Church sustenance for its earthly sojourn and the strength to live by the power of the Spirit in the interim. In this respect, the Eucharist offers believers food for the journey as they strive to realize the goals of the kingdom in the here-and-now and as they make their way toward the heavenly Jerusalem. The eschatological feature of the Eucharist does not lead believers to escape the challenges of the present, but to confront and find practical solutions for them. As they await Christ's second coming, they also strive to build up his kingdom and celebrate its presence in their midst.

As a meal shared with the crucified and risen Lord, the Eucharist is also a celebration of the power of the Spirit. If Jesus' resurrection represents an outpouring of the Spirit that conquered death and raised humanity to the level of a glorious, transformed existence, then the Eucharist is a concrete and visible sign of the Spirit's power to transform all of creation. When at Eucharist, Jesus, the New Man, shares a meal with his followers and inaugurates a New Creation by changing simple elements like bread and wine into his body and blood. Those who eat his body and blood share in that New Creation and are themselves gradually transformed. All of this comes about by the power of the Holy Spirit, who was unleashed in a powerful way at Jesus' death on the cross, at the moment of his Resurrection, and at the Church's birth on Pentecost. The Eucharist represents a continuation of this outpouring of the Spirit through history in the life of the Church and its members. Without it, the Church could not exist, and the spiritual wellspring of its faith would run dry.

The Eucharist, for Durrwell, is the height of Christian prayer, for it is the prayer of Christ himself. As members of his body, the Church, believers share in this prayer and are able to offer glory and praise to God their Father. When at Eucharist, everything is done through, with, and in Christ. Without him, we would not be able to pray in any substantial or meaningful way. The Eucharist is not just any prayer, but the prayer of

Christ to the Father in which we are allowed to share by the power of his Spirit. By sharing in this prayer, Christ's glorified existence shines through us and radiates outwards to others. The prayer of Christ transforms us and propels us to share his love with those around us. In this way, the kingdom grows in ever-widening circles of Spirit-filled friendships, which are nothing but a foretaste of things to come. The Eucharist, for Durrwell, is all about intimacy with God, which enables us to have intimate friendships with others.

For Durrwell, the Eucharist continues the redeeming action of Christ manifested in Jesus' incarnation and paschal mystery. The Word of God became flesh, lived among us, suffered, died, and rose from the death to liberate us from the slavery of sin so that we might become adopted sons and daughters of the Father. The Eucharist brings the selfless sacrifice and presence of our redeeming Lord into our midst and allows us to break bread with him and worship his Father as our own. In his mind, there is only one Christian mystery and the Eucharist encompasses it from beginning to end. This sacrament puts us in touch with Jesus, our Redeemer, who serves as both priest and victim in a sacrificial meal that releases the redeeming power of the Spirit to transform all who call upon his name. It reveals the mystery of Christ and makes it present in the concrete circumstances of space and time. It unleashes the transforming power of the Spirit upon the world and offers it space within the human heart to work its wonders.

Finally, Mary was with her Son from the beginning of his earthly sojourn to the end—and beyond. The close bond they shared during life on earth continues in his glorious life in heaven. She was the first to experience the fullest fruits of the Redemption wrought by her son by being preserved from original sin through her Immaculate Conception and experiencing the fullness of the resurrected life through her glorious Assumption into heaven. She now sits beside her Son as the glorious Queen of heaven and earth. This close relationship between Mother and Son extends to a special cooperation in the work of Redemption and in the sacraments, especially that of the Eucharist. As Mother of Our Lord, Mary is also "Mother of the Eucharist." Durrwell assigns a special role to Mary in the work of Redemption and sees her as someone whose life lies where the Eucharist lies—at the heart of the Church.

Although these observations do not exhaust Durrwell's teaching on the Eucharist, they cover its major contours and demonstrate the essential role it plays in Christ's redemptive action. They also point to the integrated nature of his theological outlook and highlight the centrality of Eucharistic worship for Catholic spirituality today.

Conclusion

F. X. Durrwell was one of the most prominent theologians and spiritual writers of his day and noted for the way he brought the Resurrection back to the center of Catholic theological reflection. He is also remembered for the connections he drew between theology and the spiritual life, most notably between mystery of Redemption and its impact on the daily life of the believer. His teaching on the Eucharist reflects these two major themes. The sacrament of the Lord's Last Supper was for him a living testimony of the Risen and Glorified Lord's presence in our midst and an essential means for entering more deeply into the redeeming love of Christ's paschal mystery.

The Eucharist, for Durrwell, lies at the very heart of the Church. It brings the reality of Christ's paschal mystery into the midst of those who celebrate it and makes them participants in the saving action of Christ's passion, death, and resurrection. As the "sacrament of the paschal mystery," it permeates the Church's proclamation and is the ultimate focus of everything the Church says and does. The Eucharist is the "sacrament of sacraments" and the Church's most prized possession. From it, she receives the daily sustenance necessary for continuing her earthly sojourn. Through it, God unleashes the power of his Spirit upon her members. With it, she proclaims the salvific message of Christ's redeeming love.

Durrwell's teaching on the Eucharist touches the heart of the Christian message. It places the sacrament at the very center of Christ's ongoing redemptive action and underscores the healing and transformative powers that lie therein. It highlights Christ's glorified presence in the consecrated elements, the sacrificial nature of the ritual, and the eschatological nature of the banquet being celebrated. At the heart of the sacrament is the visible presence of the redeeming love of Christ and the sanctifying power of the Holy Spirit. It constitutes the Church and represents all that it hopes one day to become.

Reflection Questions

- For Durrwell, the Eucharist is a ritual meal that joins Jesus' Last Supper with his apostles with the meals they shared with him as the Risen Lord. What does Durrwell mean by a "ritual meal?" What are this meal's essential elements? Do you view the Eucharist as a manifestation of Jesus' Last Supper with his disciples? Do you view it as a meal with the Risen Lord?
- Durrwell emphasizes the close connection between the Eucharist and the sacrament of Baptism. How would you describe the relationship between these two sacraments? Which, to you mind, is more necessary? How does the Eucharist carry on the work begun in Baptism?
- For Durrwell, the Eucharist is the "Sacrament of the Parousia." In what sense does this sacrament rest on the promise of Christ's Second Coming? In what ways does it

anticipate this Second Coming? In what ways does it make it present?

Voice Twenty-Three

Edward Schillebeeckx:
Transignified Meaning

Our next voice offers many challenging theological insights into the meaning of the Eucharist for today's believers. Edward Schillebeeckx, O.P. (1914-2009) was born in Antwerp, received his early education at Turnhout, and entered the Dominican Order in 1934. He was ordained to the priesthood in 1941 and studied at various philosophical and theological faculties, including Louvain, Le Salchoir, the Ecole des Hautes Etudes, and the Sorbonne (Paris). He served in the Belgian army in the early years of World War II and afterwards began a lengthy academic career first at the Theology Faculty of the Catholic University of Louvain and later, beginning in 1958, at the Catholic University of Nijmegen in the Netherlands. He was a theological expert (*peritus*) at the Second Vatican Council and drafted many texts for the Dutch bishops during its four sessions. Although trained and well versed in classical Thomism, he studied phenomenology and was deeply immersed in modern Protestant and Catholic theology. A prolific author, he dedicated his writing and research to extending the limits of Catholic theology and finding new ways of formulating the teachings of the Church that would be more accessible to the mindset and sensitivities of the modern world.

These efforts created tensions with Church authorities and led to numerous criticisms by the Congregation for the Doctrine of the Faith, the watchdog of the arm the Catholic magisterium. His books include: *Christ the Sacrament of the Encounter with God* (1963), *God and Man* (1969), *Revelation and Theology* (1979), *Ministry* (1981), *God Among* Us (1983) *Jesus: An Experiment in Christology* (1985), and *I Am a Happy Theologian* (2004). His teaching on the Eucharist appears in many of his writings, especially in *The Eucharist* (1968, 2005), where he takes up the topic of "transignification."[1]

---

[1] Edward Schillebeeckx, *Christ the Sacrament of the Encounter with God*, trans. Paul Barrett, Mark Schoof, and Laurence Bright (New York: Sheed and Ward,1963); *The Eucharist*, trans. N. D. Smith (New York: Sheed and Ward, 1968); *God and Man*, trans. Edward Fitzgerald and Peter Tomlinson (New York: Sheed and Ward, 1969); *Revelation and Theology*, 2 vols., trans. N.D. Smith (New York: Sheed and Ward, 1979); *Ministry: Leadership in the Community of Jesus Christ*, trans. John Bowden (New York: Crossroad, 1981); *God Among Us: The Gospel Proclaimed*, trans. John Bowden (New York: Crossroad, 1983); *Jesus: An Experiment in Christology*, trans. Hubert Hoskins (New York: William Collings & Sons/Crossroad, 1979); *I Am a Happy Theologian: Conversations with Francesco Strazzari*, trans. John Bowden (New York: Crossroad, 2004). Note: The original Dutch editions of these works normally appeared two to five years prior to the appearance of their English translations]. For relevant biographical information, see Schillebeeckx, *I Am a Happy Theologian*, 1-44; Edward Schillebeeckx and Johann-Baptist Metz, eds., *The Right of the Community to a Priest*, Concilium 133 (no. 3, 1980), 137; Peter Steinfels, "Edward Schillebeeckx, Catholic Theologian Dies at 95," *The New York Times* (January16, 2010), A26. For the various Church processes against Schillebeeckx, see *I Am a Happy Theologian*, 32-40.

Schillebeeckx's Theological Outlook

Throughout his writings, Schillebeeckx emphasizes the importance of having a personal encounter with Christ, especially as it is mediated through the Church and its sacraments. Reacting against the theology of the manuals of the pre-Vatican II era, he believes "[t]he intimateness of God's personal approach to man is often lost in a too severely objective examination of that which forms the living core and center of religion, the personal communion with the God who gives himself to men."[2] To counteract this tendency, he emphasizes the mode of being peculiar to human existence and seeks to present Christianity and religion in general as "...above all a saving dialogue between man and the living God."[3] Christ, in his mind, is the means through which this dialogue takes place and brings about this personal encounter between the human and the divine.

Schillebeeckx seeks to root his reflections in the Church's theological tradition, yet move it forward. He presents humanity's religious yearnings in terms of its search for a visible manifestation (or sacrament) of the divine. This holds true for pagan religion, as well as for Israel's search for God throughout salvation history. It is within this tradition that God gradually unveils himself through the Law and the prophets and whose self-revelation reaches its fullness in Jesus Christ, the primordial sacrament, who represents the epitome of divine love for man and human love for God.[4] According to Schillebeeckx, the redemptive mystery of Christ unfolds in his humiliation in the service of the Father and his heavenly

---

[2] Schillebeeckx, *Christ the Sacrament of the Encounter with God*, 3.

[3] Ibid.

[4] Ibid., 13, 17.

exaltation as it takes place in his paschal mystery. Because of his passion, death, resurrection, and ascension, he is able to impart his Spirit and begin the process of humanity's sanctification. In his mind, "we can see sufficiently clearly that the mysteries of the Passover (death, resurrection, exaltation) and of Pentecost are the representation in human form, realized in the mystery of Christ, of the mystery of the redeeming Trinity."[5]

If Christ is the "Sacrament of God" who embodies in his paschal mystery the redeeming action of the Trinity, then the Church is the "Sacrament of the Risen Christ" that continues the saving action of Christ through time.[6] With St. Augustine, Schillebeeckx affirms that "Christ dies that the Church might be born."[7] "The earthly Church, for him, "is the visible realization of this saving reality in history."[8] As such, it is a visible and concrete union in grace: "This communion itself, consisting of members and a hierarchical leadership, is the earthly sign of the triumphant redeeming grace of Christ."[9] He goes so far as to claim that the Church is more than a mere means of salvation. "It is Christ's salvation itself, this salvation as visibly realized in the world. Thus it is, by a kind of identity, the body of the Lord."[10]

In light of the above, Schillebeeckx presents the individual sacraments as "the sevenfold ecclesial realization of the one mystery of redemption."[11] They are the Church's celebration of

---

[5] Ibid., 36.

[6] Ibid., 48.

[7] Augustine of Hippo, *In Evangelium Johannis*, tract 9, 10 [PL 35.1463]; Schillebeeckx, *Christ the Sacrament of the Encounter with God*, 47.

[8] Schillebeeckx, *Christ the Sacrament of the Encounter with God*, 47.

[9] Ibid., 47-48.

[10] Ibid., 48.

[11] Ibid., 79.

the mysteries of Christ's life and the means through which the personal encounter with Christ in the Church becomes possible. As such, they represent "the ecclesial manifestation of Christ's love for men...and of his human love for God."[12] While valid when properly celebrated, they are fruitful in the lives of the faithful only when this love is reciprocated. Schillebeeckx concludes: "It is by the sacraments that we journey toward our final goal—the sacramental way is our hidden road to Emmaus, on which we are accompanied by our Lord. And even though we are not yet able to see him, we are conscious of his concealed presence near us, for when he addresses us through his sacraments, our hearts, intent upon his word, burn with longing."[13] He goes on to quote the words of St. Ambrose, "You have shown yourself to me, Christ, face to face. It is in your sacraments that I meet you."[14] Schillebeeckx believes this statement is especially true when Christians gather around the table of the Lord and recognize him in the breaking of the bread.

Schillebeeckx on the Eucharist

The Mass, for Schillebeeckx, is the point of contact where the mystery of Christ's redemption touches people in their daily lives. This process of sanctification takes place in and through the Church and does so in a way that both heals and sanctifies. For Jesus, the Last Supper represents "the unshaken assurance of salvation when face to face with death."[15] Since, "[t]here is no gap between Jesus' self-understanding and the Christ pro-

---

[12] Ibid., 63.

[13] Ibid., 222.

[14] Ambrose of Milan, *Apologia Prophetae David,* 12, p. 58 [PL 14.875]; Schillebeeckx, *Christ the Sacrament of the Encounter with God,* 222.

[15] Schillebeeckx, *Jesus,* 306.

claimed by the Church," Schillebeeckx concludes, "the memory of Jesus' life and especially of the Last Supper must have played a vital role in the process of their conversion to faith in Jesus as the Christ, the one imbued to the full with God's Spirit."[16]

That memory touches the heart of the Church's nascent faith and lies behind the central role played by the Eucharist in its life and message. Schillebeeckx recognizes that the Church has traditionally presented the sacrament as a foretaste of the heavenly banquet, which immerses the faithful in the sacrifice of Calvary, and contains the real presence of the Risen Christ. He understands that the Eucharist has typically been described as a *banquet*, a *sacrifice*, and a real *presence*. The sacrament, in this respect, gives the faithful heavenly food, makes the sacrifice of Calvary present in an unbloody manner, and brings the Risen Lord into their midst through the transubstantiated bread and wine. In his desire to move the tradition forward and to present the mystery of the Eucharist in a language that will speak to our present-day sensitivities, he eventually proposes an entirely new way of understanding Christ's presence in the Eucharist. He does so by employing the term "transignification."[17]

Schillebeeckx claims that the Church's doctrine of "transubstantiation," which teaches that, at the moment of consecration, the substance of the bread and wine are changed into the substance of Christ's body and blood, presupposes scholastic categories and distinctions that are foreign to the modern-day way of thinking and difficult to understand. Since the doctrine represents a new approach to the Eucharist in its day, he says it would be appropriate in our own day to find a new way of formulating the Church's teaching on the Lord's presence in the sacrament. The challenge, he goes on the say, is to find a way so "that the new formulation does not contradict

---

[16] Ibid. 312.

[17] Schillebeeckx, *The Eucharist*, 144-51.

the original, inviolable datum of faith or minimize it"[18] Drawing from the philosophy of phenomenology, Schillebeeckx draws the distinction between reality itself and reality as a phenomenal appearance: "The inadequacy of man's knowledge of reality accounts for a certain difference between reality and its appearance as a phenomenon."[19]

Schillebeeckx claims that the conflict between Aristotelian categories and modern physics calls for a new way of describing Christ's presence in the Eucharist, one that rediscovers the sacrament's symbolic activity and the meaning conveyed through it.[20] Transignification, he says, expresses the change in meaning which the reality of Christ's paschal mystery impresses upon the phenomenal world as represented in the sacramental bread and wine: "the usual secular significance of the bread and wine is withdrawn and these become bearers of Christ's gift of himself—'Take and eat, this is my body.'"[21] What takes place at the Eucharistic celebration is therefore a change of meaning: "In this commemorative meal, bread and wine become the subject of a new *establishment of meaning*, not by men, but by the living Lord *in* the Church, through which they become the *sign* of the real presence of Christ giving himself to us."[22] Schillebeeckx concludes that this new approach of transignification, although not identical with transubstantiation, is intimately connected with it.[23]

---

[18] Ibid., 86.
[19] Ibid., 148.
[20] Ibid., 94-96.
[21] Ibid., 137.
[22] Ibid.
[23] Ibid., 149.

Some Further Insights

This brief exposition of Schillebeeckx's teaching on the Eucharist points out its strong emphasis on the sacramental nature of Christ and the Church and underscores the important way in which the sacrament facilitates a personal encounter with God. It also shows how Schillebeeckx attempts to present the doctrine of the real presence in a way that is faithful to the tradition, yet also takes into account our present-day sensitivities and patterns of thought. The following remarks delve more deeply into Schillebeeckx's presentation and its relevance for today.

To begin with, Schillebeeckx roots his teaching on the Eucharist in the larger context of Christ and his body, the Church. By calling Christ the "primordial sacrament" and the Church, the "sacrament of the Risen Christ," he emphasizes the element of personal encounter with God as the goal of the Christian life. In this respect, the sacraments in general, and the Eucharist in particular, were instituted by Christ either explicitly or implicitly through the apostolic institution as a means of promoting throughout history the possibility of this encounter between God and man, between the human and the divine. In doing so, he seeks to avoid the reified, mechanistic rendering of sacramental grace that the scholastic formulations have, at times, tended to convey. By bringing the symbolic meaning of the sacraments to the fore and, in the case of the Eucharist, by showing how the very meaning of the elements of bread and wine have been changed to convey a sense of unshaken assurance of salvation in the face of death, he retrieves insights into the meaning of the sacrament from deep within the tradition and presents them in a way that is palatable to our present sensitivities and way of thinking. He does so, moreover, by preserving the "sign" value of the real presence itself, by focusing it not on the elements of bread and wine themselves, but on the intimate, personal encounter they sustain between God and man.[24]

Schillebeeckx makes the point that any new formulations of the Church's dogmatic teachings (in this case, its teaching on the Eucharist) must be faithful to the tradition, yet open to the experience of modern man. Although "transignification" is not identical with "transubstantiation," he affirms the two are closely related and, in fact, complement each other. In his teaching on the Eucharist, Schillebeeckx is not trying to discard the Church's teaching on transubstantiation, but simply find a new approach to the mystery of Christ's presence in the Eucharist that will make sense to our modern sensibilities. His main difficulty with the doctrine of transubstantiation is that it is rooted in medieval categories that have largely lost their meaning for modern man. If the Catholic faith is to continue to be a living faith, then theologians must strive to find new ways of understanding the mystery of the real presence. In this respect, he is attempting to do with "transignification" what medieval scholastics like Albert the Great, Bonaventure, and Thomas Aquinas, did with "transubstantiation," a teaching which in the thirteenth century was a relatively new theological concept, perceived as modernist, and which only entered gradually over time the popular imagination of the Catholic faithful.[25]

If medieval scholastic terms such as "substance," "species," and "accidents" upon which the Church bases it teaching on "transubstantiation" are difficult to comprehend today, it is also true that any new formulation will have its own limitations and, in all likelihood, one day suffer a similar fate. The history of theology reflects the changing currents of human

---

[24] See Schillebeeckx, *Christ the Sacrament of the Encounter with God*, esp. 197-222.

[25] See Schillebeeckx, *The Eucharist*, esp. 11-21.

thought in its attempt to understand the mysteries of the Christian faith. While the Church must always be open to new formulations that might better explain the mysteries of the faith and hence promote the development of doctrine, it also has the duty and responsibility of embracing those theological formulations that have served it well in elucidating the truths of the tradition. The doctrine of "transubstantiation" is one such formulation, for it stands out as the theological formulation which, to date, has best expressed the mystery of the real presence. Although it first appeared on the theological scene only on the twelfth century, it gained prominence in the thirteenth, was defined at the Council of Trent, and reaffirmed in Paul VI's encyclical, *Mysterium fidei* and his *Credo of the People of God*.[26] It was taught, still later, by John Paul II and Benedict XVI and also listed in the *Catechism of the Catholic Church*.[27] For all its strengths, "transignification," by way of contrast, has never had such success in making its way into the Church's theological imagination and official teaching.

The main difficulty with "transignification" is that it focuses on a change in the meaning of the consecrated bread and wine rather than in their substances. In making this shift from the classical category of "substance" to the present-day concern for "meaning," the argument against "transignification" states that a deeper shift is taking place from objective to subjective reality. In other words, the change that takes place is not in the bread and wine themselves, but in the meaning attached to them by

---

[26] See The Council of Trent, *Decree on the Most Holy Eucharist*, chap. 4; Paul VI, *Mysterium fidei,* Encyclical Letter (September 3, 1965), no. 11; Idem, The *Credo of the People of God*, Apostolic Letter in the Form of *Motu Proprio* (June 30, 1968) nos. 25-26.

[27] See John Paul II, *Ecclesia de Eucharistia,* Encyclical Letter (April 15, 2003), no. 15; Benedict XVI, *Sacramentum caritatis,* Post-Synodal Apostolic Exhortation (February, 22, 2007), no. 6; *Catechism of the Catholic Church*, nos. 1373-77, 1413.

those who receive it. Such an understanding expressly goes against the current teaching of the Church. In the words of Paul VI: "Every theological explanation which seeks some understanding of this mystery [the Eucharist] must, in order to be in accord with the Catholic faith, maintain that in the reality itself, independently of our mind, the bread and wine have ceased to exist after the consecration, so that it is the adorable body and blood of the Lord Jesus that from then on are really before us under the sacramental species of bread and wine, as the Lord willed it, in order to give Himself to us as food and to associate us with the unity of His Mystical Body."[28] In his encyclical letter, *Mysterium fidei,* moreover, Paul VI makes it clear that "transignification" does not provide an adequate explanation of the transformation that takes place in the Eucharistic elements.[29] Such an assessment of the limitations of "transignification" would indicate that, for all its strengths, it ultimately can be used only to complement the Church's teaching on transubstantiation in order to emphasize the element of personal encounter with God in the sacrament.

Finally, Schillebeeckx is to be commended for his attempt to find a new approach to the Catholic doctrine of the real presence that would address our present sensitivities and make them more accessible to our current modes of thought. In doing so, he represents the kind of theological thinking that seeks to delve more deeply into the mysteries of the faith and find new ways of expressing the truths they hold. It must be noted, however, that no theological formulation—be it "transubstantiation" or "transignification"—will ever fully exhaust the mysteries they seek to express. For this reason, a more suitable approach to expressing our understanding of

---

[28] Paul VI, *The Credo of the People of God*, 13.

[29] Paul VI, *Mysterium fidei*, Encyclical Letter (September 3, 1965), no. 11.

such mysteries as the Lord's real presence in the Eucharist would be to recognize the various strengths and weaknesses of the various models seeking to explain the mystery, admit that, while some are better than others, no single model will ever fully explain the mystery under consideration, and therefore use these various models in conjunction with one another. As far as "transubstantiation" and "transignification" are concerned, it bears noting that Schillebeeckx himself remarked that, although not identical, they are closely connected. Up until this point, theologians and Church authorities have largely focused on how these two approaches to the real presence differ from one another. It is incumbent for future development of our understanding of the doctrine to explore how they are connected. The place to begin would be to emphasize that the change in meaning envisioned by "transignification" occurs not merely in the human subject (i.e., those who receive the sacrament), but first and foremost in God himself (i.e., the sacrament's objective and subjective source). Such an approach recognizes that God, for whom all things are possible, has the ability to change not only what the bread and wine *are* (transubstantiation), but also what they *mean* (transignification). The objective reality and subjective meaning of the Eucharist, in other words, are determined primarily by God and only secondarily by the believing community.

Although these observations do not exhaust Schillebeeckx's teaching on the Eucharist, they cover its major themes and demonstrate how a single theologian can cause a reexamination of the Church's traditional theological formulations in an attempt to deepen the Church's understanding of the mysteries of the faith and push the tradition forward. Among other things, they bring to the fore his deep desire to present the Eucharist as an occasion for a personal encounter with Christ and to assist people in their search for ultimate meaning.

Conclusion

Edward Schillebeeckx was a seminal thinker and one of the leading Catholic theologians of the twentieth century. Throughout his writings, he was not afraid to probe the various theological formulations embedded in the tradition and seek new ways of expressing the truths they conveyed. These efforts led him to many creative insights about the nature of the Christ event and its meaning for believers today. His experiments in Christology, ecclesiology, and sacramental theology were an attempt to remain faithful to the tradition, while at the same time moving it forward. At times, these attempts led Church authorities to question the validity of his insights and even his orthodoxy.

In one of his last books, Schillebeeckx describes himself as "a happy theologian."[30] He depicts himself in this manner, because he believes he has remained faithful to his vocation as someone charged with exploring the Christian tradition and seeking out new ways through which it could remain a vital force in the lives of the faithful and present the Gospel message in a meaningful way to unbelievers. To do so, he believed it was necessary to adopt ways of thinking and categories of thought that convey the truths of the faith in a way that could be amenable to the intellectual and spiritual sensitivities of his day. His emphasis on Christ as the sacrament of encounter with God, the Church as the sacrament of the Risen Christ, and the sacraments in general as the concrete realizations of the one mystery of redemption are but a few examples of his dogged attempt to present the mysteries of the faith in a coherent, insightful, and meaningful way for today's believers. The same holds true for his attempt to understand the Catholic doctrine of the real presence.

---

[30] Schillebeeckx, *I Am a Happy Theologian*, 79-81.

Schillebeeckx proposes his theory of "transignification" in an attempt to reassess the Catholic belief that Jesus is really present in the consecrated bread and wine. He develops this approach mainly because he believes that "transubstantiation," the traditional way of explaining the doctrine, uses outmoded categories that conflict with modern physics and have little attraction for today' believers. Regardless of the truth of this assessment, Schillebeeckx works hard to present the mystery of the real presence in a way that is both understandable and palatable to the world today. For him, the two approaches— "transubstantiation" and "transignification"—while not identical are nevertheless intimately related.

Church teaching clearly gives "transubstantiation" primacy of place, because it insists upon a real, objective change in the consecrated bread and wine, rather than a mere subjective change in the mind of the believer. At the same time, it is open to the possibility that new formulations might one day arise that express the mystery of the faith even more completely than its formulations. Because "transignification" does not do this sufficiently, it can only be used in a complementary and ancillary way with "transubstantiation." It would seem that the way to move the tradition forward would be to suggest that multiple models be used to express this mystery and to affirm that God, the source of all objective and subjective reality, has the power to change not only what the bread and wine *are*, but also what they *mean*.

Reflection Questions

- For Schillebeeckx, the Eucharist is the place where the mystery of redemption touches people in their daily lives. Have you experienced the Eucharist in this way? Does it meet you where you are? Does it address your problems and difficulties? Are you allowing it to do so?

- Schillebeeckx employs the word "transignification" as a means of moving the tradition forward and presenting the mystery of the Eucharist in a language that will speak to our present-day sensitivities. Do you understand what this term means? What are its positive and negative elements? Does it move the tradition forward? Does it exhaust the meaning of this great mystery?

- Schillebeeckx claims that the new approach of transignification, although not identical with transubstantiation, is intimately connected with it. How are the two approaches connected? How do they differ? Which of them do you prefer? Is the term "substance" really an antiquated philosophical category? In what ways can "transignification" be used as a complement to the Catholic doctrine of "transubstantiation?"

Voice Twenty-Four

Avery Dulles:
Multi-Layered Symbolism

Our next voice was one of the most renowned American Catholic theologians of his generation. Avery Dulles, S. J. (1918-2008) converted to Catholicism while attending Harvard University (1936-1940), was a Lieutenant in the U.S. Navy during World War II, and entered the Society of Jesus upon his discharge in 1946. He was ordained to the priesthood in 1956 and studied theology at the Gregorian University in Rome, where he earned his doctorate in 1960.

Dulles teaching career spanned almost five decades. He served on the faculty of Woodstock College from 1960 to 1974, The Catholic University of America from 1974 to 1988, and was the Laurence J. McGinley Professor of Religion and Society at Fordham University from 1988 to 2008. He served as President of The Catholic Theological Society of America and the American Theological Society, was a member of the International Theological Commission, and was active in the Lutheran/Roman Catholic Dialogue.

In 2001, Pope John Paul II made Dulles a cardinal of the Catholic Church in recognition of his important contributions to Catholic theology. A prolific author, he is best known for his works on systematic theology such as *Models of the Church* (1974), *Models of Revelation* (1983), *The Craft of Theology*

(1992), and *The Assurance of Things Hoped For* (1994). His teaching on the Eucharist is noted for its emphasis on the real presence, its strong ecclesial dimension, and its close connection to the ministerial priesthood.[1]

Dulles's Spirituality

As a Jesuit, Dulles was deeply influenced by the *Spiritual Exercises* of St. Ignatius of Loyola (1491-1556) and its principle of thinking with the Church. This collection of meditations seeks to help people master themselves and order their lives so as not to be influenced in their decisions by any undue attachments. The person making the exercises re-imagines the Gospel stories in a personal way and then prayerfully discusses his or her experiences with a trained spiritual director. The ultimate goal of this process of discernment is to help people see God's providential plan for their lives and enable them to become contemplatives in action. Dulles's long and dedicated career as a Jesuit theologian in the area of systematic theology must be understood as a direct result of his adherence to the Jesuit ideal of doing everything "for the greater glory of God."[2]

This spiritual outlook influenced Dulles's approach to theology, which involved a prayerful, imaginative, and critical

---

[1]For more biographical information on Dulles, see Patrick W. Carey, *Avery Cardinal Dulles, S.J.: A Model* Theologian, 1918-2008 (New York/Mahwah, NJ: Paulist Press, 2010). See also Thomas G. Guarino, "Why Avery Dulles Matters," *First Things* (May, 2009), http://www.firstthings.com/article/2009/04/why-avery-dulles-matters-1243317340.

[2] For the influence of Ignatian spirituality on Dulles's life, see Carey, *Avery Cardinal Dulles, S.J.*, 94-136. For the Ignatian rules on thinking with the Church, see *The Spiritual Exercises of St. Ignatius*, trans. Anthony Mottola (Garden City, NY: Image Books, 1964), 139-42.

examination of Christian revelation found in the Scriptures and the Tradition of the Church as presented and interpreted by the Magisterium. In all of his writings, he was careful to place the subject under investigation in the context of biblical revelation and the living tradition of the Church. To aid his understanding and analysis of Catholic theology, he took care to study the thoughts of contemporary theologians, but gave priority of place to the hermeneutical role of the Church's magisterium in elucidating the meaning of God's Word for the world today. Taken together, these various strands of his approach to theology led him to formulate a creative approach to the systematic study of theology that was, at one and the same time, open to a variety of perspectives and loyal to the deepest instincts of the Catholic faith.[3]

Dulles was one of the major proponents of the "models" approach to Catholic theology, the basic idea of which was that certain images or metaphors serve as organizing principles for theological reflection on divine revelation and vie with one another to become an overarching paradigm. His fundamental insight was that each model has something to contribute to the understanding of theology and needs to be viewed in complementary fashion rather than in opposition to one another. For example, in *Models of the Church* (1974), his groundbreaking work on the ecclesiology of the Second Vatican Council, he identified five models at work in the Church's self-understanding. These were the Church as Institution, Mystical Communion, Sacrament, Herald, and Servant. Many of the tensions within the Church, he concluded, could be traced to an overemphasis of one of these models to the detriment (or possible exclusion) of one or more of the others. The key to a proper ecclesiological understanding of the Church was to place

---

[3] See Avery Dulles, *The Craft of Theology: From Symbol to System* (New York: Crossroad, 1995), 17-39, 69-118.

all of these models in a dynamic and creative tension with one another so that they correct the limitations of each other and propel the Church to a deeper appreciation of the mystery of the divine plan. Dulles would later employ this same "models" approach to theology to the notion of revelation in *Models of Revelation* (1983), the meaning of faith in *The Assurance of Things Hoped For* (1994), and to areas of pastoral concern such as catechesis and evangelization.[4] This approach to theology enabled him to sustain an underlying unity in the midst of theological pluralism without giving in to the dangerous extremes of theological relativism, on the one hand, and dogmatic fundamentalism, on the other.[5]

In addition to this approach, Dulles was also aware of two overlapping but also different "models," if you will, of Catholic theology itself: the more magisterial approach taught in Catholic seminaries and the more curious, exploratory approach found in many Catholic colleges and universities. Each of these approaches presupposes adherence to the Catholic faith, but have different points of departure related to their specific purposes. In Catholic seminaries, where the primary purpose is to train young men for the priesthood, the point of departure is the teachings of the councils and pronouncements of the magisterium. In Catholic colleges and universities, by way of contrast, professors are not bound by the rigors of seminary formation and often start at the cutting edge of theological inquiry and work their way back towards to the teachings of the magisterium. In addition to these two

---

[4] See, for example, Avery Dulles, "Historical Models of Catechesis," *Origins* 37/22(2007): 347-52; Idem, "Models of Evangelization," *Origins*, 37/1(2007): 8-11.

[5] For Dulles's "models" approach to theology and its significance for interpreting Vatican II, see Carey, *Avery Cardinal Dulles, S.J.*, 211-73; 482-83.

approaches to Catholic theology, Dulles was also very much aware of the "Catholic Studies" approach taken in many secular universities, where Catholicism is often taught outside the context of a committed faith and examined in light of the sociological and anthropological approaches used in the discipline of Religious Studies. Having taught in Catholic seminaries, colleges and universities, as well as serving as visiting professor of a number of secular universities, he was very adept at navigating the often stormy theological waters of Roman Catholicism and ecumenical dialogue in a balanced, professional, and highly competent manner. As his teaching on the Eucharist suggests, he sought to use his deep theological acumen in service of the Church he so dearly loved.[6]

Dulles on the Eucharist

In one respect, Dulles's approach to the Eucharist is a reflection of his "models" approach to theology. He sees, for example, that a person's views toward this sacrament will vary depending on whether he or she has an understanding of Church as Institution, Mystical Communion, Sacrament, Herald, and Servant—or various combinations thereof. He also recognizes that other variations are possible depending on the model(s) of revelation a person adopts (e.g., revelation as doctrine, history, inner experience, dialectical presence, or new awareness) or of faith (e.g., propositional, transcendental, fiducial, affective-experiential, obediential, or praxis). From this perspective, a person can incorporate any one or more of the above models into his or her views toward the Eucharist that, in turn, appears as an extension of his or her presup-

---

[6] For Dulles's comparison between teaching theology in the seminary and in the university, see Dulles, *The Craft of* Theology, 149-64; Carey, *Avery Cardinal Dulles, S.J.*, 427-44.

positions about the nature of faith, revelation, and Church. In such an approach, it is important, on the one hand, to prevent a single model from having undue precedence and, on the other, not to have an overabundance of models that would dilute the symbolic meaning of the sacrament and obscure its doctrinal clarity.[7]

Dulles's personal views on the Eucharist reflect the balanced approach displayed throughout his writings. In an article on Pope John Paul II's teaching on the sacrament, he affirms the famous statement by Henri de Lubac, S.J. that the Eucharist "builds the church and the church makes the Eucharist." He also affirms John Paul II's claim that the Eucharist displays the four marks of the Church as being one, holy, catholic, and apostolic. He concludes the article stating that the church is in dire need of renewal in each of these four essential marks or characteristics. Although irrevocably *holy* in its divine head and apostolic heritage, its members are sinful and in constant need of purification. The Church, moreover, is not only imperfect in holiness, but also suffers from internal ethnic, national, and ideological tensions that detract from its *unity*. If that is not enough, we often use the term *catholic* without having any sense of what it entails, and the Church's *apostolicity* is difficult to maintain when surrounded by the forces of secular culture that seek to negate all sense of the sacred in modern life and create the illusion that we can imagine a salvation of our own making. In his mind, only the Eucharist has the power to preserve these four essential marks of the Church. Only it can renew the hearts

---

[7] See Avery Dulles, *Models of the Church* (Garden City, NY: Image Books, 1978), 19-37; Idem, *Models of Revelation* (Garden City, NY: Doubleday, 1983), 19-35; Idem, *The Assurance of Things Hoped For: A Theology of Christian faith* (New York/Oxford: Oxford University Press, 1994), 170-84. For an application of the "models" approach to the Eucharist, see Kevin W. Irwin, *Models of the Eucharist* (New York/Mahwah, NJ: Paulist Press, 2005).

and minds of its members and enable them to be a force for positive change in the world today.[8]

Dulles displays his breadth of knowledge and typical clarity of expression when examining the theological basis for Catholic teaching on Christ's presence in the Eucharist. He affirms the limited capacity of the human mind to see the real presence as an ineffable mystery that should be welcomed "with wonder and amazement." He recognizes that some Catholics have inter-preted the Eucharist "either too carnally or too mystically, too grossly or too tenuously, too naively or too figuratively" and goes on to explain that "Christ's presence in this sacrament resembles that of the soul in the body. My soul is not partly in my head, partly in my heart, partly in my hands, but is entirely present in the whole and in every part." What is more, while it is true that the Second Vatican Council recognizes multiple ways in which Christ is present in the liturgy, "the presence of Christ in the eucharist surpasses them all." He summarizes the importance of the Real Presence with his customary eloquence of expression: "Although the mystery of the real presence certainly stretches our powers of comprehension to the utmost, it is not simply a puzzle. It is a consoling sign of the love, power and ingenuity of our divine Savior. He willed to bring himself into intimate union with believers of every generation and to do so in a way that suits our nature as embodied spirits. The forms of food and drink, deeply charged with memories from the history of ancient Israel, are meaningful even to the unlearned throughout the ages. They aptly symbolize the spiritual nourishment and refreshment conferred by the sacrament. On another level, they call to mind the crucifixion of Christ, who shed his blood for our redemption. And finally, they prefigure the everlasting banquet of the blessed in the heavenly

---

[8] See Avery Dulles, "A Eucharistic Church," *America* 119/20(2004): 8-12.

Jerusalem. The many-layered symbolism of the Eucharist is not separable from the real presence. The symbolism has singular power to recapture the past, transform the present and anticipate the future because it contains the Lord of history truly, really and substantially." One would be hard put to find a more balance and well-reasoned defense of Christ's presence in the sacrament.[9]

Finally, Dulles draws a close connection between the Eucharist and the priesthood. The sacrament, he believes, unfolds in three tenses: it looks back to the Last Supper; it celebrates the presence of the Holy Spirit in the believing community; and it looks forward to the eschatological banquet and Christ's return in glory. The priest, in his mind, celebrates the sacrament *in persona Christi* as priest, prophet, and king. These sanctifying, teaching, and governing offices are intimately related and cannot be separated from the person of Christ and his ministerial priesthood. Dulles believes that the reason for the loss of priestly identity in the period immediately following the Second Vatican Council was partly due to a minimizing of the sacral dimension of the priesthood. He believes that priests fulfill their highest office through the celebration of the Eucharistic sacrifice and that this sacral function must be revitalized and integrated into a single identity if priests are to minister to the Church effectively through the threefold ministry of Word, Worship, and Pastoral Care.[10]

---

[9] All quotations in this paragraph come from Avery Dulles, "Christ's Presence in the Eucharist," *Origins* 34/39(2005): 627-31.

[10] See Avery Dulles, "A Eucharistic Church," 8-12; Idem, *The Priestly Office: A Theological Reflection* (New York/Mahwah, NJ: Paulist Press, 1997), 33-34; Idem, *The Priest and the Eucharist* (Weston, MA: Blessed John XXIII National Seminary, 2000), 6-21.

Some Further Insights

This brief exposition of Dulles's teaching on the Eucharist highlights the central role it plays in his understanding of the believing community and the ministerial priesthood. The following observations highlight some of the spiritual and theological underpinnings of his view of the sacrament and their relevance for today's Catholics.

To begin with, Dulles was convinced of the centrality of the Eucharist for the life and mission of the Catholic Church. The Church, at one and the same time, both constitutes the Eucharist and is constituted by it. This sacrament, he believed, put the Church and its members in touch with the Creating, Redeeming, and Sanctifying Lord, and did so in such a way that they were divinized by it through their participation in and reception of it. The Eucharist, in other words, cannot exist without the Church, and the Church cannot exist without the Eucharist. The preeminence of the Eucharist in the Church's life and mission is the starting point from which all other theological reflection on the sacrament takes place. To overlook this fundamental point of departure for the Church's life and mission does serious damage to the Gospel message. Jesus came to this world to give life, and to give it in abundance (cf. Jn 10:10). The Eucharist, for Dulles, represents God's gift of abundant life to his people.[11]

Dulles also maintains that the Eucharist is an unfathomable mystery, one that ultimately goes beyond the limits of human comprehension. Part of the reason he adopts a "models" approach to theology is because it recognizes a gap between the particular model being employed and the mystery it seeks to express. Although employing other models simultaneously to capture different aspects of the mystery and

---

[11] See Dulles, "A Eucharistic Church," 8-12.

thus create a logical web of meaning may lessen the gap, he recognizes that, even then, a disparity will still exist and the full meaning of the mystery will remain elusive. When seen in this light, Dulles's "models" approach to the theology represents a profound sense of the limitations of human reason, while still recognizing its capacity to say something rather than nothing. Dulles successfully applies this approach to theology to such areas as revelation, faith, and ecclesiology. Although he does not apply it specifically to the Eucharist, the implications of his approach for the sacrament are clear and have been eagerly pursued by others.[12]

Dulles recognizes that the four marks of the Church are reflected in the Eucharist, but also sees the sacrament as an important instrument of renewal. In its humanness, the Church is in constant need of being purified of its sins and in desperate need of overcoming national, racial, and ideological tensions that divide it and prevent it from carrying out its universal apostolic mission in the world. Only Jesus, the God-man, the person whom God sent into the world to heal our sinful humanity and elevate it to new heights can bring about the deep changes necessary for the renewal of the Church. The Eucharist, for Dulles, is the means through which the Church remains in vital contact with the divinizing power of Christ. Through it, Christ not only enters our midst, but also gradually transforms those who receive him into Spirit-filled beings fully alive with the love for God and others.[13]

Dulles affirms the priority of the real presence and draws an intimate connection between the Eucharist and the ministerial priesthood. He recognizes a single priesthood of Christ, but makes an important distinction between the ordained priesthood and the priesthood of all believers. The

---

[12] See Carey, *Avery Cardinal Dulles, S.J.*, 211-73; 482-83.
[13] See Dulles, "A Eucharistic Church," 8-12.

character of the ministerial priesthood is intrinsically ordained to preside over the Eucharistic sacrifice and to serve the community of the faithful. In the absence of an ordained priest, the community cannot simply call forth one of its members to take his place, since the ordained priesthood represents the apostolic and catholic nature of the Church and must be exercised in unity with the apostolic succession of bishops. This sacral duty of the priest is intimately related to his teaching and governing offices and constitutes an essential part of his identity. Dulles believes the confusion in priestly identity in the period immediately following the Second Vatican Council stems, at least in part, from an unfortunate (and possibly unintended) lack of emphasis on this important and con- stitutive function of the Catholic priesthood.[14]

Dulles also emphasizes that the priest plays a twofold role of mediation at the Eucharistic sacrifice: representing Christ to the believing community (a Christological dimension), and the believing community to Christ (an ecclesiological dimension). For this very reason the Liturgy has the priest sometimes speaking in the first person singular (representing Christ to the people) and, at other times, in the first person plural (representing the people to Christ). This twofold process reflects the incarnational mediation of Christ who, as the God-man, makes it possible for humanity to enter the presence of the Father and reap the benefits of divine sonship. Because he acts *in persona Christi*, the priest both intercedes for divine mercy on behalf of his people and mediates the sanctifying grace that comes through the sacraments. Because of this, the priest fulfills the demands of Christian discipleship in a unique way. At one and the same time, he both follows in the footsteps of Christ and

---

[14] See Dulles, "Christ's Presence in the Eucharist," 627-31; Idem, *The Priestly Office*, 39-41;

finds Christ standing in the priest's own shoes.[15]

Dulles points out that the Eucharist is a sacrament of the universal Church and cannot be constituted by any human group. The priest acts on behalf of the Church and dispenses the mysteries of salvation according to those rites properly set forth to render them valid and licit. In this respect, he has a special responsibility to safeguard the integrity of the sacrament and to protect it from being defamed or denigrated in any way. While this responsibility lies at the feet of every member of the Catholic faithful, it is a special duty of the ordained priesthood, since they offer the Eucharistic sacrifice *in persona Christi* and without them the sacrament could not take place. For this reason, the Eucharistic Church relies on the priesthood of Christ as manifested through ordained priesthood in the service of the priesthood of the faithful. The latter, in turn, share in the one priesthood of Christ, by virtue of their membership in the body of Christ, the Church, and their common call to discipleship.[16]

Finally, because the Eucharist is the "sacrament of sacraments" and the primary means by which God divinizes his people, Dulles emphasizes the importance for priests to nourish their lives and ministries through prayer and the search for holiness. Because priests are public figures who stand before the people as representatives of Christ and his Church, they must be careful not to allow the trappings of their public role take center stage in their lives and devolve into a hollow clericalism and careerism. On the contrary, their desire to become holy will enliven all three aspects of their priestly office—the prophetic, the priestly, and the pastoral—and will enable them to be of greater service to the people they serve. The Eucharist, for Dulles, lies at the very heart of the priestly life and

---

[15] See Dulles, *The Priestly Office*, 35-37; Idem, *Models of the Church*, 74.

[16] Ibid., 34-35.

ministry and points the way to a priest's own personal sanctity and divinization. In keeping with his Jesuit vocation, Dulles wants all priests and the people they serve to become a Eucharistic Church "for the greater glory of God."[17]

Although these observations do not exhaust Dulles's teaching on the Eucharist, they cover its major aspects and point to the essential role it plays in his understanding of the Church and its relevance for the ordained priesthood. They also reflect the balanced approach of his theological outlook and the perennial value of Eucharistic worship for Catholic faithful.

Conclusion

Avery Dulles has left the Church a rich corpus of theological scholarship rooted in Scripture, Tradition, and teaching of the magisterium. A voice for the "moderate middle" in Catholic thought, his "models" approach to theology provided both scholars and the people in the pews alike with a valuable tool for understanding the fast moving changes in the post-Vatican II Church. He possessed a rare gift that enabled him to write in a way that was faithful to Church teaching, intellectually rigorous, and accessible on a popular level. For this reason alone, his writings will continue to be read and will impact future discussion along a wide spectrum of theological issues: the nature of faith, revelation, and the Church—to name but a few.

Dulles's balanced approach to theology is reflected in his teaching on the Eucharist, which is a logical extension of his views on fundamental theology and ecclesiology. Intrinsic to this teaching is the notion he adopts from his fellow Jesuit, Henri de Lubac, S.J., that the Eucharist both builds the Church and is made by it. This reciprocal relationship between the Church and the Eucharist is fostered by the ordained

---

[17] See Dulles, *The Priest and the Eucharist*, 18-20.

priesthood, which has been entrusted with a threefold office to teach, govern, and sanctify the Church and its faithful. Dulles believed that the reason for the decline in priestly vocations in the post-Vatican II Church was due, at least in part, to a de-emphasis of the sacral role of the priesthood in favor of its teaching and governing functions. For this reason the renewal of the Church must include, among other things, a renewed balance in the priestly office, one which restores the mediating role of the priest between God and the faithful to its rightful place.

During his lifetime, Dulles achieved both national and international acclaim as a theologian and representative of the mainstream Catholic thought. His popularity on the lecture circuit, his many visiting professorships, his thirty-three honorary doctorates, and his elevation to the college of cardinals all give witness to the high esteem in which he was held both in popular venues, ecumenical gatherings, the world of Catholic academia, and even the highest circles of the Catholic hierarchy. His writings are highly esteemed, have influenced a generation of Catholic theologians, and have even filtered into the popular Catholic imagination. His views on the Eucharist reflect his overall theological outlook and are rooted in his Jesuit spirituality, his priestly vocation, and his close adherence to the Catholic understanding of God's redeeming and divinizing love made manifest in the person of Jesus Christ.

Reflection Questions

- For Dulles, a person's views toward Eucharist will vary depending on whether he or she has an understanding of Church as Institution, Mystical Communion, Sacrament, Herald, and Servant. Which of these models do you identify with most? With which do you least identify? How has your view of Church shaped your understanding of the Eucharist? In what ways can we legitimately speak of "Models of the Eucharist?"

- Dulles believes that only the Eucharist has the power to preserve the four essential marks of the Church. How does the sacrament achieve this? What does it mean to preserve the Church's oneness, holiness, catholicity, and apostolicity? How does your participation in the Eucharist contribute to this process? In what sense are you called to help preserve (and even renew) these essential marks?

- Dulles draws a close connection between the Eucharist and the priesthood. Do you believe that the priest celebrates the sacrament *in persona Christi* as priest, prophet, and king? In what ways has the priesthood suffered from a decreased emphasis on the sacral character of the ministerial priesthood? What characteristics of priestly ministry need to be emphasized today? Have you ever encouraged anyone to consider the possibility of a priestly vocation?

Voice Twenty-Five

G. E. M. Anscombe:
Consuming Jesus

Our next voice was a British analytical philosopher and a staunch defender of the Catholic faith. G. E. M. Anscombe (1919-2001) was born in Limerick, Ireland 1919, graduated from Sydenham High School in 1937, and went on to study at St. Hugh's College, Oxford, where she graduated with First Honors in 1941. She converted to Catholicism during her undergraduate years and married philosopher Peter Geach in 1941. She pursued postgraduate studies at Newnham College, Cambridge from 1942-1945, studied under Ludwig Wittgenstein, the father of analytical philosophy, and eventually became the editor, translator, and publisher of his writings. She taught at Somerville College, Oxford from 1946-1970 and at Cambridge University from 1970-1986. Her major philosophical works include *Intention* (1957) and "Modern Moral Philosophy"(1958). She is most remembered for her criticism of the state of modern philosophy, her work on intention, and her reintroduction of virtue ethics into the philosophical discussions of the day. A devout Catholic and critical thinker, she was a strong advocate of the Catholic stance against abortion and birth control, and was arrested several times for protesting in front of abortion clinics. Although she was primarily a Catholic philosopher, she did, at times, discuss more strictly theological matters. Her teaching on the Eucharist offers one such instance.[1]

Anscombe's Spiritual Outlook

Anscombe would be the first to point out that Catholic thought had an enormous influence on her own life. During her high school years, she was known to have been an avid reader of theological works and was particularly influenced by the writings of G.K. Chesterton. Her curiosity about matters of faith and her spiritual and intellectual dissatisfaction with Anglicanism led to inquiries with the Dominicans of Blackfriars College, Oxford, who facilitated her conversion to Catholicism in 1938. It was at Blackfriars College, moreover, where she met Peter Geach, a fellow philosopher and convert to Catholicism, whom she married and raised a family of seven children. It is also significant that she collaborated on a number of occasions with her husband, whose specialty was logic and the history of philosophy and who was an influential figure in what later came to be known as Analytical Thomism.[2]

It is important to note that Anscombe, who wrote what is arguably the most important work on human intention of the

---

[1] See Alan Vincelette, *Recent Catholic Philosophy: The Twentieth Century* (Milwaukee, WI: Marquette University Press, 2011), 184; Luke Gormally, "Introduction," in *Moral Truth and Moral Tradition: Essays in Honor of Peter Geach and Elizabeth Anscombe*, ed. Luke Gormally (Dublin: Four Courts Press, 1994), 1-5. For a complete Anscombe bibliography, see L. Gormally, C. Kietzmann, and J. M. Torralba, "Bibliography of Works by G. E. M. Anscombe (7th version, June 2012), http://www.unav.es/filosofia/jmtorralba/anscombe/G.E.M._Anscombe_Bibliography.htm.

[2] For an example of a collaborative effort by Anscombe and Geach, see G.E.M. Anscombe and Peter Geach, *Three Philosophers* (Ithaca, NY: Cornell University Press, 1961).

twentieth century (*Intention*, 1957), was for all practical purposes what we might call an "intentional Catholic." A disciple of Ludwig Wittgenstein who succeeded him in his chair at Cambridge and who as his translator and one of his literary executors was probably most responsible for making him known in the English-speaking world, she was a serious and devout convert to the Catholic faith. Her conversion to the Catholic faith, her vocation to the lay state, specifically to married and family life, and her profession as a philosopher, were deeply intertwined with the Catholic intellectual tradition. This was a tradition that touched her deeply, shaped her convictions about the nature of truth, and to which she was intensely loyal. It gave her a unique vantage point from which to survey the philosophical problems of her day and served as the backdrop against which she lived out her vocation and conducted her philosophical research. It also propelled her to live out her moral convictions in the public square even when those convictions ran against the tide of public opinion and got her into trouble with legal authorities, as in the case of her arrests for anti-abortion protests in the 1970s.

Like many other well-known converts—John Henry Newman, G.K. Chesterton, Frederick Copleston, Ronald Knox, Jacques Maritain, Dietrich von Hildebrand, Avery Dulles, and Alasdair MacIntyre (to name but a few)—her journey to Catholicism involved a carefully reasoned search for truth which brought her to belief in Jesus Christ as the Son of God and Redeemer of the human race. It also involved a journey of the mind that led to a deep understanding and conviction that the Catholic Church was established by Christ to safeguard the deposit of faith and promulgate the Gospel message throughout history. As a philosopher, she understood the limitations of human reason and did her best to insure that its conclusions were well argued, based on solid evidence, and to the point. She had little patience with poorly constructed arguments (whether for or against the faith) and took them apart with precise reasoning that both went to the core of the problem and pointed the way to a possible resolution. Her famous debate with C.S. Lewis at the Oxford Socratic Club in 1948 about his assertion in the book *Miracles* (1947) that "Naturalism" is self-refuting is a case in point, as was her active and lively participation in Catholic philosophical discussions at the Spode House Conference Center, Straffordshire from 1942-1972.[3]

We cannot speak of the influence of the Catholic intellectual tradition on Anscombe without adverting at some point to her understanding of the lay vocation and its role in the Church's life and mission. The theology of the various states of life within the Church—priestly, religious, and lay—forms a part of this rich intellectual tradition, and we would be remiss to think that Anscombe was unaware of its general contours and how it impacted her vocation within the Church and her profession as a Catholic philosopher. Indeed, it goes without saying that, as an intentional convert to Catholicism who took her faith seriously, she saw her primary responsibility before God as working out her salvation as a married Catholic lay woman by participating in the sacramental life of the Church, being faithful to her duties to her husband and family, and bringing the Gospel into the marketplace of the temporal sphere of life. She understood that the specific vocation of the laity was "to make the Church present and fruitful in those places and circumstances where only through them can it become the salt

---

[3] See G. E. M. Anscombe, "A Reply to Mr. C.S. Lewis's Argument that 'Naturalism' is Self-Refuting," in *The Collected Philosophical Papers of G.E.M. Anscombe*, vol. 2, *Metaphysics and the Philosophy of Mind* (Oxford: Basil Blackwell, 1981), 224-32. See also Alister McGrath, *C.S. Lewis: A Life* (Carol Stream, IL: Tyndale House Publishers, 2013), 250-59; Vincelette, *Recent Catholic Philosophy*, 184.

of the earth."[4] To this end, she used her skills as an analytical philosopher to seek the truth about some of the most basic (and controversial) issues of her day—the purpose of modern moral philosophy, the role of intention in the moral act, the proper use of the principle of double effect, the dignity of the human being, the spirituality of man, the role of the state, the use of contraception, abortion, euthanasia, the just war—to name but a few. In examining these issues, she sought the truth of the matter at hand and, in serving the truth, believed she was breaking open the Wisdom of God and thus participating in the mission of the Church. Her teaching on the Eucharist is a specific instance where she employs it in the service of theology.[5]

Anscombe's Teaching on the Eucharist

In 1974, Anscombe published a pamphlet with the Catholic Truth Society entitled, *On Transubstantiation*.[6] In it, she discusses this Eucharistic doctrine from the perspective of what it means (and does not mean) and how it can be taught. She begins with these words, "It is easiest to tell what transubstan-

---

[4] Second Vatican Council, *Lumen gentium* ("Dogmatic Constitution on the Church," November 21, 1964), no. 33. For an expanded treatment of the vocation of the laity, see John Paul II, *Christifideles laici* ("Post-Synodal Apostolic Exhortation on the Vocation and the Mission of the Lay Faithful in the Church and in the World, December 30, 1988).

[5] For an expanded treatment of Anscombe's contribution to the Catholic intellectual tradition, see Dennis J. Billy, "G. E. M. Anscombe and Catholic Moral Thought," in *G.E.M. Anscombe and the Catholic Intellectual Tradition*, eds., John Mizzoni, Philip Pegan, and Geoffrey Karabin (Aston, PA: Neumann University Press, 2016), 25-48.

[6] G. E. M. Anscombe, "On Transubstantiation," in *The Collected Philosophical Papers of G. E. M. Anscombe*, 3:107-12.

tiation is by saying this: little children should be taught about it as early as possible."7 By this statement, she does not mean to imply that a child can understand the word 'transubstantiation" itself, but only that it can comprehend that something mysterious is taking place at Mass. All that is necessary is for its parent to whisper in the child's ear at the moment of consecration: "Look! Look what the priest is doing...He is saying Jesus' words that change the bread into Jesus' body. Now he's lifting it up. Look! Now bow your head and say 'My Lord and my God,'" and then "Look now he's taken hold of the cup. He's saying the words that change the wine into Jesus' blood. Look up at the cup. Now bow your head and say, 'We believe, we adore your precious blood, O Christ of God.'"8 She goes on to say that the worship we render God at the moment of the consecration contains an implicit belief in the death and resurrection of the Christ. "Thus by this sort of instruction," Anscombe claims, "the little child learns a great deal of the faith. And it learns in the best possible way: as part of an action; as concerning something going on before it; as actually unifying and connecting beliefs, which is clearer and more vivifying than being taught only later, in a classroom perhaps, that we have these beliefs."9 She speaks of teaching little children "both because it is important in itself and because it is the clearest way of bringing out what 'transubstantiation' means.10

The word, transubstantiation, she says, was developed first in Greek and later in Latin translation to convey the idea "that there is a change of what is there, totally into something else. A conversion of one physical reality into another *which already*

---

7 Ibid., 3:107.
8 Ibid.
9 Ibid.
10 Ibid.

exists."[11] It does not refer to a new substance coming out of an already existing one, nor is it like digestion where a person becomes what he or she eats. These are changes in matter, but the word refers to something else: "When one says 'transubstantiation' one is saying exactly what one teaches the child, in teaching it that Christ's words, by the divine power given to the priest who uses them in his place, have changed the bread so that it isn't there any more (nor the stuff of which it is made) but instead there is the body of Christ."[12] Anscombe says that the doctrine does not refer to a "dimensive" way of being in a place (as if the physical dimensions of Christ body could occupy those of the bread of wine), but in a "non-dimensive" way. She says there are other ways of being in a place and uses the example of a thousand pieces of mirror "each of which reflects one whole body, itself much bigger than any of them and itself not dimensively displaced."[13] When applied to the Eucharist, she states: "*That* which the bread has become, the place where we are looking has become (though not dimensive) the place where it is: a place in heaven."[14] Even so, Anscombe says that it would be a mistake to think that the doctrine of transubstantiation could ever be fully understood: "It was perhaps a fault of the old exposition in terms of a distinction between the substance of a thing (supposed to be unascertainable) and its accidents, that this exposition was sometimes offered as if it were supposed to make everything intelligible."[15] An element of mystery will always remain: "When we call something a mystery, we mean that we cannot iron out the difficulties about understanding it and demonstrate once for

---

[11] Ibid., 3:108.
[12] Ibid.
[13] Ibid.
[14] Ibid.
[15] Ibid., 3:108-9.

all that it is perfectly possible."[16]

Anscombe goes on to offer three reasons why we celebrate the Eucharist: (1) he tells us to do so; (2) it is his way of being with us until he comes again; and (3) he wants to nourish us with himself.[17] The first, she claims, is reason enough; the second concerns the doctrine of transubstantiation; the third, for her, "is the greatest mystery of all about the Eucharistic sacrifice, a greater mystery than transubstantiation itself, though it must be an essential part of the significance of transubstantiation."[18] She spends the remainder of her pamphlet exploring this mystery of mysteries. At his Last Supper with his disciples, Jesus was celebrating a Passover meal and, in addition to the traditional Jewish grace, then added the words over the bread, "This is my body," and over the cup of wine "This is my blood." She points out that, of the two types of Jewish sacrifice—the holocaust, in which the whole of the sacrificial victim is destroyed, and the other, in which the people eat the sacrificial victim—Jesus at the Last Supper is enacting the latter: "[H]is first command in his grace saying was to eat; it subsequently emerges that he is making a sacrificial offering and that he is superseding the paschal lamb, assuming its place."[19] Jesus gives his flesh and blood to us as food. On one level, Anscombe claims that what Jesus is doing is clearly symbolic: "we are not physically nourished by Christ's flesh and blood as the Jews were by the paschal lamb."[20] On another level, however, she says that taking part in Holy Communion is more than just a symbolic action (a typically Protestant notion), but that we actually are consuming Jesus, that is to say *"eating*

---

[16] Ibid., 3:109.

[17] Ibid.

[18] Ibid.

[19] Ibid., 3:109-10.

[20] Ibid.

him."[21]

In reflecting on why anyone would want to eat someone's flesh and drink his blood, Anscombe points out that Christians are not like savages who were known to eat the flesh of a brave adversary to acquire his virtue. The eating and drinking of Christ's flesh and blood is a symbol of something deeper, but is unlike other symbolic gestures with clear meanings such as "kissing the feet of the savior" or "binding oneself to him." She delineates the difference in this way: "Certainly this eating and drinking are themselves symbolic. I mean that, whether this is itself literal or is a purely symbolic eating of his flesh and drinking of his blood, that is in turn symbolical of something else. So if we only symbolically (and not really) eat his flesh, our action is the symbol of a symbol. If we literally eat his flesh our action is a direct symbol. The reason why the action is in any case strange and arcane is this: it is not a natural or easily intelligible symbol. How, and what, it symbolizes—that is deeply mysterious."[22]

Anscombe then deals with the concept of "trans-signi-fication, a concept which holds that the "substance" of a thing is the meaning it has in life. Some theologians say this is a better term that "transubstantiation," since bread and wine are not single substances and it would therefore be misleading to speak of a change in substance. She defends transubstantiation in this way: "the bread and wine that are fit to use at Eucharist are defined by the natural kinds they are made from, by wheat and grape."[23] Her main criticism of this "trans-signification," however, is this: "the odd thing, which apparently is not noticed, is that what gets trans-signified in the Eucharist is not the bread and wine, but the body and blood of the Lord, which are trans-

---

[21] Ibid., 3:110.

[22] Ibid., 3:110-11.

[23] Ibid., 3:111.

signified into food and drink. And that is the mystery."[24] When we receive Holy Communion, we eat the body and drink of the blood of Christ and share in the life of God himself. She ends her treatment of the Eucharist with a quotation from St. Augustine: "He gives us his body to make us into his body."[25] The sacrament, for him as well as for her, "effects the unity of the people who join together to celebrate the Eucharist and to receive communion."[26] It is "the mystery of the faith which is the same for the simple and the learned. For they believe the same, and what is grasped by the simple is not better understood by the learned: their service is to clear away the rubbish which the human reason so often throws in the way to create obstacles."[27]

Some Further Insights

Although much more could be said, the above presentation highlights many of the main contours of Anscombe's spiritual outlook and teaching on the Eucharist. If nothing else, it demonstrates that her reflections on the Eucharist are critical, creative, and concise. What follows are some remarks concerning the depth of her insights and their relevance for believers today.

To begin with, Anscombe claims that even a small child is capable of understanding what the Church is teaching through the doctrine of transubstantiation. She employs her analytical method to uncover what we might call the "teaching behind the teaching:" a change of one concrete reality (the bread and wine) into another that already exists (flesh and blood of the Risen

---

[24] Ibid.

[25] Ibid., 3:111-12.

[26] Ibid.

[27] Ibid., 3:112.

Lord). The doctrine, she maintains, unifies and connects beliefs, since it implies belief in the divinity and resurrection of Christ. She reminds us that no formulation of the faith will ever fully be able to explain what takes place.

Anscombe refuses to separate her work as an analytical philosopher from her Catholic belief system. She uses the analytical method to probe many of the doctrinal and moral teachings of the faith in order to deal with the intellectual obstacles the believing community may be facing and so arrive at a deeper understanding of the issue at hand. In the case of the Church's teaching on the Eucharist, she points out both the strengths and weaknesses of terms such as "transubstantiation" and "trans-signification" and goes to the very heart of what takes place at the Eucharist: the change of bread of wine into the body and blood of the Risen Lord.

Anscombe says that one of the weaknesses in the traditional doctrine of transubstantiation is that it sometimes gives the impression of being a comprehensive explanation with no room for development. Although she points out that even classical Aristotelian thought would not consider the notion of transubstantiation tenable, she says that the way the doctrine is sometimes presented deprives the sacrament of its sense of mystery. As a philosopher, she has a very good sense of what human reason can and cannot do. In the case of the Eucharist, she underscores the point that no theological formulation will ever exhaust the mystery of the change that takes place during Mass.

In her analysis of "trans-signification," the idea that what takes place at the consecration is not a change of "substance," but a change in "meaning," she recognizes the difficulty with using the term "substance," since the bread and wine are multiple rather than not single substances. At the same time, she says that the bread and wine fit to be used at Eucharist (there can be no additives) are *defined* by what they are made from: wheat and grape. More importantly, she identifies a weakness in applying the notion of "trans-signification" to the Eucharist, since the transformation of meaning is not that in the bread and wine, but in the body and blood of Christ himself.

Anscombe recognizes that the Eucharist is both a symbol and yet more than a symbol. She points out the weakness in some Protestant understandings of the Eucharist being merely a symbolic eating of the body and blood of Christ. The difficulty with such positions, she maintains, is that the eating and drinking are themselves symbolic, and those who hold this position run the risk of turning the Eucharist into a "symbol of a symbol." For this reason, the Catholic position that communicants consume the *real* flesh of their Savior, Jesus Christ, is more tenable, since it preserves both the mystery and the authentic symbolism of what takes place at Mass.

The purpose of the Eucharist, for Anscombe, is to make us into the body of Christ. While the image of the "body," she maintains, is a metaphor, the unity of life to which the metaphor points is no metaphor, but very much a reality. At Eucharist, Christ gives us his flesh and blood so that we might become one with him by sharing in his very life. When seen in this light, the Eucharist is an expression of our real and authentic union with him and one another. The sacrament, in other words, both symbolizes and effects the unity with Christ of all who gather around the table of the Lord and celebrate the Lord's redeeming love.

Finally, as a Catholic philosopher Anscombe uses reason to explore the meaning of the Catholic doctrine of transubstantiation and come to a deeper understanding of the mystery of the sacrament. She uses reason to explain this teaching in a way that is intelligible and easy to understand and yet also preserves its sense of mystery. In doing so, she is not engaging in apologetics, nor attempting to exhaust the meaning of the sacrament, but simply demonstrating the reasonableness of the

Catholic faith, while at the same time emphasizing that what takes place at the consecration must always be open to further possible formulations. In the end, she recognizes that the sacrament is one of the great mysteries of the faith that belongs to both the simple and the learned.

Conclusion

In a piece for the New York Times marking the tenth anniversary of her death, Mark Oppenheimer described G. E. M. Anscombe as an "outspoken Catholic philosopher," considered by some "the greatest postwar English philosopher, and the greatest female philosopher ever (a superlative she would loathe)," whose "fearless thinking and uncompromising Christian writing" was "enjoying a renaissance." He further asserts that her views "are inseparable from her biography."[28] She was not a philosopher who simply happened to be a Catholic and whose faith had little (if anything) to do with her program of philosophical inquiry. On the contrary, her faith informed her reasoned search for truth, while at the same time enabling her to remain true to the strictest standards of her profession. She herself saw no contradiction between her Catholic faith and analytic philosophy's careful examination of language as a preferred method for doing philosophy.

Anscombe's teaching on the Eucharist is a clear example of her willingness to apply the analytical method to the tenets of her Catholic faith. "Analytical philosophy," she once wrote, "is more characterized by styles of argument and investigation than by doctrinal content. It is thus possible for people of widely different beliefs to be practitioners of this sort of philosophy. It ought not to surprise anyone that a seriously believing Catholic

---

[28] Mark Oppenheimer, "Renaissance for Outspoken Catholic Philosopher" *New York Times*, January 7, 2011.

Christian should also be an analytical philosopher."[29] Rather than being a hindrance to her philosophical endeavors, Anscombe's Catholicism gave her a unique vantage point from which to view the issues at hand, see them in perspective, and identify angles that many of her contemporaries either over-looked or simply could not see. Her explanation of the doctrine of transubstantiation, for example, combines critical analysis and an openness to mystery. It points out the doctrine's strengths and weaknesses, examines critically the alternative explanation of "trans-signification," and focuses on the underlying teaching that the Church is trying to convey: that at the words of consecration the bread and wine become the body and blood of Our Lord Jesus Christ.

Anscombe viewed her role as a Catholic philosopher as clearing away the debris that human reason had often put in the way. She anticipated John Paul II's challenge in *Fides et ratio* "to trust in the power of human reason and not to set themselves goals that are too modest in their philosophizing."[30] She also recognized, as John Paul himself asserts, that "[p]hilosophical thought is often the only ground for understanding and dialogue with those who do not share our faith."[31] She did, in other words, what she knew how to do best: philosophize! She did not see any contradiction between her Catholic faith and her analytical approach to philosophy, but saw them as mutually enriching. If nothing else, her teaching on the Eucharist reminds today's believers of the reasonableness of the Catholic faith and its capacity to withstand the critical gaze of careful

---

[29] G. E. M. Anscombe, "Twenty Opinions Common among Modern Anglo-American Philosophers," in *Faith in a Hard Ground: Essays in Religion, Philosophy and Ethics by G.E.M. Anscombe*, eds. Mary Geach and Luke Gormally (Exeter, UK: Imprint Academic, 2008), 66.

[30] John Paul II, *Fides et ratio*, no. 56.

[31] Ibid., no. 104.

philosophical analysis. It also highlights the limitations of human reason and its inability to fully articulate (let alone exhaust) the sacramental mysteries that touch the very the foundations of the Catholic theological tradition.

Reflection Questions

- Anscombe was a philosopher who used the tools of rational analysis to explore the mysteries of the Catholic faith. How do you view the relationship between faith and reason? How are they compatible? How are they not? Does reason have its limitations when exploring the mysteries of the faith? If so, how do we know when we have reached them?
- Anscombe maintains that even a small child is capable of understanding the basic idea behind the doctrine of transubstantiation. Do you agree that the doctrine is easy to understand? Do you agree with the way Anscombe explains it? Do you agree that the transformation that takes place at the consecration will always remain a mystery and thus can never be fully explained?
- For Anscombe, the purpose of the Eucharist is to make us into the body of Christ. Do you believe that the bread and wine are transformed into Christ's body and blood so that when we receive them we become more deeply incorporated into him? Do you think that this transformation is more than a metaphor? Do you believe that it points to a sharing in his resurrected life that is very much a reality?

Voice Twenty-Six

Jean Corbon:
Fontal Energy

Our next voice comes from one of the Eastern Catholic traditions. Jean Corbon, O.P. (1924-2001) was born in Paris, entered the Dominicans at a young age, and went to the Middle East soon after ordination. He settled in Lebanon in 1959 and became a priest of the Melkite Greek-Catholic eparchy of Beirut. He was a professor of Liturgy at the University of St. Joseph in Beirut and University of the Holy Spirit in Kalik, and the secretary of the commission for ecumenical relations of the Assembly of the Catholic Patriarchs and Bishops of Lebanon. He is most remembered for his modern-day classic on the Liturgy, *Liturgie de Source* (1980), which was translated and published in English as *The Wellspring of Worship* (1988). This book was a major source for the opening liturgical section in Part Two of *Catechism of the Catholic Church* (CCC 1066-1209). His influence is especially evident in the subsection entitled, "The Liturgy: Work of the Holy Trinity" (CCC 1077-1112). He was also the primary author of the fourth section of the *Catechism* on prayer, which he wrote in Beirut in the face of tense political, even violent circumstances. [1]

---

[1] See Cassian Folsom, "The Holy Spirit and the Church in the Liturgy," *Homiletic and Pastoral Review* 96/7(April, 1996): 15-23,

Corbon's Theological Outlook

For Corbon, the Trinity is the ultimate reality and lies at the heart of his of theological vision. All things have their *source* in the Triune God, their *place* in his plan for creation, and their *end* in his heavenly kingdom. The Liturgy, for him, is Trinitarian in scope and must be understood against the backdrop of the whole of salvation history. He sees it as the means chosen by God to pour himself into creation and bring about its transformation.[2]

Corbon believes it is a mistake to limit the Liturgy to the rituals themselves or to think of it as essentially a human activity. Instead, it is a life-giving river with its source in the Heavenly Liturgy continually celebrated by Christ in the presence of the Father. The Church's sacraments are earthly manifestations of this one, continuous, and eternal Liturgy. As a result of his Incarnation, Passion, Death, Resurrection, and Ascension into heaven, Christ has divinized human nature and, through his Holy Spirit, now offers us the opportunity to share in his Divine Sonship. The Liturgy we celebrate is an earthly manifestation of this Heavenly Liturgy. When we celebrate it, our humanity undergoes a gradual process of *theosis* or divinization, which heals our wounds and elevates us to a new level of existence. Through the Liturgy, the Old Adam becomes the New. The wellspring of worship rises up within our hearts and makes us "christs in Christ."[3]

---

http://rumkatkilise.org/corbon.htm; See also the brief biographical note on the back cover of Jean Corbon, *The Wellspring of Worship*, 2nd ed., trans. Matthew J. O'Connell (San Francisco: Ignatius Press, 1988).

[2] See Corbon, *The Wellspring of Worship*, 29-35.

[3] Ibid., 216-23.

For Corbon, the Liturgy represents a movement from mystery to celebration to life. Rooted in the mystery of the Triune God, it is celebrated in heaven and on earth, and manifested in the Church and in the lives of ordinary believers. This movement from mystery to celebration to life is accomplished by a threefold synergy of the Holy Spirit: to manifest Christ to us (*anamnetic* synergy), to transform us into the glorious body of the Lord (*epicletic* synergy) and to bring us into the communion of Christ with the Father (synergy of *communion*). The Liturgy, for him, is all about manifesting Christ, divinizing us, and bringing us into communion with the Father. The purpose of this communion is for God to dwell in us and for us to dwell in God.[4]

Deeply connected with this threefold synergy of the Spirit is the threefold self-emptying (*kenosis*) of God in creation, the incarnational/paschal mysteries, and the liturgical mysteries. God's economic plan of creation, redemption, and sanctification is unified in the single goal of divine and human communion. God creates, becomes human, and undergoes the paschal mystery in order to divinize humanity and bring it into the presence of the Father through Christ by the work of the Spirit. In this way, the historical realism of creation and incarnation leads to the sacramental realism of the Liturgy, and culminates in the mystical realism of *theosis* or divinization.[5] The Eucharist, for Corbon, plays an essential role in this process.

Corbon on the Eucharist

Corbon calls the Eucharist "the 'sacrament of sacraments' in which the body of Christ brings to bear all the energies contained in his transfiguration and 'accomplishes' his mystery

---

[4] Ibid., 100-102.

[5] Ibid., 17-18; 46-51; 216-23.

in the Church."[6] He considers the Holy Spirit the "principal liturgist" for it is he who "enables us to experience the Eucharist as the mysterious symphony of the incarnate Word."[7]

According to Corbon, "the Church celebrates the Eucharist, and the Eucharist 'accomplishes' the Church."[8] The other sacraments are not to be set alongside the Eucharist, but are a way in which the body of Christ grows in maturity and reaches the fullness of communion with the divine. In his mind, "Christ and his Spirit gradually gave them to the Church on the basis of its life, to meet the structural and vital needs of the body as it grew."[9] In this sense, all the sacraments are oriented toward the Eucharist and flow from it.

In the celebration of the Eucharist, Corbon identifies a *prelude*, where the Spirit opens us up to what is to be celebrated; a *liturgy of the Word*, where he shows the Lord who is coming; an *anaphora* (the Eucharistic prayer), where he shows us who is coming; a *communion*, where we receive the Body and Blood of Christ; and a *finale* where everything begins anew.[10] The Holy Spirit is at work throughout the entire process, divinizing us in the body of the Lord and in a transforming union of the human and the divine. It is especially present in the threefold movement of the Liturgy of the Word, the Anaphora and, Holy Communion: "By this threefold influence the Holy Spirit permeates our being and makes us experience Christ, our Passover. He reveals him to us, actualizes him for us, and makes us participate in him."[11] In the first movement, the Father gives us his Word. In the second, Jesus' paschal mystery becomes

---

[6] Ibid., 146.

[7] Ibid.

[8] Ibid., 159.

[9] Ibid., 160.

[10] Ibid., 146.

[11] Ibid., 147.

ours. In the third, the Spirit illumines our eyes of faith.[12]   The
Liturgy thus moves from Word to Presence to Transformation.
The Liturgy of the Word leads to the Liturgy of the Eucharist,
which, in turn, leads to the Liturgy of Life.[13]

The Eucharist, for Corbon, gives us the human face of the
Heavenly Liturgy. It is the supreme celebration of the Church,
one that both establishes the Church and points to its
consummation at the end of time. Its goal is to bring us into a
living union with the Blessed Trinity, that deep communion of
love existing at the very ground of all reality. The celebration of
the Eucharist immerses us in the new creation established by
Christ's paschal mystery; it celebrates not only the transformation of time and space, but also the conversion of the
human heart and the ultimate divinization of the human family.
The Eucharist puts us in touch with the fontal liturgy offered by
Christ in the presence of his Father. It brings heaven to earth
and earth to heaven. In doing so, it pours God's mercy and
compassion into the lives of those who celebrate it.[14]

The Eucharist, in other words, must not only be celebrated,
but also lived. It provides the fontal energy of the Spirit that
enables believers to follow the call of their Master and walk in
his footsteps. It divinizes our human nature, sanctifies our
hearts, and enables us to carry the transforming presence of
Christ in all we do. Nothing escapes its influence: our work, our
community, our culture, our world, all things meet in the glory
of God and find their end in him. The Eucharist is the wellspring
of worship, the wellspring of life, the wellspring of our
transformation in Christ through the power of his Spirit.[15]

---

[12] Ibid., 154.
[13] Ibid., 146-58; 199-205.
[14] Ibid., 62-63; 241-48.
[15] Ibid., 224-48.

Some Further Insights

This brief exposition of Corbon's teaching on the Eucharist focuses on the Holy Spirit's central role in the Liturgy for bringing about humanity's divinization (*theosis*). The following remarks seek to develop some of his key insights into the Liturgy as the "wellspring of worship" and what it means to be other "christs in Christ" and to celebrate "life in the Spirit."

To begin with, Corbon comes from an Eastern rite and represents that second lung of spirituality so important to the Catholic faith. His insights into the Eucharist provide a refreshing counterbalance to the Western theological mindset, which analyzes everything, sometimes to the detriment to the faith and the divine mysteries it seeks to convey. The influence of his thought on the writing of the *Catechism of the Catholic Church* reveals a marked sensitivity to the importance of integrating the Western and Eastern streams of Catholic spirituality so that believers would be able to come to a deeper appreciation of the meaning and purpose of the Liturgy in their lives. The reintegration of these two traditions within the supernatural organism of Christ's body, the Church, enables believers to be more at home in the faith and to experience the Gospel of Christ on an even deeper level of consciousness. From this perspective, the marriage of East and West within Christianity will do much to further the goals of new evangelism of the Church of the new millennium.

Corbon emphasizes the role of mystery in the Divine Liturgy much more than his counterparts in the West. To do so, he brings to the discussion a wealth of vocabulary and liturgical terminology rarely used in the West. His decision to open his book with a liturgical vocabulary or glossary of terms illustrates how foreign this language has become to Western Christian sensitivities and reveals our need to learn it so we too might be able to understand something of the movement of the Spirit in the rituals we celebrate and in the liturgy of worship and praise our lives are called to become. At the same time, Corbon is very conscious of the limitation of words and their inability to capture the totality of the mystery they seek to convey. He understands the power words have to reveal and conceal and knows that, in the end, only the Holy Spirit himself can plumb the depths of the mystery of divine love contained in the Liturgy and reveal God's Word to the Church.

Corbon points out that the Liturgy makes two demands of us: (1) faith and conversion and (2) authenticity of life.[16] These demands are intimately related. The Church's celebration of the Eucharist requires faith and the recognition of our need to grow in it. Faith is a gift and not something we can create or manufacture on our own. God's grace penetrates the human heart and reveals his presence in mysterious ways. When we celebrate the Liturgy, we are brought face-to-face with the weakness of our faith and our need to deepen its influence in our lives. Once we get in touch with our need to grow in faith, we can humbly ask God for the grace to "walk by faith" (2Cor 5:7). To be authentic disciples of Christ, we must come to terms with our present experience of faith, ask God to deepen it, and allow it to flow from the Liturgy into the warp and woof of our daily live. In this way, we gradually come to enjoy an intimate communion with the Holy Spirit and are able to live the Gospel on a deep level of awareness.

Corbon likens the Eucharist to a river of life that flows upon the earth from the eternal Liturgy celebrated in heaven. As such, it is the "wellspring of worship" from which all authentic Christian life and action flow. To experience the full effects of this sacrament, however, we must open their hearts to the movement of Spirit and allow his energies to irrigate our souls with the water of its abundant graces. For this to happen, we

---

[16] Ibid., 129-30.

must identify and pull down whatever obstacles prevent us from receiving the life-giving water of divine grace. We must also recognize that we are incapable of doing so on our own. Only the Spirit can pull down our destructive tendencies and inclinations toward sin. Only he can water the seeds of faith planted deep in our hearts at the moment of our baptism. Only he can transform the human heart and shape it into the dream the Father has for it. For this reason, we must approach the Eucharist with humility and a deep sense of gratitude for the gift of this sacrament and the transformation it promises to bring about in our lives.

For Corbon, the Liturgy consists of much more than the Church's sacramental rituals. The sacraments are earthly manifestations of the one Heavenly Liturgy eternally offered by the risen and glorified Christ in the presence of the Father. They are "masterpieces of creation" that come down from eternity and spill into life itself to form the beginning of the new creation envisioned by God for the world's redemption and sanctification.[17] This wider perspective enables him to affirm the movement from mystery to celebration to life that pervades his entire theological outlook. As the "sacrament of sacraments," the Eucharist reflects the Heavenly Liturgy in a unique way, for the Church, at one and the same time, both celebrates and is established by it. His theological vision is such that, after Christ's ascension to the Father's right hand, everything in space and time has a sacramental dimension to it and is oriented toward the mystical realism of humanity's divinization.

Corbon's understanding of the Eucharist steers clear of the dry forensic legalism characteristic of so much of Western moral teaching. Rather than focusing on our obligations before the law, he focuses on how the Holy Spirit communes with our spirits and empowers us to follow the way of Jesus in a way that

---

[17] Ibid., 137.

is free, spontaneous, and faithful to the New Law of grace given us through Christ's paschal mystery. By drawing a close bond between spirituality and morality, grace and freedom, and liturgy and life, he brings out the deeper currents of the Gospel message that can be easily overlooked and, in some instances, entirely forgotten. The Eucharist, for him, is the center of our lives and is present at both the beginning and the end of our spiritual pilgrimage. When seen in this light, morality is not something added to the Liturgy, but flows from its very heart. The way we worship, in others words, has everything to do with the way we live our lives. Life in the Spirit embraces the moral life and transforms it from a list of laws and obligations to a deep personal and communal embrace of God's will for us as individuals and as a Church.

Finally, for Corbon, the heart of the Eucharist lies in the threefold movement of the Spirit in the liturgy of the Word, the anaphora *(Eucharist Prayer), and communion.* In this process, we listen, remember, and receive as the Spirit celebrates Christ's Pasch and makes it present to us by immersing us in its ineffable mystery. The power of the Eucharist to divinize us comes from the Triune God who creates, redeems, and sanctifies humanity. The Eucharist, for Corbon, exists to give glory and praise to the Father and to divinize us in the process so we might enter into his presence. This mystery of our *theosis* points to the deeper mystery of God's compassionate love and mercy for all humanity. God manifests his love for us by entering our world, giving himself to us to the point of dying for us, to become our nourishment and source of hope. The Eucharist thus plays a central role in this providential plan for our lives. Through it, the risen and glorified Lord enters within us, transforms our humanity by the power of his Spirit, and brings us into the presence of the Father as a new creation.

Although much more can be said about Corbon's teaching on the Eucharist, these brief remarks bring out its central themes and point to their relevance for the faithful following of Christ in today's world. His teaching touches the very heart of Christ's paschal mystery and highlights its relevance for the Christian proclamation for the world today. It demonstrates why the Eucharist is so vital to the Church and its mission and why Catholics should place it at the heart of their spiritual outlook and make it the centerpiece of their life and worship.

Conclusion

Jean Corbon highlights the intimate connection between the heavenly and earthly liturgies, and insists that our celebrations must spill over into and become the liturgy of life. The connections he draws between mystery, celebration, and life lie at the heart of the Church's understanding of the Liturgy and place the sacraments at the very center of its moral and spiritual life. The Liturgy, for him, is an action of the Triune God and the principle means by which he divinizes our humanity and allows us to enter God's presence. As the "wellspring of worship," it's principal purpose is to give honor and glory to God, and its secondary purpose is to make us other "christs in Christ."

According to Corbon, the Holy Spirit operates throughout the Liturgy and acts as its principal celebrant. It does so especially in the Eucharist, which as the "sacrament of sacraments" represents the point at which the divine communes with the human in an intimate fellowship (*koinonia*) of love. The Spirit's divinizing energy is at work in the threefold epiclesis of Word, *Anaphora*, and Communion, and by them manifests the love of the Triune God to those participating. This divine synergy affects us by revealing the Father's Word to us, making Christ's paschal mystery our own, and allowing the Spirit to illumine our faith. As a result, it heals our wounded nature and divinizes it to become part of a new creation in Christ enabling us, like him, to empty ourselves for others in a kenotic expression of selfless love. As a result, the Eucharist does not merely teach us about the spiritual moral life, but empowers us to live it by reconstituting our nature according to the humanity of the risen and glorified Christ.

Corbon's teaching brings many valued insights from the Eastern Christian tradition to our understanding of the Eucharist. By focusing on the power of the Spirit to transform us into other christs, he brings to the sacramental realism of the liturgy the important mystical realism of divinization. The result is a deeper appreciation of the relevance of the Eucharist for our spiritual moral lives and the possibility of living the Gospel on a deep level of awareness. The Eucharist, for Corbon, is meant to penetrate every aspect of our being and to flow into our work, family relations, community, society, and our culture at large. If it is true that "God became human so that humanity might become divine," then, in Corbon's eyes, the Eucharist is the primary means through which the Spirit makes this process of divinization a concrete reality in our lives.

Reflection Questions

- For Corbon, all the sacraments are oriented toward the Eucharist and flow from it. In what sense is the Eucharist the primordial sacrament? Why does it have precedence over all the other sacraments? Why is the Eucharist called the "sacrament of sacraments?"
- For Corbon, the Holy Spirit uses the Eucharist to divinize us through a transforming union of the human and the divine. In what sense is the Eucharist a continuation of the incarnating process of the Word becoming flesh initiated in the person of Christ? In what sense is it not? Does the Eucharist assimilate our humanity into the divinized humanity of Christ? Is this what it means to be a member of the Body of Christ?

- For Corbon, the Eucharist is the wellspring of worship that must not only be celebrated, but also lived. Is the Eucharist the center of your life? Do you allow it to enter into every aspect of your daily existence? Do you allow it to enter at all? What areas of your life are you keeping from God? What areas do you need to let go of and allow God to touch with his gentle transforming power?

Voice Twenty-Seven

Walter Kasper:
Sacrament of Unity

Our next voice has dedicated much of his life to promoting Christian unity. Walter Kasper (1933-) was born in Heidenhein an der Brenz, Germany, and ordained a priest in 1957. After serving two years as a parochial vicar in Stuttgart, he went on to earn a doctorate in dogmatic theology at the University of Tübingen and served on the faculty there at the outset of his academic career. From 1964-1970 he taught dogmatic theology at the Westphalian University of Münster and became dean of the theological faculty both there in 1969 and upon his return to Tübingen in 1970. During this time, he was also the editor of *Lexikon für Theologie und Kirche* and, in 1983, a visiting professor at The Catholic University of America in Washington, D.C. In 1989, he was named bishop of Rottenburg-Stuttgart and in 1994 was named co-chair of the International Commission for Lutheran-Catholic Dialogue. He was appointed President of the Pontifical Council for Christian Unity and also of the Commission for Religious Relations with the Jews in 1999 and made a cardinal by John Paul II in 2001. An active member of The International Theological Commission, his best known theological works include *Jesus the Christ* (1976), *The God of Jesus Christ* (1984), *Theology and Church* (1989), and *That*

They All May Be One: The Call to Unity Today (2004), and *a Celebration of Priestly Ministry* (2007). His view on the Eucharist flows from these works and is best expressed in his book *Sacrament of Unity: The Eucharist and the Church* (2004).[1]

Kasper's Theological Outlook

Kasper has written extensively in the field of systematic theology and throughout his career has sought to present a cohesive vision of the Catholic faith, one rooted in the mystery of the Trinity and its revelatory self-disclosure in the person of Jesus Christ, the unique mediator between God and humanity, who has established the Church as the universal sacrament of salvation, and given us the Eucharist as the means of entering into and maintaining communion with his love.

In his exposition of the doctrine of the Trinity, Kasper maintains "[t]he God of Jesus Christ...is the ultimate, eschatological and definitive determination of the indeterminant

---

[1] Walter Kasper, *Jesus the Christ*, trans. V. Green (London/New York: Burns & Oates/Paulist Press, 1976); Idem, *The God of Jesus Christ*, trans. Matthew J. O'Connell (New York: Crossroad, 1984); Idem, *Theology and Church*, trans. New York: Crossroad, 1989); Idem, *That They May All Be One: The Call to Unity Today* (London/New York: Burns & Oates, 2004); Idem, *Sacrament of Unity: The Eucharist and the Church*, trans. Brian McNeil (New York: Crossroad, 2004); Idem, *A Celebration of Priestly Ministry: Challenge, Renewal, and Joy in the Catholic Priesthood*, trans. Brian McNeil (New York: Crossroad, 2007) [Note: The original German editions of these works normally appeared one or two years before their English translations]. For the major details of Kasper's life, see the website of the Holy See. See also the Catholic-pages Internet site: http://www.catholic-pages.com/hierarchy/cardinals_bio.asp?ref =167.

openness of man."[2] The Christian God, in this respect, is both the origin of our deepest yearnings and desires and the goal toward which they tend. The intimate community of divine persons—Father, Son, and Spirit—pours itself out in creation and draws its creation back to itself. Humanity was created by God out of love and seeks to return to the source from which it came. Kasper believes that the proclamation of the Triune God is of the greatest pastoral importance in today's world, for it represents the fulfillment of humanity's deepest dreams and aspirations, and provides an answer to the situation created by modern atheism.[3]

This pastoral importance is rooted in the Christian conviction "...that there is only one instance in history where the Spirit found acceptance in a unique way, totally, undistorted and untarnished—in Jesus Christ."[4] For this reason: "Light falls from Jesus Christ on the rest of history.... Only through him and in him is it possible to share in the complete fullness of the Spirit."[5] The universal activity of the Spirit culminates in his paschal mystery and, in the course of history, has been "sublated" in his body, the Church, which draws its very life and being from Christ.[6] For Kasper, the mystery of the Trinity has revealed itself fully, uniquely, and totally in the Spirit-filled Christ, and continues its creative, redemptive, and sanctifying mission throughout history in the mystery of his body, the Church.

Kasper's understanding of the Church flows from his understanding of Christ: "Jesus Christ alone is the primal sacrament: the church is a sacrament only 'in Christ;' and that

---

[2] Kasper, *The God of Jesus Christ*, 315

[3] Ibid., 315-16.

[4] Kasper, *Jesus the Christ*, 267

[5] Ibid.

[6] Ibid.

means that it is a sign and an instrument, both of which by definition point beyond themselves. The Church is the sign which points beyond itself to Jesus Christ, and it is an instrument in the end of Jesus Christ, since he is the real author of all saving activity in the church."[7] For Kasper, Christ is the head of his body, the Church, and cannot be separated from it. The universal sacrament of salvation cannot exist apart from the primal sacrament of salvation. His teaching on the Eucharist flows from these fundamental theological insights.

Kasper's Teaching on the Eucharist

Kasper believes "the mystery of Jesus Christ can only be understood as a revelation of the Trinitarian mystery; and the same is true for the Eucharist."[8] The sacrament, in his mind, "...is directed toward the Father, the source and origin of all being, and of the whole of salvation; in thanksgiving, the church also receives in the Eucharist the unique gift of God to human beings, his communication of himself in Jesus Christ, so as to be joined with him in innermost communion."[9] What is more, "both movements...take place in the power of the Holy Spirit, who also prepares us for fellowship with Christ and allows this fellowship to become fruitful Christian living."[10]

Belief in the Trinity and the celebration of the sacrament are thus intimately related: "the Eucharist is *the sacramental summing up* of that mystery (the Trinity). Both in their different ways are a 'symbol'—both creed and emblem—of the one mystery of God's salvation through Jesus Christ in the Holy

---

[7] Kasper, *Theology and Church*, 116.
[8] Ibid., 194.
[9] Ibid.
[10] Ibid.

Spirit."[11] When seen in this light, an authentic Eucharistic spirituality "would have to be the most intimate unity of receiving and giving, contemplation and action. It would have to be strong enough to overcome the disastrous antitheses and conflicts in the present life of the church, conflicts which actually threaten the understanding and practice of the Eucharist itself. It would have to enable us to understand as a single unity the gathering for worship *and* the sending forth into the world of that gathered congregation."[12]

Kasper points out that table fellowship lies at the very heart of this Eucharistic spirituality and that, even today, believers recognize Jesus as he accompanies them on the road and reveals himself to them in the breaking of the bread. This presence is the Risen Lord himself who has undergone death, been raised by the Father, and imparts his Spirit to the community of believers. When seen in this light, Jesus' paschal mystery is intimately related to the Eucharistic mystery—and vice versa. When they gather at the table of the Lord, Christians are immersed in his paschal mystery. There, at their celebration of table fellowship, the Lord quenches their hunger for life by giving them his body and blood as food for eternal life.[13]

The Eucharist, in this respect, is the "sacrament of unity," for through it God descends into our world, unites himself to the members of his body, the Church, and dwells within them. The Eucharist, for Kasper is a living memorial of the Christ event which immerses the believing community in the sacrifice of Golgotha, points it to empty tomb of Easter morning, and offers to those who receive it the intimate communion of love of the Father, Son, and Spirit. As such, it is a foretaste of the heavenly banquet and an eschatological sign of the transformation of

---

[11] Ibid.

[12] Ibid.

[13] Kasper, *Sacrament of Unity*, 38-56.

creation into the fullness of God's kingdom. "The Eucharist," in his mind, "makes present and synthesizes the entire mystery of salvation in a sacramental manner."[14] It exists as sacrifice for the unity of the Church: "If we were to abandon the sacrificial character of the Eucharist and its intimate link to the cross, we would also lose the seriousness which is inherent in its character as a fellowship meal. Eucharistic community means community under the cross."[15] Kasper accentuates the intimate connection between the Eucharist and the Church and says the sacrament must therefore lie at the heart of the Church's efforts for genuine unity and authentic apostolic mission. He insists *ubi eucharistia, ibi ecclesia* ("Wherever the Eucharist is celebrated, there is the church").[16] "The Church," in his mind, "is not something we 'make' and 'organize.' It is the Eucharist that makes the church, just as it is the church that celebrates the Eucharist."[17] In celebrating this sacrament, moreover, priests are called to embrace a Eucharistic existence and be ministers of unity.[18]

Some Further Insights

This brief exposition of Kasper's teaching on the Eucharist highlights how the unity of the Church reflects the intimate love the Trinity and how the fellowship of believers is rooted in the mystery of the cross and the Risen Lord's presence to them in the breaking of the bread. The following observations highlight some of the spiritual underpinnings of his view of the Eucharist as the "sacrament of unity" and its relevance for today's

---

[14] Ibid., 113.
[15] Ibid., 132.
[16] Ibid., 139.
[17] Ibid., 139.
[18] See Kasper, *A Celebration of Priestly Ministry*, 143-75.

Catholics.

To begin with, Kasper's presentation of the Eucharist flows from his understanding of the mysteries of the Trinity, Jesus Christ, and the Church. His Trinitarian theology, Christology, and Ecclesiology are intimately related and overflow into his understanding of the Eucharist as the "sacrament of unity." At the center of his theology is the insight that an intimate communion of love (*communio*) underlies all of reality and rests in the very heart of God himself.[19] This intimate love of Father, Son, and Spirit pertains not only to God's inner relationships but also to his outer (or economic) relationships with his creation as manifested in the threefold work of creation, redemption, and sanctification. When seen in this light, the Eucharist is the "sacrament of unity," because it establishes this intimate communion of love in the new creation (as an eschatological sign), in the redeeming action of Christ (as a real, albeit sacramental, representation), and in the sanctifying work of the Spirit (as a concrete expression of God's transforming and divinizing love). The Eucharist thus brings the creative, redemptive, and sanctifying work of the Trinity to the believing community and empowers it to carry on Christ's evangelizing mission in the world.

Kasper points out that we recognize Jesus in the "breaking of the bread" even today, especially when we gather at Mass for Sunday worship. The experience of Emmaus in the testimony of the Church tells us that Jesus not only accompanies us often unrecognized during our sojourn through life, but also reveals himself to us as the Risen Lord in the breaking of the bread. This recognition deepens our commitment to build up the community of faith and to give witness to his love in our

---

[19] For Kasper, the concept of *communio* also lies at the heart of the Church's ecumenical efforts. See Kasper, *That They May All Be One*, 50-74.

own lives. As the disciples recognized him when they broke bread at table together at Emmaus, the believing community proclaims Christ's presence in their midst whenever they gather to offer this sacrifice of praise and thanksgiving to God the Father, through Christ, and in the Spirit. In doing so, their hearts burn within them as they read the Scriptures and interpret them in the light of his paschal mystery. What is more, the sacrament deepens their commitment to life in community and confirms their conviction that they never walk alone but that Christ is always with them, both walking beside them and being present to them in the deepest recesses of their hearts.[20]

Kasper maintains that the Eucharist "makes present and synthesizes the entire mystery of salvation in a sacramental manner."[21] For this reason, the sacrament lies at the very heart of the Church and its Gospel proclamation of Christ coming to redeem the world and make all things new. The Eucharist, in his mind, constitutes the Church and is constituted by it. The sacrament exists for the Church—and vice versa. By immersing itself in Eucharistic worship, the believing community renders glory and praise to the Father, is renewed interiorly so that it may deepen its relationship to Christ and his Spirit, and is empowered to go out and make disciples of all men by living out in their lives the Gospel of love. As a summary of Christ's salvific message, it brings together the mysteries of the Trinity, the Incarnation, Christ's passion, death and resurrection, and the Church and, in doing so, offers believers a concrete way of affirming their love for God and actually participating in the communion of love that overflows in the mission of love. In this respect, the Eucharist is not only the "sacrament of unity," but also the "sacrament of communion" and the "sacrament of mission."

---

[20] See Kasper, *Sacrament of Unity*,
[21] Kasper, *Theology and Church*, 194.

If, as Kasper claims, Christ is the "primal sacrament" and the Church, the "universal sacrament of salvation," then the Eucharist is the basic means by which the community of believers gains access to these saving mysteries in the concrete circumstances of their everyday lives. It is through the Church and its sacraments that Christ sheds light on the rest of history and brings about its transformation along with the rest of creation. As the preeminent sacrament of the Church, the Eucharist plays a special role in the world's ongoing redemption, for it makes the Christ-event present within the ordinary confines of space and time and, in doing so, gives those who participate in it the opportunity to cross over into the threshold of eternity and receive the divinity into their very selves. In this sense, the Eucharist is the "sacrament of unity" because of the communion it brings about between God and man, the human and the divine. Rooted in the intimate *communio* of divine love, this unity empowers the community of believers to extend its circle of love to others and build up the kingdom of God.

Like the wood of the cross itself, the Eucharist, as the "sacrament of unity," has both vertical and horizontal dimensions which, although not identical, are themselves intimately related. The upright dimension is the unity the sacrament brings about between God and man; the horizontal, the unity it effects among the community of believers and, from them, outward towards others and humanity at large. The point of intersection is Jesus Christ himself, who has embraced our humanity and taken it into the presence of the Father. The Eucharist, in other words, is a celebration of both God and humanity, of Jesus, the God-Man, and of the Church, in its divinized humanity. It brings together our yearning for transcendence and our desire to live in peace with one another. What it more, it affirms without any hesitation that such peace is not possible apart from Christ and that to achieve it, one must embrace the sacrifice of the cross and walk with it along the path of discipleship. When seen in this light, the Eucharist, as the "sacrament of unity" is also the "sacrament of discipleship" and the "sacrament of the cross."

Kasper also points out that the Eucharist is not an individual act of worship, but a celebration of the community of believers. This communal dimension flows from the very source of the God himself who, as an intimate community of love, sustains the uniqueness of each of the Divine Persons, while at the same time maintaining the divine *communio* of the Father, Son, and Spirit. Because the Eucharist reflects this intimate communion of divine love, it seeks to maintain a balance in the community of believers between the common welfare of the Church and the dignity of the human person. It seeks, in other words, to avoid the extremes of excessive individualism and collectivism by maintaining a delicate balance between the identity of the person and the identity of the community. This delicate balance should be reflected not only in the theology of the sacrament itself, but also in the way it is explained to believers, and especially in the way it is celebrated. The Eucharist, in other words, is not a private devotion but an act of worship of the community as a whole (both local and universal) that includes the various needs of the individuals gathered there. The extent to which the celebrating community maintains this delicate balance in its liturgical life says a great deal about the depth of its understanding of the underlying mystery from which it flows.

Finally, the eschatological focus of the Eucharist orients the entire believing community toward the heavenly banquet and gives it a foretaste of it in their breaking of the bread. This foretaste is rooted in the experience of faith and blesses the community with the hope that God's love abides in it and will not abandon it during its earthly sojourn. When seen in this light, the sacrament is a celebration of faith that makes love possible in the present moment and promises to carry the community of believers into the very heart of God himself. This eschatological orientation of the community of believers enables it to view things in their proper perspective and to live their lives according to the values of the kingdom. These values are rooted in the life of the Spirit and give a witness to an unbelieving world of the community's hope in the beyond and its willingness to both live and die for its coming. As such, the community itself becomes a eucharistic foretaste of the coming of the kingdom and the values it seeks to promote.

Although these observations do not exhaust Kasper's teaching on the Eucharist, they convey its major contours and demonstrate the important role it plays as a force of unity in the community of believers (both Catholic and non-Catholic) and in the entire human community. Among other things, they demonstrate the intimate *communio* that flows from the Trinity itself to Jesus, our Incarnate Lord, to his body, the Church, and those who gather for Eucharist. They also affirm Jesus' real presence and sacrificial offering in the breaking of the bread and the passing of the cup that takes place at the celebration of every Eucharistic banquet.

Conclusion

Walter Kasper is one of the most profound Catholic thinkers of his generation and has dedicated his life to the exploring the mystery of *communio* as it exists in the mystery of the Trinity, God's self-revelation in the person of Jesus Christ, the universal sacrament of salvation of the Church, and especially in the "sacrament of unity" known as Eucharist. Because of his deep love for the Church, he has also striven throughout his life to promote the cause of Christian unity and, as a result, has become a prominent voice in ecumenical dialogue at the highest levels.

Kasper's teaching on the Eucharist flows from his understanding of the intimate communion (*communio*) of love existing in the very heart of the Godhead and flowing into the visible world though his creative, redemptive, and sanctifying actions. This *communio* exists in Jesus' intimate relationship with the Father, is imparted to the community of believers through the sending of the Holy Spirit at Pentecost, pours into the confines of space and time at the celebration of the Eucharist, is the guiding concept in Catholic ecumenical theology, and forms the basis of what Kasper calls "spiritual ecumenism."[22] For Kasper, the Eucharist is the sacramental summing up of the mystery of the Trinity and represents the origin and source, the beginning and end, of the entire Christian sojourn. It both constitutes the Church and is constituted by it. It brings the divinizing power of Christ's sacrificial death on the cross into our midst and points to a world beyond the grave and a transformed existence rooted in the intimate communion of the Godhead.

For Kasper, the Church is most itself at the celebration of the Eucharist. This celebration represents all that the Gospel stands for and all that the Church exists for. Without it, the Church would not exist; with it, the Church not only exists, but is also empowered to bear the sufferings of the world upon its shoulders until the end of time. This eschatological orientation of the sacrament enables the faithful to savor the past, live in the present, and yearn for the coming of the new creation and ultimate consummation of all things in Christ. As a foretaste of the heavenly banquet, the Eucharist inspires the members of the believing community to forge bonds of loving communion with those around them. In doing so, it helps to build God's kingdom on earth and looks forward to the time when the communion of divine love has fully taken root in the hearts of men. Until that

---

[22] See Kasper, *That They May All Be One*, 50-74, 155-72.

time, the Church continues its earthly sojourn and seeks to remain faithful to the Gospel message proclaimed by Christ and his Church. As an action of Christ, this "sacrament of unity" continues to forge bonds of friendship with all who listen to the Word of God as it is proclaimed from the pulpit, sacrificed at the altar, and planted in the depths of the human heart.

Reflection Questions

- Kasper maintains that the mystery of the Eucharist must be understood as a revelation of the mystery of the Trinity. What roles do the Father, Son, and Holy Spirit play in the celebration of the Eucharist? What role do you play in it? In what sense does the mystery of the Eucharist give us access to the unity within the Trinity?

- According to Kasper, the Eucharist "makes present and synthesizes the entire mystery of salvation in a sacramental manner." How would you describe the "mystery of salvation?" What does Kasper mean by a "sacramental manner?" What are the benefits of our gaining such access to this mystery of salvation? What does it mean for you?

- Kasper emphasizes both the communal and the eschatological nature of the Eucharist. Do you consider the sacrament an action of the Whole Church, or as a time for private worship? In what sense does the sacrament orient us toward the heavenly? Who is present at this banquet?

Voice Twenty-Eight

Josef Ratzinger (Pope Benedict XVI): Sacrament of Charity

Our final voice stands out as a learned theologian and a wise, discerning pope. Joseph Ratzinger (1927-) was born at Marktl am Inn in the diocese of Passau, Germany on April 16, 1927. Ordained in 1951, he taught fundamental and dogmatic theology at various German universities from 1952-1977, was consecrated Archbishop of Munich and Freising in 1977, made cardinal in the same year, and served as Prefect of the Congregation for the Doctrine of the Faith and President of the Pontifical Biblical Commission and of the International Theological Commission from 1981-2005. Elected Pope on April 19, 2005, he took the name Benedict XVI and spent his pontificate reinforcing the fundamental truths of the Catholic faith and emphasizing the need for a new evangelization in the face of secularism and religious oppression. He announced his resignation nearly eight years later on February 11, 2013, becoming the first pope to do so in nearly six centuries. His teaching on the Eucharist appears in many of his writings, but is the main focus of his attention in *Sacramentum Caritatis* (2007), his Apostolic Exhortation on the Eucharist as the source and summit of the Church's life and mission.[1]

Sacramentum Caritatis

In the Introduction to his exhortation, Benedict calls the Eucharist the "sacrament of charity" through which the Lord "becomes our companion along the way" (nos. 1-2). He says the Holy Spirit has guided the Church throughout its history in an "orderly development of the ritual forms" through which she commemorates the saving event of Christ's paschal mystery (no. 3). The Year of the Eucharist (October 2004-October 2005), which began during the reign of Pope John Paul II and ended in the early months of his own pontificate, was the occasion for his writing this apostolic exhortation. More specifically, it is a response to the XI Synodal Assembly, which took up the theme of the Eucharist at the close of that Year. His purpose in writing the exhortation is "to take up the richness and variety of the reflections and proposals which emerged from the recent *Ordinary General Assembly of the Synod of Bishops*...and to offer some basic directions aimed at a renewed commitment to Eucharistic enthusiasm and fervor in the Church" (no. 5). He also wishes to encourage "the Christian people to deepen their understanding of the relationship between the Eucharistic mystery, the liturgical action, and the new spiritual worship which derives from the Eucharist as the sacrament of charity" (no. 5).

Benedict divides his exhortation on the Eucharist into three parts. In the first, *The Eucharist, A Mystery to Be Believed*, he brings out the Trinitarian (nos.7-8), Christological (nos. 9-11),

---

[1] Both Benedict XVI's biography and the text of *Sacramentum caritatis* ("Apostolic Exhortation on the Eucharist as the Source and Summit of the Christian Life," February 22, 2007) can be found on the website of the Holy See (See Acknowledgments page).

Pneumatological (nos. 12-13), Ecclesiological (nos. 14-15), Sacramental (nos. 16-29), Eschatological (nos. 30-32), and Mariological (no. 33) dimensions of this great mystery of faith. In doing so, he provides a sound doctrinal basis for the sacrament and enables his readers to see its ramifications for the Church's entire belief system. Among other things this important doctrinal context presents the Eucharist as "a free gift of the Trinity" (no. 8), a manifestation of "the new and eternal covenant of the blood of the Lamb" (no. 9), which through the power of the Spirit sanctifies and completely transforms bread and wine into the body and blood of Christ (no. 13). It also presents the Eucharist as the causal principle of the Church and ecclesial communion (nos. 14-15), the end of all the sacraments and ecclesial ministries of the Church (no. 16), a foreshadowing of the messianic banquet (no. 31), and the embodiment of Christian life as seen in the life of the Blessed Virgin Mary (no. 33). In this section of the exhortation, the pope devotes most of his time relating the Eucharist to the other sacraments (nos. 16-29). He places the Eucharist at the center of the whole initiation process (no. 18), sees an intrinsic relationship between it and the sacrament of Reconciliation (no. 20), draws a connection between its healing power and the Anointing of the Sick (no. 22), and emphasizes its deep significance for the vocational sacraments of ordination (no. 23) and marriage (no. 27). The centrality of the Eucharist for the life of the Church, he maintains, stems from the Church's identity as the "universal sacrament of salvation" (no. 16).

In the second part, *The Eucharist, A Mystery to Be Celebrated*, Pope Benedict emphasizes the important role played by the liturgy in the sacramental life of the Church, especially in the Eucharist. He uses the theological principle of *lex orandi, lex credendi* to point out the intrinsic unity of the Church's faith and worship (no. 34) and shows how both converge in the liturgical category of beauty (no. 35). "The 'subject' of the liturgy's intrinsic beauty," he maintains, "is Christ himself, risen and glorified in the Holy Spirit, who includes the Church in his work" (no. 36). For this reason, the Eucharistic celebration is the work of *"Christus Totus,"* including the head and all the members of his body (no. 36). Since the Eucharistic celebration is essentially an action of God who manifests the presence of the Risen Lord to the believing community, its basic structure is not subject to change (no. 37). He stresses "the need to avoid any antithesis between the *ars celebrandi* (the art of proper celebration) and the full, active and fruitful participation of all the faithful" (no. 38). He goes on to identify the bishop as the celebrant par excellence (no. 39), to call for a respectful use and selection of liturgical books, art, and song (nos. 40-42), and to examine the structure of the Eucharistic celebration (nos. 43-51). He spends a considerable amount of time looking at the question of authentic participation, treating such subjects as priestly ministry, incul- turation, necessary personal requisites, ecumenical sharing, the media, care for the sick, prisoners, and migrants, large-scale celebrations, the use of Latin, and the celebration of the Eucharist in small groups (nos. 53-63). In all of these considerations, he insists on a proper interior participation in the celebration (nos. 64-65) and emphasizes the important link between the celebration and Eucharistic adoration (nos. 66-69).

In the third part, *The Eucharist, a Mystery to Be Lived*, Pope Benedict focuses on the intrinsic relationship between the Eucharist and Christian living. He points out that, when we eat and drink Christ's body and blood, "[i]t is not the eucharistic food that is changed into us, but rather we who are mysteriously transformed by it" (no. 70). This "new worship includes and transfigures every aspect of life"(no. 71). For this reason, the Christian life has an intrinsically Eucharistic aspect to it, one that encompasses every dimension of human existence: the physical, emotional, intellectual, spiritual and social (no. 71). He emphasizes the importance of living the Sunday obligation (no. 73) and underscores the relationship between the Eucharistic celebration and the Sabbath day of rest (no. 74). In developing the link between spirituality and Eucharistic culture, he points out the importance of the Eucharist for the evangelization of cultures, vocations to the priestly, consecrated, and lay states, and its role in the moral transformation of the faithful (nos. 77-83). What is more, he emphasizes the importance of "eucharistic consistency" in the private and public spheres of life and points out the need for politicians and public officials to form their consciences and make decisions based upon the values inherent in the sacrament (no. 83). To this end, he points out that the Church in its mission, witness, life, and worship breaks bread for the life of the world (nos. 84-88) and seeks to promote through its social teaching "the sanctification of the word and the protection of creation" (nos. 91-92). To further these ends, he has directed the appropriate offices of the Roman Curia to publish a Eucharistic Compendium that will encourage believers to make their Eucharistic celebration the center of their lives and a true act of spiritual worship (no. 93). In his concluding paragraphs, Pope Benedict reminds his readers that "the Eucharist is at the root of every form of holiness" and points to the many saints who advanced in the way perfection through their deep Eucharistic devotion (no. 94). He closes his exhortation by asking for the intercession of Mary, the Immaculate Virgin who, as the ark of the new and eternal covenant, is seen by the Church as the "Woman of the Eucharist" (no. 96).

Some Further Insights

Despite its brevity and schematic nature, the above presentation of Pope Benedict's apostolic exhortation, *Sacramentum Caritatis*, covers the main contours of his teaching on the sacrament and the comprehensive character of his approach. The following insights seek to probe his teaching in more detail and offer some points of departure for a continuing discussion on the role of the Eucharist in the life and worship of the church.

To begin with, an examination of the structure of the exhortation sees a movement from belief (Part One) to worship (Part Two) and then to action (Part Three). From the perspective of size, the document also shows that Benedict spends twenty-six paragraphs dealing with belief, thirty-five with worship, and twenty-three with action. Taken together, these two insights indicate that the second part is the centerpiece of the entire work, with the first part providing the theological context for the Eucharistic celebration and the third, its moral ramifications. This centrality of worship for understanding the nature of the Eucharist and its influence on Christian faith and action adds a new dimension to the *lex orandi, lex credendi* principle mentioned by Benedict in no. 34. The law of prayer is not only the law of faith, but also the law of action, *lex vivendi*. As the central act of Christian worship, the celebration of the Eucharist is presented as a divinely inspired action that guides the Church in its teaching and practice of faith and morals.

The intimate relationship between faith, worship, and action converges in what Pope Benedict calls the liturgical category of beauty (no. 35), which is manifested in the ars celebrandi, *or art of celebrating (no. 38).* Because the Eucharist is "a radiant expression of the paschal mystery" (no. 35), it must be celebrated in a dignified and orderly fashion and in a way that is worthy of its divine origins. For this reason, every aspect of the liturgical celebration must be prepared for with care and approached with the proper interior dispositions on the part of both the priest and faithful. Since the Eucharist is the means by which "we contemplate beauty and splendor at their source" (no. 35), those who share in it must be willing to enter into its mystery and allow it to penetrate every aspect of their lives, especially in what they profess and in how they conduct themselves. In this respect, the "Beauty of the Eucharist," is a dynamic, living presence that seeks to transform the minds and hearts of those who celebrate it.

The intimate relationship between spirituality and morality also shines through in Benedict's exhortation. Rather than containing a tension or, in some instances, even a sharp divide between what it means to be a spiritual person and an ethical one, the Eucharist presents Catholic spirituality and morality as inextricably connected. For Catholics, it is impossible to be a truly spiritual person without being ethical—and vice versa. This is so because the Eucharist is the causal principle of the Church and the spiritual and moral values it generates are meant to embrace not only the whole of human existence, but the whole of creation. The Eucharist transforms the moral sense and, through the presence of the Risen Lord in our lives and the power of His Spirit, enables us to live up to it. Without it, we have little, if any hope, of responding fully to our call of being sons and daughters of God. That is not to say that natural law and the moral sense it instills in each person is not operative in all people, but only that without the grace available to us through the Eucharist and the other sacraments it is impossible for us to live up to all the standards of the moral law.

The purpose of the Eucharist is to bring about a transformation in the lives of those who share in it. As Benedict so eloquently reminds his readers, unlike ordinary food, it does not become a part of us, but we are changed into it (no. 70). As a result of our participation in the celebration of the Eucharist, and especially through our sharing in Christ's body and blood, we realize our baptismal promises as living members of his body, the Church, and become more deeply immersed in his paschal mystery. This transformation embraces the whole of human existence and has repercussions for all creation. For this reason, the Eucharist cannot be relegated to a merely private affair or thought of as something peripheral or accidental to the faith, but lies at the very heart of what it means to be a follower of Christ. On the contrary, the Eucharist is the gift par excellence of Christ to his Church for, through the power of his Spirit, it provides the daily sustenance for her to live out her prophetic mission to the world.

In his exhortation, Pope Benedict points out that the Eucharist constitutes the Church in both her being and action (no. 15). As such, it is the principle of unity that gives the followers of Christ their unique identity. This "mystery of communion" (no. 15) enables the Church to bring together people of diverse races and cultural backgrounds around the table of unity, while at the same time seeking to inculturate Christ's message throughout the world and preserve in local cultures whatever is consistent with authentic Gospel values. For this reason, the Eucharist lies at the heart of the fellowship (*koinonía*) present in the Church since her origins and provides the impetus for the "spirituality of communion" with which it seeks to draw all peoples to Christ's embrace. As the pope points out, "Christian antiquity used the same words, *Corpus Christi* to designate Christ's body born of the Virgin Mary, the eucharistic body and his ecclesial body" (no. 15). This close connection between the historical Jesus, the Eucharist, and Christ's mystical body lies at the heart of the ecclesial concept of *communion* and the call to discipleship.

This ecclesial communion, the pope points out, is reflected in the very structure and makeup of the Eucharistic celebration itself and should be one of the major values upheld by and sustained by the ars celebrandi. The pope asserts that there is "an inherent unity in the rite of the Mass" and that "[t]he liturgy of the word and the Eucharistic liturgy, with the rites of introduction and conclusion 'are so closely interconnected that they form but one single act of worship'" (no. 44). This "inherent unity" in the very order of the Mass is a reflection of the order that exists within the body of Christ, the Church. In accordance with one's state in life and ministry in the life of the Church, each person participating in the Mass has an important role to fulfill in making the celebration a true act of spiritual worship. The dignity with which we celebrate the Eucharist reflects the dignity of our status as sons and daughters of God, our anticipation of the messianic banquet, and the unique role we place in the coming of the kingdom.

Finally, the "inherent unity" of the Eucharist not only reflects the Church's koinonía and its place in God's kingdom, but also her transforming mission to the world. As God's Spirit hovered over the face of the waters to bring order out of chaos at the time of the first creation, it now works through the Church to sow the seeds of love in a world overrun with hatred to bring about a new creation. This creative action is a divine action made manifest through the work of human hands. As members of Christ's body, the Church, we are called to do our part establishing God's kingdom on earth. The success of this creative process is assured by Christ's victory over death and is hastened by our willingness to cooperate with his divine plan. We cooperate with God's plan to the extent that we work together to establish peace and justice in the world. In this respect, the Church's teaching on peace and social justice is intimately related to its Eucharistic life and mission.

Although these insights in no way exhaust the theological richness of the exhortation, they do reveal some of the pope's deepest concerns about the Eucharist and show how central it is to the Catholic tradition. Through this document, the pope wishes to renew the "eucharistic wonder" of the faithful and show how it is "the efficacious sign of the infinite beauty of the holy mystery of God" (no. 97).

Conclusion

Although Pope Benedict XVI's teaching on the Eucharist appears elsewhere in his magisterial writings,[2] its presentation in *Sacramentum Caritatis* is the most comprehensive treatment he offered during his pontificate. Based on the insights garnered from the Eleventh Ordinary General Assembly of the Synod of Bishops, it seeks to point out a way for a renewal of Eucharistic fervor and devotion in the Church. It does so by looking to doctrinal, liturgical, spiritual, and moral bases of authentic Eucharistic worship.

One of the keys to understanding Benedict's teaching is the theological and liturgical category of *communio*, the notion that the sacrament constitutes the Church and sustains its communion with Christ, the believing community, and all humanity. This deep bond of unity overflows into a deep sense of mission, one that reflects the creative, redemptive, and sanctifying mission of the Holy Trinity. For this reason, the "spirituality of communion" lies at the heart of Benedict's teaching and offers the faithful a solid grounding for a renewal of enthusiasm for and devotion to the sacrament.

The Eucharist, for Benedict is "the food of truth" and the means God chose to become "our companion along the way." It is the "sacrament of charity," which reveals not only the true meaning of love as embodied in Christ's sacrificial death on Calvary, but also a way of being thoroughly transformed by this love. It is a work of God that empowers us to love as Christ loved and to be loved as Christ was and is loved by the Father. It is the "mystery of faith" at the very heart of the Church's identity and

---

[2] See, for example, the encyclical *Deus Caritas Est* in The Holy See *http://www.vatican.va/holy_father/benedict_xvi/biography/doc uments/hf_ben-xvi_bio_20050419_short-biography_en.html*.

mission of bringing Christ to others. It is a mystery to be proclaimed, a mystery to be lived, and a mystery to be offered for the world's salvation.

Reflection Questions

- Benedict maintains that the purpose of the Eucharist is to bring about a transformation in the lives of those who share in it. Is this always the case? If not, why not? Have you found your participation in the Eucharist transformative? If so, in what ways?

- Benedict maintains that the Eucharist constitutes the Church in both her being and action. In what sense does the life of the Church flow from the Eucharist? Can the Church exist without the sacrament? Can you? Have you found that your participation in the Eucharist empowers you to live the Gospel?

- According to Benedict, the "inherent unity" of the Eucharist reflects both the unity of the Church and its transforming mission in the world. In what sense is the Church's mission a call to build bonds of unity in the world? What impact has this call had on your own life? In what ways have you built unity within your family, community, society, and the larger world around you?

Conclusion

The Eucharist is a sacrament of beauty, mystery, and meaning. Its beauty both attracts and transforms. It leads us into the mystery of God, the Church, and our very selves. It reveals to us the meaning of who we are and the world in which we find ourselves. Most of all, it shows us the face of Christ and invites us to share in his passion, death, and resurrected life. In the words of the Apostle Paul, "I have been crucified with Christ, and it is no longer I who live, but it is Christ who lives in me" (Gal 2:20).

The authors presented in this volume encountered the sacramental Christ and saw in him not a faded memory of his earthly past, but the transforming presence of his risen and glorified existence. In this encounter, they sought to understand the meaning of the sacrament instituted by Christ the night before he died, when he broke bread with his disciples and passed around a cup of wine saying, "This is my body...This is the chalice of my blood...Do this in memory of me."[1] That single moment transcended both time and space, and has had repercussions for all ages, for all men and women, indeed, for all creation.

Although they were not always in agreement, these voices had a direct impact on Catholic thought and helped to prepare the way for the Second Vatican Council's challenge to the

---

[1] *The Roman Missal*, Eucharist Prayer II (Magnificat-Desclée, 2011), 630-31.

Church to engage the world, enter into dialogue with it, and help in its ongoing transformation. In their love for the Eucharist, they brought a message of hope to a time that was arguably one of the bloodiest, most violent in human history. Their theological work of *fides quaerens intellectum* ("faith seeking understanding") led to a deeper understanding the *mysterium fidei* ("the mystery of faith"), of which the Eucharist was the most real and visible sign. They were also keenly aware that no theological formulation, however creative and innovative, could exhaust the full meaning of this sacrament. For this reason, they understood that the theology of the Eucharist, while always continuous with the tradition of the Church, must always be open to reformulation and further development. For them, it was this challenge and call to a faith that would lead believers to a deeper understanding of the sacrament and reveal something of their origins and final destiny. They reminded believers that they were all pilgrims on the way and that Christ himself was "the way, and the truth, and the life" (Jn 14:6). The Eucharist, for them, was a sacrament of Christ and his Body, the Church. It lit up the path to life and led those who followed it to the truth of Christ himself. It posed deep, heart-probing questions that could be answered only by sound conviction and an active stillness of mind and heart.

Even today, these twentieth-century voices remind us that, in the end, the Eucharist itself—its preparation, celebration, and consummation—embodies the process of "faith seeking understanding." This great *sacramentum caritatis* ("sacrament of love") points out the way of the Lord Jesus and invites us to share in his life of humble, selfless service. When we receive the Eucharist, we affirm its meaning for our lives as it gently shapes our souls to be one with the heart and mind of Jesus. In celebrating it, we acknowledge our limitations and encounter the limitless mystery of a loving God. Through it, we ponder the truth about ourselves and delve into the depths of our souls to find there our inability to make things right. The Eucharist bids us to recognize that only God can undo the knots wrought by humanity's wrongs. It invites us to behold him, the "Bread of Life," and to feed on his loving, life-giving nourishment. This nourishment, the Eucharist, is nothing other than the glorified body of Jesus Christ himself. The two are one and the same. There is no separation between them.

God speaks to us in the Eucharist. His voice moves our hearts and sets them ablaze with the fire of divine love. Through this sacrament, he reveals his love for us and manifests his desire to heal us and make us whole. He tells us that he loves us more than we could ever imagine. The voices in this volume affirm again and again that the Eucharist is the visible, palpable sign and reality of God's continual and ongoing presence with his people. They remind us that, in the end, God asks of us nothing more than to let go of ourselves and allow him to enter the warp and woof of our daily lives. To do so would be to set out on an adventure that no one could dare imagine.

Acknowledgments

Parts of this book were previously published as: "Dom Columba Marmion on the Eucharist," *Emmanuel* 121(no. 3, 2015), 157-65 [Voice One]; "Karl Adam on the Eucharist," *Emmanuel* 122(no. 6, 2016): 379-88 [Voice Two]; "Reginald Garrigou-Lagrange on the Eucharist," *Emmanuel* 121(no. 5, 2015): 289-97 [Voice Three]; "Teilhard de Chardin on the Eucharist," *Emmanuel* 121(no 6, 2015): 357-67 [Voice Four]; "Romano Guardini on the Eucharist,' *Emmanuel* 123(no. 6, 2017): 370-79 [Voice Five]; Ronald Knox on the Eucharist," *Emmanuel* 122(no. 5, 2016): 305-13 [Voice Six]; "Josef A. Jungmann on the Eucharist," *Emmanuel* 123(no. 2, 93-100): 93-100 [Voice Seven]; "Dietrich von Hildebrand on the Eucharist, *Emmanuel* 119(no. 3, 2013): 233-39, 245-47 [Voice Eight]; "Fulton Sheen on the Eucharist," *Emmanuel* 124(no. 6, 2018): 368-76[Voice Nine]; "Henri de Lubac on the Eucharist." *Emmanuel* 120(no. 6, 2014): 425-33 [Voice Ten]; "Dorothy Day on the Eucharist," *Emmanuel* 123(no. 4, 227-36): 227-36 [Voice Eleven]; "Frank Sheed on the Eucharist," *Emmanuel* 124(no. 3, 2018): 159-66; "Adrienne von Speyr on the Eucharist," *Emmanuel* 117(no. 6, 2011): 486-95 [Voice Thirteen]; Dom M. Eugene Boylan on the Eucharist," *Emmanuel* 123(no. 5, 2017): 308-18 [Voice Fourteen]; "Yves Congar on the Eucharist," *Emmanuel* 121(no. 4, 2015): 223-30 [Voice Fifteen]; "Josef Pieper on the Eucharist," *Emmanuel* 123(no. 3, 2017): 155-64 [Voice Sixteen]; "Karl Rahner on the Eucharist," *Emmanuel* 122(no. 2, 2016): 80-89 [Voice

Seventeen]; "Jean Daniélou on the Eucharist," *Emmanuel* 120(no. 2, 2014): 73-81 [Voice Eighteen]; "Hans Urs von Balthasar on the Eucharist," *Emmanuel* 119(no. 4, 2013): 324-33 [Voice Nineteen]; "Bernard Häring on the Eucharist," *Emmanuel* 120(no. 4, 2014): 303-10 [Voice Twenty]; "Louis Bouyer on the Eucharist," *Emmanuel* 122(no. 3, 2016): 158-67 [Voice Twenty-One]; "F.X. Durrwell on the Eucharist," *Emmanuel* 119(no. 5, 2013): 408-17 [Voice Twenty-Two]; "Edward Schillebeeckx on the Eucharist," *Emmanuel* 120(no. 3, 2014): 144-5 [Voice Twenty-Three]; "Avery Dulles on the Eucharist," *Emmanuel* 120(no. 5, 2014): 364-73 [Voice Twenty-Four]; "G. E. M. Anscombe on the Eucharist," *Emmanuel* 124(no. 2, 2018): 78-89 [Voice Twenty-Five]; "Jean Corbon on the Eucharist," *Emmanuel* 119(no. 6, 2013): 519-27, 31 [Voice Twenty-Six]; "Walter Kasper on the Eucharist," *Emmanuel* 122(no. 1, 2016): 14-23 [Voice Twenty-Seven]; "Benedict XVI on the Eucharist," *Emmanuel* 119(no. 2, 2013): 127-35 [Voice Twenty-Eight]. Except for those within direct quotations from the authors studied, all Scriptural citations come from *Holy Bible: New Revised Standard Version with Apocrypha* (New York/Oxford: Oxford University Press, 1989). All Vatican documents are available on the website of the Holy See at: http://w2.vatican.va/content/vatican/en.html. In keeping with the book's popular tone, footnotes have been kept to a minimum. The strictly historical material in the book is not original to the author.

Postscript

Therefore the Eucharistic Celebration is much more than a simple banquet: it is exactly the memorial of Jesus' Paschal Sacrifice, the mystery at the center of salvation. "Memorial" does not simply mean a remembrance, a mere memory; it means that every time we celebrate this Sacrament we participate in the mystery of the passion, death, and resurrection of Christ. The Eucharist is the summit of God's saving action: the Lord Jesus, by becoming bread broken for us, pours upon us all of His mercy and His love, so as to renew our hearts, our lives, and our way of relating with Him and with the brethren. It is for this reason that commonly, when we approach this Sacrament, we speak of "receiving Communion," of "taking Communion": this means that by the power of the Holy Spirit, participation in Holy Communion conforms us in a singular and profound way to Christ, giving us a foretaste already now of the full communion with the Father that characterizes the heavenly banquet, where together with all the Saints we will have the joy of contemplating God face to face.

Pope Francis, Papal Audience
February 5, 2014

www.ingramcontent.com/pod-product-compliance
Lightning Source LLC
Chambersburg PA
CBHW030856270326
41929CB00008B/445